SALTWATER
Flies:
OVER 700 OF THE BEST

SALTWATER
Flies:
OVER 700 OF THE BEST

Deke Meyer

Fly Plates Photographed by Jim Schollmeyer

A Frank
Amato
PORTLAND

DEDICATION:

This book is dedicated to the tiers who contributed
flies for this endeavor.
Without you there would be no book.

A TRUE SALTWATER DRY FLY— PETE PARKER'S HELICOPTER FLY

A friend asked Pete if he could come up with a dry fly for saltwater. Pete says, "The only incident I could recall of a saltwater denizen taking a dry was when the big shark ate the helicopter in the movie JAWS II. The fly is a little difficult to cast. However, once you get it out there, it will auto-rotate down for a nice gentle presentation."

©1995 by Deke Meyer

Published in 1995 by Frank Amato Publications, Inc.
P.O. Box 82112, Portland, Oregon 97282
(503) 653-8108

Softbound ISBN: 1-57188-020-8

All photographs taken by Jim Schollmeyer except where noted.
Frontispiece photograph: Tony Oswald
Title Page photograph: Brian O'Keefe

Book Design: Tony Amato

Printed in HONG KONG

1 3 5 7 9 10 8 6 4 2

CONTENTS

INTRODUCTION

These seven hundred plus fly patterns are the direct consequence of thousands of hours spent fishing and tying flies by hundreds of saltwater fly fishing men and women. Some patterns are classics or derivations of classics, but many are pioneering efforts by anglers whose flies have never been described in print or photographed before.

In a sense, when you read this book you are glimpsing this process of fishing and tying, of trying new patterns and fine tuning favorites. On the one hand, this is the fly-tying pinnacle in the art of chasing the tremendous variety of salty critters that swim the estuaries, coves, inland seas and the great briny blue that blankets this planet. On the other hand, fly tying and fishing is an ongoing voyage of exploration, and as such, will never be complete—which means you can take part in this trek to discover new salty horizons.

How *Saltwater Flies: Over 700 of the Best* is Laid out

I've tried to track down the originator of each pattern listed, and have engaged in a lively philosophical discussion with some of the contributors. Going on the premise that knowledge is cumulative, I believe in giving credit to the person who first devised a fly design, but since our knowledge is collected and then modified as we push forward in time, at some point the modifier should get credit, too. The challenge is this: When do you begin attaching credit to the modification of an original fly via the name of the modifying tier? In almost all cases, I had the contributing tier name the fly. If a second name is listed, then that is the business name of the professional tier or the company marketing the fly commercially.

In the "Classics" chapter we look at traditional flies that are part of the history of saltwater fly fishing and fly patterns. Also, they illustrate some of the radical changes in saltwater fly fishing and how we approach designing flies.

In simplistic terms, the main criteria for a fly to be included in the "Bluewater" chapter is that the fly must be big and meant to be fished offshore. However, that doesn't take into account that sometimes bigwater fish such as tuna will feed on 6-inch baitfish, demanding a fly of the corresponding size. Conversely, some of the flies in the "Inshore" chapter are 8 or 10-inches long, a real rod full when casting from shore or a small boat.

This is not a fly tying book, but a reference for those curious about the latest in saltwater patterns. Certainly, you may be talented or bold enough to tie from these recipe listings without tying instructions, but that wasn't the intent. I've added the "Sources" chapter for those wishing to obtain flies for an upcoming trip, or to get an in-hand pattern to tie copies to fish with, or for those seeking wholesale distributors.

Naming Materials

In recent years, the most profound influence on saltwater flies is the overwhelming use of iridescent plastics in wing, tail and body materials. I encountered an overwhelming variety of brand names; I attempted to list the correct name of material the tier used. In some cases, the materials might seem interchangeable and the tiers didn't mind, but often the tier had specific reasons for using a specific brand name material. I leave that for you to investigate; one thing is certain—glittering plastics will shine in front of salty gamefish on into the next century, and as such will play a major role in fly tying.

GUIDO RAHR

FLIES THAT GLOW

1

Fluorescent and Phosphorescent

Fly tiers have used fluorescent materials for a number of years now, mainly because the added brightness of fluorescent components often makes the fly more effective in low light conditions and in murky water.

Under normal lighting conditions this streamer tied with phosphorescent materials appears similar to many other flies.

After being energized by a strong light source, such as a camera flash, phosphorescent flies glow for a few moments.

Fluorescent fly tying materials glow only when light is applied; they glow during the day in full sun, but we don't see the fluorescence. It only becomes visible to us in dim light. An excellent example is the fluorescent dye in the finish of many of our fly lines. The advantage to the fisherman becomes obvious when fishing in the fading light of evening or on an overcast day: Because the line will fluoresce or gleam a bit in the dimness, it's much easier to see, which allows the angler to quickly approximate where the fly is tracking the water. The same principle holds true for fish tracking a fly tied with fluorescent elements—the fish can see your fly from farther away—which can make an immense difference in subdued light or when water clarity is less than ideal.

Like fluorescent materials, phosphorescent or glow-in-the-dark tying materials are also fueled by light energy and shine in dim light. But the major difference is that phosphorescent ingredients continue to glimmer for a few moments after the light source is taken away. So to that degree, phosphorescent materials are not dependent on the continuous application of light.

Glow-in-the-dark fly tying components include body tubing and Flashabou. The tubing can be split out and unraveled to make wing and tail material, but it's coarser and stiffer than Flashabou. Glow-in-the-dark Flashabou is a bit coarser than regular Flashabou but still moves well in the water. The tubing comes in small, medium and large, and both materials come in white, yellow, green, blue, orange and pink. However, when energized with bright light all these glow-in-the-dark phosphorescent elements radiate a yellowish-green glint.

I was curious as to how glow-in-the-dark materials worked—how they store and release light over a span of minutes—but the supplier wouldn't tell me for fear of others copying what is a trade secret. At any rate, I suspect that light energy changes certain chemical properties of the material on a molecular level and somehow that energy is retained a few moments and then quickly dissipates. It's called cold light because unlike a light bulb, it generates no heat.

Phosphorescent substances gleam under the low light conditions of evening or when fishing on an overcast day, and they offer the advantage of providing the angler with the choice of energizing them to shine when needed. The beam from a flashlight just isn't intense enough to work well for glow-in-the-dark flies at night. One of the most efficient ways to energize phosphorescent materials for night fishing is to zap the fly with a camera flash. The phosphorescent ingredients will then remain luminescent for several moments.

Lightsticks

Another option is to design a fly that incorporates a glow-in-the-dark Cyalume lightstick, sold in sporting goods stores as "Lunker Lights" which include three lightsticks in blue, green or pink, and clear plastic tubing. Some novelty or party supply shops carry lightsticks in green or blue, but without tubing. Surgical, aquarium or gas line tubing for model airplanes will hold these smaller lightsticks.

Lightsticks generate light from a chemical reaction caused when two solutions mix inside the lightstick. One of the solutions is stored in a very thin ampule within the lightstick housing. To start synthesizing light, you flex or bend the lightstick, which breaks the inner ampule, mixing the solution. Like phosphorescent materials, lightsticks are not a source of heat, but of cold light. They cannot be recharged, but continue to generate a cold luminescence in green, blue, pink, etc. for 10-12 hours.

The challenge in tying flies incorporating a lightstick is designing the fly so that the lightstick can first be flexed to begin generating light, then added to the fly so the lightstick won't fall out when casting or fishing. The lightstick shouldn't impede the hook from nailing the fish, and if possible the fly design should allow for replacement of the lightstick.

Traser Lights

Traser Lights are made by AVRO, UK, and called self-activated light. Trasers are sealed hollow glass tubes internally coated with phosphor and filled with tritium gas. When the decay electrons of tritium reach the phosphor their energy is converted into light, similar to the mechanism used to produce a television picture. The process converts tritium gas to helium gas; it takes over ten years for the tritium to decay to the point of not producing light.

Trasers are: Self-activated, requiring neither power supply or wiring; a cold light source; without filaments, so they are highly resistant to shock and vibration; unaffected by water, oil and most corrosives; intrinsically safe, with no risk of fire or explosion. The electron energy is so low that the electrons cannot escape their container. Since the tritium becomes helium, (a large part of the breathing mixture for deep-sea divers) there is no adverse effect on the environment. Tritium is commercially

In normal light, the Traser-installed fly appears as any other fly. (David Woodhouse's Labraxus fly is named for the Latin nomenclature for the European sea bass, see page 70).

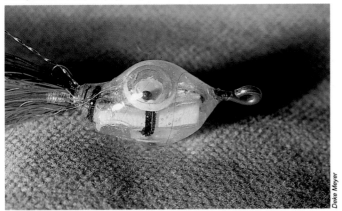

The Traser capsule is contained in the lower half of the body of the fly, centered between the eyes.

available as a by-product of nuclear power reactors.

Trasers glow in varied colors, such as red, blue, green, yellow, white, etc. and measure from .030" diameter up to 1" diameter and from fractions of an inch to several inches long. They are used in illumination of watches, panels, dials, LCD displays, etc. and for industrial and military uses.

David Woodhouse of England, who contributed some Traser-installed flies, says, "Saltwater fly fishing is pretty much in its infancy in the U.K.; however, there are certain areas it is practiced with great effect by a few anglers wishing to experiment and put in the time. We mainly fish in the cleaner saltwater in southwest England, Wales and Scotland.

In dim light you can see the glow of the self-activated Traser Light.

"We fish with a floating 7 to 9 weight line and a six to ten pound leader about six to ten feet in length. The method is to cast as far as possible and allow varying sink times and strip back in short bursts or occasionally slow winding works well. The Labraxus fly imitates the sand eels that live in the sand and rocks and are a major part of the sea bass's diet. It can be quite

Traser Lights glow in varied colors, such as red, blue, green, yellow, white, etc. and measure from .030" diameter up to 1" diameter and from fractions of an inch to several inches long.

exciting to wade quietly thirty yards into a light surf before dawn and have a bass of six to eight pounds chasing your fly almost to your feet.

"A lot of the sea trout we catch are from the estuaries in Wales and Scotland; fishing is generally from dusk to dawn with small shiny flies. Whilst bass fishing with our flies we regularly had pulls from sea trout, so we made smaller flies and when the opportunity came along we added the light source. It has many advantages to the night fisher, one being that you can retrieve your flies from the trees after a bad cast, and also you can actually see the light disappear when a fish swallows the fly."

Woodhouse reports Florida tarpon to 80 pounds on Traser flies—there may be no limit to the applications for Traser Lights in saltwater flies. (For more information, see Traser Lights in the "Sources" chapter, page 116.)

Bioluminescence

The idea of incorporating artificial light in a fly may seem alien, but the glow-in-the-dark notion is not new. Scientists call it bioluminescence, the emission of light by living organisms, caused by a conversion of chemical energy to light energy. Bioluminescence doesn't come from light absorbed by the organism or depend on light absorbed. It's a special kind of biological chemical reaction that produces a cold light without giving off heat.

The flash of the firefly, the brilliant "phosphorescence" of the ocean, or the glimmer of Jack-my-lantern or foxfire mushrooms in the forest at night are examples of bioluminescent organisms. Certain bacteria, fungi, worms, crustaceans, insects, jellyfish, squid, shrimp, clams, and fish are bioluminescent. Some emit light to frighten or confuse predators, some to attract prey, and some to attract mates. Bioluminescent fish include the dogfish shark, luminous shark, pony fish, flashlight fish, angler fish, dragon fish, viper fish, hatchet fish, and lantern fish.

One of the truly fascinating aspects of fly tying and fishing is the constant carousel of changes in materials, tying techniques, and tactics associated with new approaches to fly fishing puzzles. Perhaps this glow-in-the-dark approach will light your way to new fishing horizons.

CLASSIC
SALTWATER FLIES

2

Arbitrarily, I selected these classics based on the books I had available that date back 20 or so years, and through interviews conducted during the course of research for this book. If you have access to other books or tiers, you might compile a different selection.

However, almost any collection of classic saltwater flies will offer us a handle on the fly tying tradition laid down in previous years. Besides imparting a sense of history, looking at these flies supplies us with some basic designs that still catch fish, and shows us how saltwater fly design has changed over the years.

The first saltwater patterns were either bucktail or bucktail and feather creations, still necessary components for many of today's best flies. And some of these classic designs, such as Lefty Kreh's Deceiver and Dan Blanton's Whistler series, have changed little over the years because they are still effective fish-taking flies. Some of these classics have fallen out of favor because they use feathers from protected birds such as swan and jungle cock.

The most important change in the direction of saltwater fly design is our concept of the fishing itself: not unlike trout fly fishing, salt rodders have tuned into more of a match-the-hatch strategy, presenting the fish with a particular simulation of its prey. Where fly rodding pioneers cast generalist bucktail and chenille flies at bonefish, permit, bluefish and stripers, now we present specific crustacean or baitfish patterns, matched to the size, shape and coloration of the prey. But that is not to say that generalist designs such as the Deceiver or the Whistler won't catch fish, because that isn't true. In fact, in many fishing situations, you search the water with a generalist pattern to better appeal to predator gamefish that feed on a wide range of baitfish. A generalist pattern offers the built-in advantage of enticing gamefish because once the fly is working in the water, the bucktail and marabou undulates, mimicking baitfish, imparting that elusive sense of lifelike prey to the searching predator gamefish.

The Lefty's Deceiver of 20 years ago depicts the latest development of that time, the use of silver or gold flat Mylar tinsel, a great improvement over metallic tinsels. Today, the most profound impact on saltwater fly design is the volcanic fireworks of sparkle plastic in its many forms, offering the tier incredible options when designing flies. The tier can incorporate just a bit of flash in a crustacean pattern, a swath of light reflection that mimics a bright baitfish, or go all-out with an iridescent bluewater fly designed to pull gamefish to the strike from yards away. Whether used for the body, tail or wing material, these sparkling new plastics open wide horizons for the saltwater tier.

Mark Sosin and Bub Church's Blockbuster featured its thread body encased in epoxy, a common approach now. In fact, tiers use various types of epoxy, hot glue and silicone to form new styles of flies that result in flies that are extremely durable, and can be formed into specific shapes not otherwise achieved. Also, many tiers use plastic or doll eyes, attaching them to the fly or encasing them within the fly via these adhesives. The effect is eyes that seem lifelike, yet remain impervious to the rigors of saltwater fishing.

Possibly the arena that has changed the most is bluewater fishing, where the fly angler pits muscle, stamina and fly tackle endurance against jumbo fish. Although spartan when compared to many contemporary bigwater flies, Winston Moore's Billfish Fly remains an effective pattern. Bluewater fishing tackle has certainly altered in the last 20 years.

Although chasing record fish may not be the game for every angler, Lee Wulff's quest for a record striped marlin off the coast of Ecuador in April, 1967, was chronicled on ABC's "American Sportsman's Show" and later in his book, THE COMPLEAT LEE WULFF, 1989, Truman Talley Books, E.P. Dutton.

Lee tells of fishing with a $12 glass 9-foot fly rod and click-drag single-action Farlow Python reel, and a 15-foot boat with a thirty-three-horsepower outboard.

He wrote, "My fly was a big one, a 4/0 tandem made with long rooster feathers in a mixture of red, white, and yellow. Guide Woody Sexton had dubbed it the Sea Wulff—a bulky fly that cast about as easily as the average bass bug." Incidentally, Wulff tied all of his flies in his hands, without a vise, including the tandem 4/0's he used for this adventure.

After a day and a half of countless presentations, Wulff finally hooked the fish he sought. The battle started at noon; the fish eventually came to the gaff over four hours later. Wulff had set a new record for striped marlin at 148 pounds on a 12-pound tippet. As a sidenote, the fish was 129 inches long, about 13 feet, almost as long as the boat.

Woody Sexton told me that they almost landed a fish he estimated at 250 pounds, but he just couldn't get close enough to gaff it. Woody said, "The guy was really a marvel at fighting fish; I learned a lot; you'd almost have to see the finesse and the power and the durability of the guy."

When reminiscing about that adventure and the boat and tackle they used, Woody said, "Listen, this was primitive—very, very primitive. There wasn't a bit of sophistication, except I think the angling was. I think what we did, with the limitations that we were working with, was rather extraordinary."

All human knowledge is a pyramid of accumulated bits and pieces, piled on top of the previous bits and pieces, the history or tradition of any human endeavor. You can dust yourself with a bit of saltwater fly fishing tradition when you catch a salty gamefish on a Joe Brooks Blonde or any of the classic patterns. In a sense, every time you tie a fly or cast it on the briny blue, you take part in the history of salt fly rodding.

I wish you good luck.

AGENT ORANGE—Winston Moore

Hook: Mustad 34007/3407; Daiichi 2546; Tiemco 811S; sizes 2-8
Thread: Orange
Body: Orange chenille
Wing: Orange fine hair; two grizzly hackle tips on each side of hair
Variations: Weighted with lead wire, denoted with orange enamel paint on orange thread head
TIED BY WINSTON MOORE

HISTORY: Winston told me, "Thirty years ago when I first used the fly there weren't that many flies with much color in them. I used to fish it a lot in Belize, in small sizes, in 6's and 8's and it was absolutely deadly. I hooked so many hundreds of bonefish down there on that fly that you wouldn't believe it, on any kind of a bottom, grassy, sand, or mud or whatever. So when I started fishing the Bahamas at Andros Island with Bonefish Charlie, I naturally had some of these with me. He'd never seen it and I'd never fished it in the Bahamas. It was so effective down there; I remember one day he and I were out in his skiff and I was taking fish after fish and he said, "Mon, you don't need no guide, all you needs is that orange fly."

"In the Bahamas I tie it weighted with lead wire and paint the head with orange enamel over the orange thread. Down there you use a larger hook size, with 4's and sometimes 2's because you've got such large fish there. That fly is very effective anywhere in the Bahamas, Belize, all over the Yucatan Peninsula north of Belize, Ascension Bay and around there; it is not worth a hoot at Los Roques or any place I've fished in Venezuela, and I

don't know why. But any fly that has orange on it, at least in my experience at Los Roques, scares the fish, it spooks them. So I don't even take it with me down there when I go."

Winston's not sure why he picked orange. He says, "That's been so long ago I'd be guessing; I don't really know. That was back, not quite in the infancy of fly fishing for bonefish, but pretty close to it. Most of the flies were pretty drab, you know, a lot of browns and just really dull, drab colors. And I knew that a lot of the time the fish weren't seeing the fly.

"That's one of the best flies I've ever used; I've taken over 6,000 bonefish on a fly. I don't know what percentage of them have been taken with that fly, but a lot of them, anyway."

APTE TARPON FLY—Stu Apte

Thread: Red
Tail: Saddle hackle, red, yellow
Body Hackle: Red, yellow
Variations: There are many color variations to the original theme. In SALT WATER FLIES, 1972, Kenneth Bay wrote that Stu Apte preferred the red and yellow color combination, saying, "This particular pattern...stirs the tarpon's memory of his favorite food, the palolo (red) worm".
TIED BY AUTHOR

BAY TERN—Bob Nauheim

Hook: Mustad 34007/3407; Daiichi 2546; Tiemco 811S; sizes 2/0-3/0
Thread: White
Tail: White hair; pink pearl Flashabou
Body: Braided silver tinsel
Wing: White hair; pink pearl Flashabou; pale green FisHair
Beard: Red kip tail
Variations: Nacht Tern, Sea tern
TIED BY BOB NAUHEIM

HISTORY: Bob wrote me, "The Terns are among my favorite patterns. I developed the series in the early 1960's because there were no West Coast striper flies that I was aware of in Sonoma County (California) at the time. Modeled basically after the Gibbs Striper Fly, I refined it as I went along. The Terns are the only striper flies I have ever used."

BLOCKBUSTER—
Mark Sosin And Bub Church

Hook: Mustad 34007/3407; Daiichi 2546; Tiemco 811S
Thread: Red
Tail: White bucktail; gold or silver flat Mylar
Body: Thread under epoxy
Wings: White bucktail; gold or silver flat Mylar
TIED BY AUTHOR

HISTORY: In his book SALT WATER FLIES, 1972, Kenneth Bay wrote that Mark Sosin said, "My favorite pattern is fashioned from bucktail and Mylar and appropriately named the Blockbuster. It was designed on my bench with Bub Church at the vise and me over his shoulder. I told Bub what I wanted to accomplish, and we worked out the pattern together... People who visit Bub are constantly amazed to learn that he employed many of the techniques that we know so well today, before most fishermen knew anything about saltwater fly rodding. You might

talk to him about a "new" pattern and he'll show you flies he tied thirty years ago that are almost identical."

BLONDE (HONEY)—Joe Brooks

Thread: Black
Tail: Bucktail, yellow
Body: Silver tinsel
Wing: Bucktail, yellow
Variations: Platinum, strawberry, Argentine, black, pink, etc.
TIED BY AUTHOR

HISTORY: In his book SALT WATER FLIES, 1972, Kenneth Bay quoted Lefty Kreh, "There have been a few people fly fishing in saltwater for more than 100 years, but it was Joe Brooks, more than any other man, who opened this exciting new world of fly fishing to the average fisherman. Just after World War II, Joe began to experiment seriously and write about saltwater fishing. The returning soldiers, starved for a chance to fish again, read almost with disbelief Joe's reports of the accomplishments of the pioneer fishermen with whom he fished."

BLONDE (PLATINUM)—Joe Brooks

Thread: Black
Tail: Bucktail, white
Body: Silver tinsel
Wing: Bucktail, white
Variations: Honey, strawberry, Argentine, black, pink, etc.
TIED BY AUTHOR

HISTORY: In his book SALT WATER FLIES, 1972, Kenneth Bay quoted Joe Brooks, "I think that the Platinum Blonde which I use for striped bass, jack crevalle, spotted sea trout, channel bass, bonefish, and tarpon (the fly I designed more than 20 years ago) has proven the best all-around saltwater fly I have ever used."

BLUEFISH STREAMER (YELLOW/RED)— C. BOYD PFEIFFER

Hook: Eagle Claw 66SS, straightened; Mustad 34011
Thread: Yellow
Tail: none
Body: Red Mylar tubing
Wing: Yellow bucktail
Variations: Wing: white, blue, black, green; body: silver, gold, yellow, black
TIED BY C. BOYD PFEIFFER
HISTORY: This pattern is included in SALT WATER FLIES, 1972, Kenneth Bay. Boyd wrote me, "The wing of bucktail (synthetics can also be used) is tied to the rear most part of the hook shank so that you have a long shank to serve as a shock leader for toothy fish."

BONBRIGHT TARPON FLY— Howard Bonbright

Thread: White
Tail: Hackle tips, white, red
Body: Silver tinsel
Wing: White hackle
Hackle: White
Cheeks: Red swan; jungle cock eye
TIED BY JIM SYNDER
HISTORY: In his book SALT WATER FLY FISHING, 1969, George X. Sand wrote, "Bonbright's popular tarpon fly, which was sold by Abercrombie & Fitch as far back as the early 1920's, is still listed in most reference books on popular US patterns."

CATERPILLAR—John Fabian

Hook: Long shank, nickel plate, bent straight, size 2/0
Thread: Black
Tail: Bucktail, orange
Body: White deer hair
Wing: Clipped hackle, orange
Front Hackle: Orange
Variations: Red or yellow tail and hackle
TIED BY JOHN FABIAN
HISTORY: John tied this original in the early 1960's for tidewater stripers in the Umpqua and Coos River estuaries, for fishing on the surface. He set the 1970 Saltwater Fly Rodders of America world records for 6 and 10-pound tippets with his fly.

COCHROACH—Lefty Kreh

Thread: Black
Tail: Grizzly hackle
Body: none
Body Hackle: Brown bucktail
TIED BY JIM SYNDER

CRACKER—George Trowbridge

Hook: Atlantic salmon, black
Thread: Red
Tag: Small gold tinsel; yellow floss
Tail: Swan, blue, yellow; peacock sword
Body: Blue floss; silver tinsel rib
Wing: Swan, red, blue; turkey; peacock sword
Hackle: Orange
TIED BY JIM SYNDER

HISTORY: In her book FAVORITE FLIES AND THEIR HISTORIES, 1892, Mary Orvis Maybury wrote of George Trowbridge's luck with his Cracker, which he used for various saltwater critters, including a 23-pound channel bass. (From AMERICAN FLY FISHING, Paul Schullery, 1987)

CRAZY CHARLIE—Bob Nauheim

Hook: Mustad 34007/3407; Daiichi 2546; Tiemco 811S; sizes 2-6
Thread: White
Tail: Silver Flashabou
Body: Silver tinsel; mono
Wing: Creme hackle
Eyes: Silver bead chain
TIED BY BOB NAUHEIM

HISTORY: Bob told me, "I came up with the original Crazy Charlie on Andros Island in the Bahamas in the late '70's and named it for Bonefish Charlie Smith. I originally tied it to emulate glass minnows but we soon realized that the bonefish were taking it as a shrimp. Originally the fly was called the "Nasty Charlie" because Charlie had said, "Dat fly nasty!" when we first took fish on it.

"I took the pattern to Key West and showed it to Capt. Jan Isley, who was then guiding there, and Jan had great success with the pattern on fussy Keys bonefish. Jan was the first to tie the fly with a hair wing. We next took it to Christmas Island when that mid-Pacific atoll first opened to bonefishing. The first fly fishermen who fished the island told us that the bonefish there had refused all of their offerings and they didn't think they would take a fly. Don't forget, this was the first time anyone had ever seriously fished for bonefish in the Pacific with a fly.

"But we were very successful with the Crazy Charlie, and when

we got back, Leigh Perkins of Orvis called me. Perkins was planning a trip to the island and wanted the pattern with which we had been so successful. When he returned after a successful trip to Christmas Island he had the fly dressed commercially for Orvis, and inadvertently changed the "Nasty" to "Crazy", hence the Crazy Charlie. The fly marketed through Orvis was a huge success and soon others began tying the pattern commercially. The Crazy Charlie was well on its way to becoming the most popular bonefish pattern ever to come down the pike!"

FRANKEE-BELLE BONEFISH FLY—Frankee Albright/Belle Mathers

Hook: 2-1/0
Thread: White
Tail: none
Body: White chenille
Wing: Brown bucktail; grizzly hackle
TIED BY AUTHOR

HISTORY: In his book SALT WATER FLIES, 1972, Kenneth Bay wrote that Joe Brooks said, "It was one of the earliest patterns tied for bonefish and, to my mind, one of the very greatest. I used it only a month ago, in size 4, to take a ten-pound bone at Key Biscayne." Bay also wrote, "Among the sportsmen who have added to the glory of the Frankee Belle Bonefish Fly are the renowned dry-fly fresh water authority, George L.M. LaBranche, who fished it in 1947; Bart Foth (who set the 1968 world record for bonefish at 12-pounds, 10-ounces on a 12-pound tippet); Lefty Kreh; and Lee Cuddy, who has a record catch of 2,000 bonefish for his time at it."

In his book SALT WATER FLY FISHING, 1969, George X. Sand

wrote of the sisters Frankee and Bonnie, "It was Frankee who after the war guided George LaBranche, by then quite elderly, when the old gentleman finally took his first bonefish on a fly. Bonnie, meanwhile, had become the first woman to take a permit on regulation fly tackle."

HISTORICAL NOTE, ORIGINS OF FLY FISHING FOR BONEFISH:

In his book LEE WULFF ON FLIES, 1980, Wulff wrote, "In 1947, when fly fishing for bonefish was just beginning, I took one of my first fly-rod bonefish on the surface with a bass bug. Still, the best place to put a fly is where the fish is looking for food, and with bonefish that means on the bottom."

In his COMPLETE BOOK OF FLY FISHING, 1958, Joe Brooks wrote, "In 1947, while I was attending an Outdoor Writers Association of America convention in St. Petersburg, Allen Corson, Fishing Editor of the Miami Herald, told me about bonefish and asked if I thought they could be taken on a fly—fly fishing being my specialty. I opined that it was worth a try, journeyed down to Islamorada, went out with Captain Jimmy Albright, who said right off that he thought it was possible, and took two tailing bonefish on streamer flies. As far as is known, that was the first deliberate attempt to take bonefish on flies, and it was successful."

GALLI-NIPPER—J. EDSON LEONARD

Thread: Black
Tail: Red wool
Body: Silver Mylar piping
Wing: Yellow bucktail; grizzly hackle
Throat: Red wool
Head: Gold chenille
TIED BY AUTHOR
HISTORY: In his book THE ESSENTIAL FLY TIER, 1976, J. Edson Leonard wrote, "The Galli-Nipper is a good example of a bucktail with overwings of hackle. I claim only part authorship for this creation because its principles are almost as old as the wet fly itself."

GIBBS STRIPER FLY—Harold Gibbs

Thread: Black
Tail: none
Body: Silver tinsel
Wing: White bucktail
Throat: Red hackle
Cheek: Jungle cock breast feather over blue swan
TIED BY JIM SYNDER
HISTORY: In his book THE ESSENTIAL FLY TIER, 1976, J. Edson Leonard wrote, "The Gibbs' Striper caught stripers everywhere, when they were responding to streamers. I still have a Gibbs' Striper that Hal gave me in 1949."

HORROR—P. Perinchief

Hook: 1/0-3/0
Thread: Red
Body: Yellow chenille
Wing: Brown bucktail
TIED BY AUTHOR

LEFTY'S DECEIVER (WHITE)—Lefty Kreh

Hook: Mustad 34007/3407; Daiichi 2546; Tiemco 811S
Thread: White
Tail: White saddle hackle
Body: Silver tinsel or Mylar
Collar: White bucktail; silver Mylar
Variations: Variations abound for this fly design, incorporating varied color schemes and new plastic materials.
TIED BY AUTHOR
HISTORY: This is probably the most famous saltwater fly of all time, and still accounts for as many fish as any other pattern in use today. In the book MASTER FLY TYING GUIDE, 1972, Art Flick has Lefty describe his Deceiver: "This fly, which swims with a fishlike motion, is of the general shape of a baitfish, and is non-fouling and offers little air resistance. It is a general-purpose fly for either coast and almost any saltwater fishing situation; only the size or color need be altered. It is generally tied in all white,

or with white hackles and red collar, or yellow hackles and red collar."

LOVING BASS FLY—Tom Loving

Thread: Black
Tail: none
Body: none
Wing: White bucktail
Hackle: Red
TIED BY AUTHOR
HISTORY: In his book SALT WATER FLIES, 1972, Kenneth Bay wrote, "This fly, the first known to be designed for striped bass, was used in the Chesapeake Bay in the 1920's, according to Joe Brooks."

LYMAN'S TERROR (GREEN)—Hal Lyman

Thread: Black
Tail: none
Body: Silver tinsel
Wing: White over green over white bucktail
Cheeks: Jungle cock breast feather
Variations: Red bucktail in wing instead of green
TIED BY JIM SYNDER
HISTORY: A variation of Gibbs' Striper developed by Hal Lyman, long-time editor of SALT WATER SPORTSMAN magazine. In his book SALT WATER FLY FISHING, 1969, George X. Sand wrote, "The actions of sea birds should always be carefully noted, of course, since they will usually become aware of the presence of game fish long before humans." However, he reported that Lyman refers to gulls sitting at the surf's edge as probably engaged in "avian gossip".

LYMAN'S TERROR (RED)—Hal Lyman

Thread: Black
Tail: none
Body: Silver tinsel
Wing: White over red over white bucktail
Cheeks: Jungle cock breast feather
Variations: Green bucktail in wing instead of red
TIED BY JIM SYNDER

NACHT TERN—Bob Nauheim

Hook: Mustad 34007/3407; Daiichi 2546; Tiemco 811S; sizes 2/0-3/0
Thread: Black
Tail: Black bucktail
Body: Braided silver tinsel
Wing: Black bucktail; gray squirrel
Variations: Bay Tern, Sea Tern
TIED BY BOB NAUHEIM
HISTORY: Bob wrote me, "Without exaggeration, I have taken over 200 striped bass with the Nacht Tern (named after my German born wife, Helena) using a floating line and fishing after sundown. There's no doubt that black has the highest visibility of any color and this is especially true at night when big fish search for bait fish looking up from a truly dark environment into a lighter one. I originally developed the Nacht Tern in the mid-1960's for fishing the lights of the bridges in San Francisco Bay.

The pattern is especially effective when fishing near bridge lights, or at dusk or dawn."

PALMER DILLER—Harvey Flint

Thread: Black
Body: Silver tinsel
Wing: Bucktail, blue, red, white
TIED BY AUTHOR
HISTORY: In his book SALT WATER FLY FISHING, 1969, George X. Sand wrote: "It was Harold Gibbs of Barrington, Rhode Island, still an ardent fly rod bassman at 82, who introduced the use of streamers for stripers in that state. World War II gasoline rationing would shortly take place. Travel to Canada for salmon would be halted, and Gibbs prepared for a substitute. In the spring of 1940 he tied a 5/0 bucktail wing streamer that imitated a small silverside bait fish and used this successfully late one afternoon on a large year-class of bass that roamed Narragansett Bay and the Barrington and Warren Rivers that year.

"Gibbs was so happy that he phoned his brother, Frank, who joined him the following evening with some experimental flies he had made up meanwhile. Harold's pattern, still used today, became known as the Gibbs Striper. This fly worked so well, as did one of Frank's, that the Gibbs brothers were able to catch some 800 stripers in the year that followed. A fishing partner of the brothers, not to be outdone, tied the Harvey Flint Palmer Diller. These three pioneering salt-water streamers continued to take striped bass along the New England coast."

PIGTAILS—Edward A. Materne

Thread: Black
Tail: none
Body: Silver tinsel
Wing: Bucktail, green, yellow, white; peacock herl
Throat: Red hackle
Variations: Optional cheeks, teal
TIED BY AUTHOR

RHODE TARPON STREAMER— Homer Rhode

Thread: Red
Tail: White hackle
Body: none
Body hackle: Red
TIED BY AUTHOR

HISTORY: Homer Rhode is probably better known for his Homer Rhode loop knot which provides an open loop knot that won't slip up against the eye of the hook, allowing maximum fly movement. In his book SALT WATER FLY FISHING, 1969, George X. Sand wrote, "Another outstanding pioneer salt-water flycaster and experimenter was Homer Rhode. Rhode tells of taking his first bonefish and permit on regulation tackle in 1930. The author first fished Florida waters in 1935 and recalls this Everglades naturalist in those days as a tall, straight, and very thin flycaster; a loner with thoughtful, perceptive eyes shaded by an inevitable

broad-brimmed hat. Homer Rhode roamed the Florida back country canals and boated and waded the shallow waters of Florida Bay, often for months without letup."

SANDS BONEFISH FLY—Hagen Sands

Thread: Black
Tail: none
Body: none
Wing: White bucktail; grizzly hackle over yellow
TIED BY AUTHOR

SEA TERN—Bob Nauheim

Hook: Mustad 34007/3407; Daiichi 2546; Tiemco 811S; sizes 2/0-3/0
Thread: White
Tail: White hair; pink pearl Flashabou
Body: Braided silver tinsel
Wing: White hair; pink pearl Flashabou; royal blue hair or FisHair
Beard: Red kip tail
Variations: Nacht Tern, Bay Tern
TIED BY BOB NAUHEIM

HISTORY: Bob wrote me, "The Terns are among my favorite patterns and I'm quite proud of the results had with this easy dressing which is simple to tie, enhanced with the advent of Flashabou."

SILVER OUTCAST—Ralph Daugherty

Thread: Black
Body: Silver tinsel
Wing: Bucktail, white, completely around the hook; peacock herl over light purple over yellow bucktail
Cheeks: Jungle cock eye
TIED BY JIM SYNDER

HISTORY: Charlie Waterman has popularized this fly through his writing, crafting stories about he and his wife Debie (who does most of the tying) catching diverse fish in tremendously varied locales with the Silver Outcast. Charlie told me this story about his coming across this streamer, some 25 years ago.

He said, "Rocky Weinstein was guiding Ralph Daugherty, a retired doctor from New England, down in the Everglades. I met them in a boat in a narrow creek and Daugherty said this fly had been working well on snook, and he gave me the streamer. Later on, I caught some big trout in Montana, and Dan Bailey, who was in the tying business, asked me what I caught the trout on, and I said I caught them on a Silver Doctor. He looked at the thing and he said, that's not the way we tie Silver Doctors. Of course, what he meant was, the materials weren't the same, and

I started calling it the Silver Outcast after that. It's a good streamer and it's caught all kinds of fish; it's actually a simplified Silver Doctor. I don't know whether it was Daugherty or Weinstein that tied the thing, but apparently they didn't have all the materials for a Silver Doctor and that's the way it came out."

SIMPLE ONE (WHITE)—C. Boyd Pfeiffer

Hook: Eagle Claw 254SS; Mustad 34007/3407; Daiichi 2546; Tiemco 811S, sizes 6-3/0
Thread: White
Tail: none
Body: Silver Mylar tubing
Collar: White bucktail
Variations: Wing/body: white/silver, white/black, white/yellow, white/blue, yellow/gold, yellow/red, black/black, black/silver
TIED BY C. BOYD PFEIFFER

HISTORY: Another fly from SALT WATER FLIES, 1972, Kenneth Bay. Boyd wrote me, "An important aspect of the tying is that the wing is tied so that it completely encircles the hook shank, allowing the body to show through, rather than the wing on top as with most streamers."

WINSTON'S BILLFISH FLY (ORANGE/RED/YELLOW)— Winston Moore

Hook: Tandem, mono snelled
Slider Head: Red foam; plastic tube
Thread: Red
Body: Silver tinsel
Underwing: Yellow hair
Wing: Red and orange hair
Variations: Blue/white/green
TIED BY WINSTON MOORE

HISTORY: Winston says, "This fly, in various colors, has taken 138 Pacific sailfish, 3 striped marlin, 2 blues and 2 blacks. It's not a work of art, but it's certainly effective." Winston places its origins around the late 1950's or early 1960's (about the same time as he developed his Agent Orange bonefish fly). Of his fly and fishing for billfish, he says, "You know, there weren't too many of us that

were doing it in those days; I don't know if there was a dozen people in the world that had done it; there may have been less than that—that had actually perfected the teasing technique."

BLUEWATER FLIES

3

ALF (BLUE)—Bill and Kate Howe

Hook: Tiemco 800S, 3/0
Thread: White or pale yellow
Body: Coated thread
Wing: Super Hair, white; Ultra Hair, smoke, clear yellow, smoke; Flashabou, silver; Ultra Hair, purple, olive; Ocean Hair, light blue; Krystal Flash, gray ghost; Ultra Hair, olive; Krystal Flash, peacock; Ocean Hair, red, white; Ultra Hair, royal blue, polar bear; Ocean Hair, black
Head: Thread colored with black felt tip, coated with Hot Stuff Special T glue with Kick-it accelerator, Jolly Glaze
Eyes: 10 mm doll eyes, black on yellow
Variations: ALF TOO
TIED BY BILL HOWE

BABY DOLL-RADO—Mark Petrie

Hook: Tandem, 5/0 cadium, 100-pound mono snell
Tail: Saddle hackle, yellow, green; gold saltwater Flashabou
Wing: Saddle hackle, yellow, green; gold saltwater Flashabou
Collar: Yellow wool
Head: Yellow wool
Eyes: 12mm doll eyes
TIED BY MARK PETRIE/SALTWATER SPECIALTIES

BABY DORADO—Pete Parker

Hook: Mustad 34007; Tiemco 811S; 4/0
Thread: 3/0 Dynacord
Wing: Super Hair, yellow, olive, chartreuse; Fire Fly, green; Flashabou, peacock; 5-minute epoxy
Glitter Head: Thread covered with hot glue, silver glitter; marker pens or lacquer for top; 5-minute epoxy
Eyes: 10mm doll eyes or decal
Gills: Red marker
TIED BY PETE PARKER

BALEO (BLEEDING CUT BAIT)—Bill & Kate Howe

Hook: Gamakatsu Octopus, 4/0; snelled Mason 40-60#
Thread: White
Tube: Clear or transparent, 3 1/2"; pearl Mylar; Ocean Hair, black; holographic powder
Tail: Ocean Hair, pearl, smoke, red, black; Krystal Flash, pearl; Flashabou, silver; Sharpie water proof red pen
Eyes: Doll eyes, black on yellow
Variations: Wahoo, blue, green
TIED BY KATE HOWE

BALEO-WAHOO (RED)—Bill & Kate Howe

Hook: Gamakatsu Octopus, 4/0; snelled Mason 40-60# wire
Thread: Red
Tube: Clear or transparent, 3 1/2"; pearl Mylar; Ocean Hair, black; holographic powder

Tail: Ultra hair, fluorescent pink, pink, light purple, red, bright red, black; Everglow tubing, pink; Holographic Mylar tape 1/32"; silver Mylar
Head: Thread coated with Hot Stuff Special T glue with Kick-it accelerator, Jolly Glaze
Eyes: Adhesive Mylar, 4 1/2mm; 2mm black on fluorescent red
Variations: Blue, green, cut bait
TIED BY KATE HOWE

BBB (BILL'S BONZA BAITFISH)—Bill Howe

Hook: Mustad 34007/3407; Eagle Claw 254/354; Tiemco 800S/811S; Pate; Owner SSW; size 1/0-9/0, single or double
Thread: Hot pink
Wing: Flashabou, pearl, silver; 1/32" prismatic tape; crinkle nylon, yellow, red, black
Head: Thread colored with black felt tip, coated with Hot Stuff Special T glue with Kick-it accelerator, Jolly Glaze
Eyes: Prismatic, painted black on fluorescent pink added
TIED BY BILL HOWE

BIG GAME TUBE FLY (BLOOD SQUID)—Cam Sigler

Hook: Not rigged; tandem tube flies
Tube: 1/8" O.D. NyLaflo High Pressure tubing; 1/8" I.D. PVC tubing glued to hard tubing
Thread: White
Tail: Marabou, white, red; Hackle, white, red; Witchcraft Witchhair mini-fish, red
Head: 5-minute epoxy; red top
Foam Head: Edgewater white foam; silver glitter line; top painted red
Eyes: Rear, 15mm oval doll eyes, black on white; front, plastic black on amber
Variations: Optional split shot in foam head; Blue Mackerel, Dorado, Green Mackerel, Mullet, Pink Squid
TIED BY CAM SIGLER/OFFSHORE ANGLERS

BIG GAME TUBE FLY (BLUE MACKEREL)—Cam Sigler

Hook: Not rigged; tandem tube flies
Tube: 1/8" O.D. NyLaflo High Pressure tubing; 1/8" I.D. PVC tubing glued to hard tubing
Thread: White
Tail: Marabou, white, blue; Hackle, white, blue; Witchcraft Witchhair mini-fish, blue
Head: 5-minute epoxy; blue top
Foam Head: Edgewater white foam; silver glitter line; top painted blue
Eyes: Rear, 15mm oval doll eyes, black on white; front, plastic black on amber
Variations: Optional split shot in foam

head; Blood Squid, Dorado, Green Mackerel, Mullet, Pink Squid
TIED BY CAM SIGLER/OFFSHORE ANGLERS

BIG GAME TUBE FLY (DORADO)—CAM SIGLER

Hook: Not rigged; tandem tube flies
Tube: 1/8" O.D. NyLaflo High Pressure tubing; 1/8" I.D. PVC tubing glued to hard tubing
Thread: White
Tail: Marabou, green, yellow, blue; Hackle, green, yellow, blue; Witchcraft Witchhair mini-fish, yellow
Head: 5-minute epoxy; blue top
Foam Head: Edgewater yellow foam; silver glitter line; top painted blue
Eyes: Rear, 15mm oval doll eyes, black on white; front, plastic black on amber
Variations: Optional split shot in foam head; Blue Mackerel, Blood Squid, Green Mackerel, Mullet, Pink Squid
TIED BY CAM SIGLER/OFFSHORE ANGLERS

BIG GAME TUBE FLY (GREEN MACKEREL)—Cam Sigler

Hook: Not rigged; tandem tube flies
Tube: 1/8" O.D. NyLaflo High Pressure tubing; 1/8" I.D. PVC tubing glued to hard tubing
Thread: White
Tail: Marabou, white, green; Hackle, white, green; Witchcraft Witchhair mini-fish, green
Head: 5-minute epoxy; green top
Foam Head: Edgewater white foam; silver glitter line; top painted green
Eyes: Rear, 15mm oval doll eyes, black on white; front, plastic black on amber
Variations: Optional split shot in foam head; Blood Squid, Dorado, Blue Mackerel, Mullet, Pink Squid
TIED BY CAM SIGLER/OFFSHORE ANGLERS

BIG GAME TUBE FLY (MULLET)—Cam Sigler

Hook: Not rigged; tandem tube flies
Tube: 1/8" O.D. NyLaflo High Pressure tubing; 1/8" I.D. PVC tubing glued to hard tubing
Thread: White
Tail: Marabou, white, black; Hackle, white, black; Witchcraft Witchhair mini-fish, silver
Head: 5-minute epoxy; black top
Foam Head: Edgewater white foam; silver glitter line; top painted black
Eyes: Rear, 15mm oval doll eyes, black on white; front, plastic black on amber
Variations: Optional split shot in foam head; Blue Mackerel, Dorado, Green Mackerel, Blood Squid, Pink Squid
TIED BY CAM SIGLER/OFFSHORE ANGLERS

SALTWATER FLIES

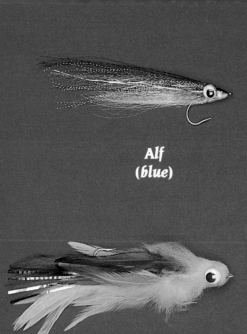

Alf
(blue)

Big Game Tube Fly
(dorado)

BBB
(Bill's bonza baitfish)

Baby Doll-Rado

Big Game Tube Fly
(green mackerel)

Baby Dorado

Big Game Tube Fly
(blood squid)

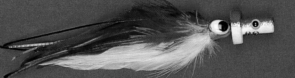

Baleo
(bleeding cut bait)

Big Game Tube Fly
(mullet)

Baleo-Wahoo
(red)

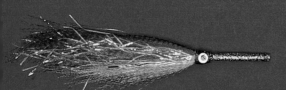

Big Game Tube Fly
(blue mackerel)

BIG GAME TUBE FLY (PINK SQUID)— Cam Sigler

Hook: Rigged tandem tube flies; Owner SSW 5/0-6/0
Tube: 1/8" O.D. NyLaflo High Pressure tubing; 1/8" I.D. PVC tubing glued to hard tubing
Thread: White
Tail: Marabou, white, pink; Hackle, white, pink; Witchcraft Witchhair mini-fish, silver
Head: 5-minute epoxy; pink top
Foam Head: Edgewater white foam; silver glitter line; top painted pink
Eyes: Rear, 15mm oval doll eyes, black on white; front, plastic black on amber
Variations: Optional split shot in foam head; Blue Mackerel, Dorado, Green Mackerel, Blood Squid, Mullet
TIED BY CAM SIGLER/OFFSHORE ANGLERS

BIG WALLY—Pete Parker

Hook: Mustad 34007 or Eagle Claw 8/0
Thread: Dynacord or Kevlar
Body: Silver Mylar braid
Lateral: Holographic tape or silver Mylar
Wing: Super Hair, white, polar bear, smoke, gray, chartreuse, green chartreuse, olive, fluorescent bright green
Gills: Super Hair, red
Glitter Head: Thread covered with hot glue, silver glitter; marker pens or lacquer for top; 5-minute epoxy
Eyes: 10mm doll eyes or decal
TIED BY PETE PARKER

BILLFISH FLY—John Barr

Hook: Mustad 3407, size 7/0, opened slightly; rear hook Mustad 9175; 80-pound Mason hard mono
Thread: White
Tail: White bucktail
Wing: White schlappen; Flashabou, pearl, silver
Collar: White bucktail
Cheeks: Red marabou
Topping: Krystal Flash, light blue, dark blue
Eyes: Doll eyes
TIED BY JOHN BARR

BILLFISH STREAKER

Hook: Mustad 34007/34011; Tiemco 800S/811S, size 3/0 and larger, stinger hook loop optional
Thread: 3/0 monocord or uni-thread
Tail: Bucktail; Flashabou, Crystal Hair to match mid-wing
Body: Braided tinsel or wool yarn with wide tinsel rib
Flash: Flashabou or Crystal Hair tied in beneath hook
Underwing: Bucktail; select colors to match bait fish being imitated

Midwing: Bucktail; select colors to match bait fish being imitated
Overwing: Peacock sword
Head: Overlay thread with micro tinsel
Eyes: Large doll eyes, round or oval
Finish: Devcon 5-minute epoxy
TIED BY RON AYOTTE

BUTORAC'S PIPELINE SPECIAL— Joe Butorac

Hook: Mustad 34007/3407; Daiichi 2546; Tiemco 811S; various sizes
Tube: 1/8" diameter hard plastic tube 3" long inserted 1/4" into a 1" long piece of 1/8" diameter soft plastic tubing
Wing: 6 yellow hackles on each side; 6 green on top
Sides: Unravelled pearl Mylar piping
Head: Thread under epoxy; green and yellow permanent markers
Eyes: Painted, black on yellow
Variations: All white, pink/white, green/white, red/white, red/pink, blue/pink
TIED BY JOE BUTORAC

BUTORAC'S POP-EYE POPPER— Joe Butorac

Hook: Mustad 34007/3407; Daiichi 2546; Tiemco 811S; various sizes
Tube: 1/8" diameter hard plastic tube 3" long inserted 1/4" into a 1" long piece of 1/8" diameter soft plastic tubing
Wing: 6 white hackles on each side; 6 blue on top
Sides: Unravelled pearl Mylar piping
Head: Closed cell foam glued to hard tube with Aquaseal, painted to match hackles
Eyes: Solid plastic, black on yellow
Variations: All white, pink/white, green/white, red/white, green/yellow, red/pink, blue/pink
TIED BY JOE BUTORAC

BUTORAC'S SAILFISH SPECIAL— Joe Butorac

Hook: Mustad 34007, 5/0 front; 4/0 back; tied tandem on 100 pound mono or nylon coated wire
Thread: White size A rod winding thread
Tail: Back hook; white bucktail
Lower Wing: 20 White saddle hackles
Upper Wing: 8 Blue saddle hackles
Sides: Unravelled large pearl Mylar piping
Head: Thread colored with blue permanent marker; epoxy
Eyes: Painted, black on yellow
Popper Head: Closed cell foam 7/8" diameter, 1 1/2" long; 1/8" diameter plastic tube
Variations: All white, pink/white, green/white, red/white, green/yellow, red/pink, blue/pink
TIED BY JOE BUTORAC

CATHERWOOD'S FLYING SQUID (PINK)—Bill Catherwood

Hook: Tandem
Thread: Pink
Tentacles: Hackle, pink, variant
Head: Brown hen body feather
Eyes: Hen body feather, black on white
Body: Pink deer hair
Mantle: Scottish Black Face sheep hair, pink
Fins: Square tipped turkey clipped flat, pink
Variations: White, rusty
TIED BY BILL CATHERWOOD

CATHERWOOD'S TINKER MACKEREL—Bill Catherwood

Hook: Tiemco 811S
Tail: Hackle, green, blue, grizzly; marabou, white
Body: Deer hair, blue, green
Body HACKLE: Blue deer hair
Eyes: Plastic, black on amber
TIED BY UMPQUA FEATHER MERCHANTS/ HUNTERS ANGLING SUPPLIES

COMBS' SEA HABIT, 4-5" (ANCHOVY)—Trey Combs

Hook: Tube type
Thread: White
Body: Plastic tube
Wing: Ocean Hair, white, green, blue; Krystal Flash, silver, yellow, rainbow
Head: Epoxy over pearl Mylar tubing; top, green permanent marker
Eyes: Adhesive, black on silver
Variations: Ballyhoo, flying fish, sardine
TIED BY UMPQUA FEATHER MERCHANTS

COMBS' SEA HABIT, 6-7" (GREEN MACHINE)—Trey Combs

Hook: Tube type
Body: Plastic tube; green foam
Wing: Hackle, white, green, blue; Crystal Flash, blue; pearl Flashabou
Eyes: Adhesive, black on silver
Variations: Pink squid
TIED BY UMPQUA FEATHER MERCHANTS

CURCIONE'S BIG GAME FLY— Nick Curcione

Hook: Tandem
Thread: White
Tail: Hackle, white, blue; Fish Hair, white; Flashabou, blue, gold
Eyes: Doll eyes, black on yellow
Head: Epoxy over thread
TIED BY ORVIS

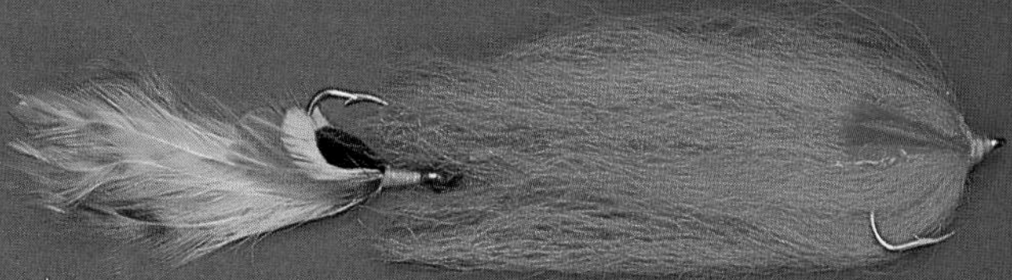

**Catherwood's Flying Squid
(pink)**

**Big Game Tube Fly
(pink squid)**

Catherwood's Tinker Mackerel

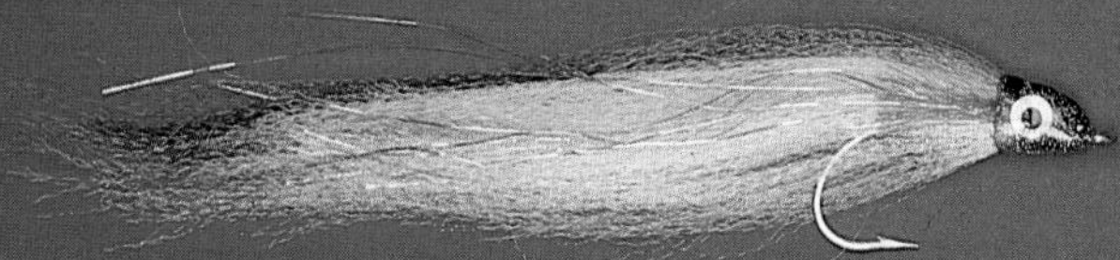

Big Wally

Butorac's Pipeline Special

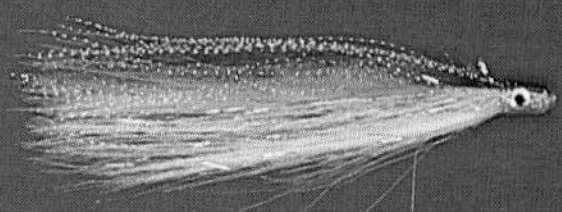

**Combs' Sea Habit, 4-5"
(anchovy)**

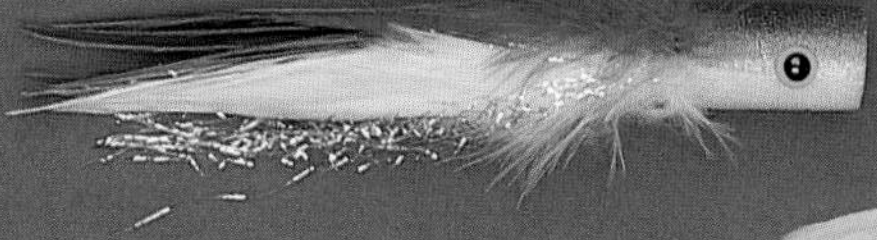

Butorac's Pop-Eye Popper

Billfish Fly

**Combs' Sea Habit, 6-7"
(green machine)**

Butorac's Sailfish Special

Billfish Streaker

Curcione's Big Game Fly

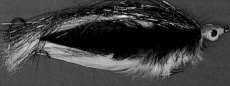

DEEPSALT BUCKTAIL (LT BLUE/DARK BLUE)—Bighorn Fly Trading

Hook: Gamakatsu O'Shaunessey Siwash 1/0-5/0
Tail: Bucktail, white
Body: Pearl braid
Underwing: Bucktail, white
Wing: Bucktail, light blue, dark blue; pearl Flashabou; peacock
Gills: Red yarn
Head: Blue Krystal Flash; pearl braid; epoxy
Eyes: Adhesive, black on silver
Variations: White, chartreuse/blue
TIED BY BIGHORN FLY TRADING

DEEPSALT CRYSTAL BAITFISH (PURPLE/BLACK)—Bighorn Fly Trading

Hook: Gamakatsu O'Shaunessey Siwash 1/0-5/0
Tail: Bucktail, white
Body: Blue pearl braid
Underwing: Bucktail, white
Wing: Bucktail, white; silver Krystal Flash; Ultra Hair, purple, black; peacock
Gills: Red yarn
Head: Blue braid; epoxy
Eyes: Adhesive, black on silver
Variations: Blue, chartreuse/blue, pink/black
TIED BY BIGHORN FLY TRADING

DEEPSALT DECEIVER (CHARTREUSE)—Bighorn Fly Trading

Hook: Gamakatsu O'Shaunessey Siwash 1/0-5/0
Thread: Chartreuse
Tail: Chartreuse hackle
Body: Chartreuse pearl braid
Collar: Bucktail, chartreuse
Wing: Chartreuse Fire Fly; peacock
Head: Thread; epoxy
Eyes: Adhesive, black on chartreuse
Variations: White/blue, white, white/chartreuse, white/red, yellow/red, yellow/green
TIED BY BIGHORN FLY TRADING

DEEPSALT MAD FLASHER (GREEN/BLUE)—Bighorn Fly Trading

Hook: Gamakatsu O'Shaunessey Siwash 2-3/0
Tail: Bucktail, white
Body: Silver braid
Underwing: Bucktail, white
Wing: Bucktail, white; silver Flashabou; Krystal Flash, silver, peacock, dark blue; peacock herl
Gills: Red marabou
Head: Blue Krystal Flash; silver braid; epoxy
Eyes: Adhesive, black on silver
Variations: White/blue
TIED BY BIGHORN FLY TRADING

DEEPSALT SQUID (PINK)—Bighorn Fly Trading

Hook: Tandem Gamakatsu O'Shaunessey Siwash 3/0-5/0
Tail: Hackle, grizzly, white; Krystal Flash, pearl, pink; white marabou
Body: Pearl Mylar tubing
Collar: White Polar Hair; pink FisHair
Wing: FisHair, white, pink
Eyes: Plastic, oval black on yellow
TIED BY BIGHORN FLY TRADING

#EL SQUID—Mark Petrie

Hook: Tandem, 5/0 cadium, 100-pound mono snell
Thread: Red
Tail: Saddle hackle, white; pearl Crystal Flash
Body: White chenille
Body HACKLE: White marabou
Eyes: 12mm doll eyes
TIED BY MARK PETRIE/SALTWATER SPECIALTIES

GRAY'S OFFSHORE POPPER (DORADO, GREEN/YELLOW)—Lance Gray

Tail: Hackle, yellow, chartreuse, chartreuse grizzly; frayed pearl Mylar tubing
Body: Plastic tube; 1" foam, green top, yellow bottom; epoxy face
Eyes: Moveable doll eyes, black on yellow
Variations: White/blue, white/pink, white
TIED BY RIVERBORN FLY COMPANY/THE FLY SHOP

GRAY'S OFFSHORE POPPER (WHITE/PINK)—Lance Gray

Tail: Hackle, hot pink, white, grizzly; frayed pearl Mylar tubing
Body: Plastic tube; 1" foam, hot pink top, white bottom; epoxy face
Eyes: Moveable doll eyes, black on yellow
Variations: White/blue, yellow/green, white
TIED BY RIVERBORN FLY COMPANY/THE FLY SHOP

GREG'S BILLFISH FLY—Greg Miheve

Hook: Mustad 3407SS (SUPER STRONG), sizes 3/0-6/0; Tandem, 100-pound mono
Thread: White flat waxed nylon; Kevlar; super glue or epoxy
Tail: FisHair or substitute, blue, white; blue hackle; saltwater Flashabou, blue, silver
Body HACKLE: Hackle or schlappen, blue, blue grizzly; saltwater Flashabou, blue
Gills: Red tinsel or Flashabou
Beak: Pearl Flashabou; epoxy
Eyes: 10 or 12mm doll eyes
Variations: Green/yellow, green/white, orange/purple, purple/blue, blue/black, red/white, red/yellow
TIED BY GREG MIHEVE

HBL (HUGE BUT LIGHT) BLUEWATER SQUID—Terry Baird

Hook: Tandem Gamakatsu O'Shaunessey Short Shank 8/0
Thread: White, flat waxed nylon
Tail: Hackle, grizzly, white; Krystal Flash, pearl, pink; white marabou
Body: Rolled Shimmerskin, pearl; plastic tube; surgical tubing; 80-pound cable
Finlet: Rolled Shimmerskin, pearl
Wing: FisHair, pink; pink Krystal Flash
Eyes: Adhesive black on silver
TIED BY TERRY BAIRD/BIGHORN FLY TRADING

LANCE'S OFFSHORE POPPER (WHITE/BLUE)—Lance Gray

Tail: Hackle, blue, white, blue grizzly; frayed pearl Mylar tubing
Body: Plastic tube; 3/4" foam, dark blue top, white bottom; epoxy face
Eyes: Moveable doll eyes, black on yellow
Variations: White/pink, yellow/green, white
TIED BY LANCE GRAY/RIVERBORN FLY COMPANY

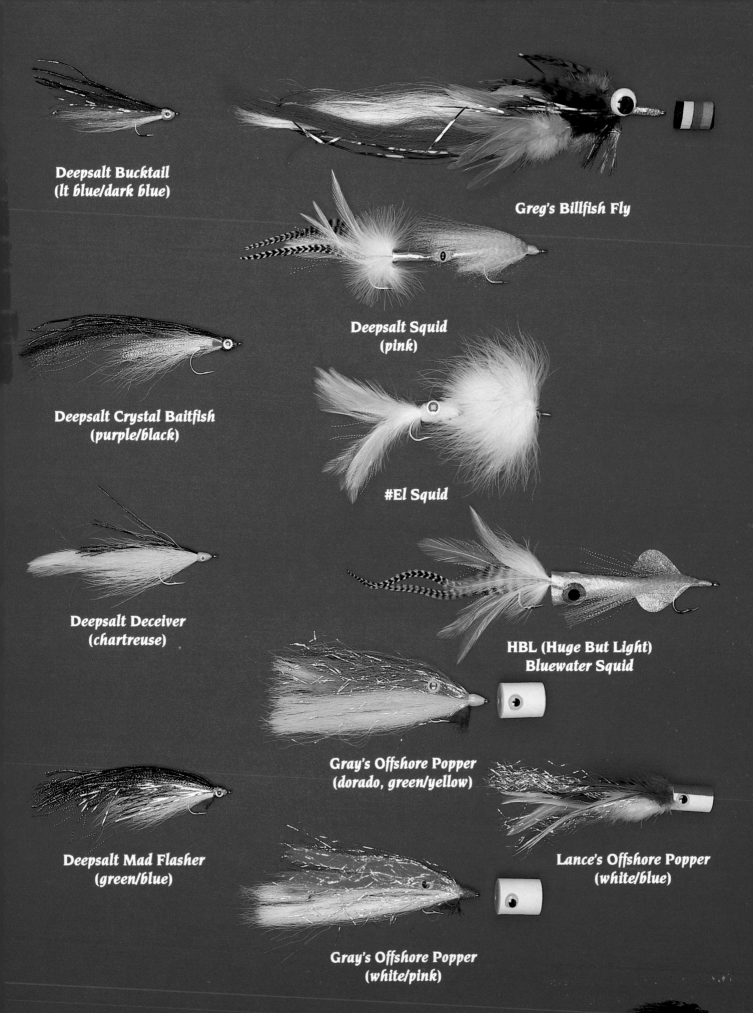

Deepsalt Bucktail
(lt blue/dark blue)

Greg's Billfish Fly

Deepsalt Squid
(pink)

Deepsalt Crystal Baitfish
(purple/black)

#El Squid

Deepsalt Deceiver
(chartreuse)

HBL (Huge But Light)
Bluewater Squid

Gray's Offshore Popper
(dorado, green/yellow)

Deepsalt Mad Flasher
(green/blue)

Lance's Offshore Popper
(white/blue)

Gray's Offshore Popper
(white/pink)

LANCE'S OFFSHORE POPPER (DORADO, GREEN/YELLOW)—Lance Gray

Tail: Hackle, yellow, chartreuse, chartreuse grizzly; frayed pearl Mylar tubing
Body: Plastic tube; 1" foam, green top, yellow bottom; epoxy face
Eyes: Moveable doll eyes, black on yellow
Variations: White/blue, white/pink, white
TIED BY RIVERBORN FLY COMPANY/THE FLY SHOP

LANCE'S OFFSHORE POPPER (WHITE/PINK)—Lance Gray

Tail: Hackle, hot pink, white, grizzly; frayed pearl Mylar tubing
Body: Plastic tube; 1" foam, hot pink top, white bottom; epoxy face
Eyes: Moveable doll eyes, black on yellow
Variations: White/blue, yellow/green, white
TIED BY RIVERBORN FLY COMPANY/THE FLY SHOP

MASTER BLASTER FLAT (WHITE)— Edgewater

Hook: Mustad 34007, tandem
Tail: Saddle hackle, white; breast feathers, white; Flashabou, pearl; Krystal Flash, pearl
Body: Foam, white
Eyes: Black on yellow post
Variations: Chartreuse, blue, yellow, black, purple
TIED BY EDGEWATER

MASTER BLASTER MYLAR (RED)— Edgewater

Hook: Mustad 34007, tandem
Tail: Saddle hackle, red; breast hackle, red; Flashabou, pearl; Krystal Flash, pearl; witch hair, red
Body: Foam; witch tape, red
Eyes: Black on silver
Variations: Light blue, silver, electric blue, chartreuse, green, pearlescent, translucent, peacock black, electric blue/light blue skirt, silver swirl, light blue/electric blue skirt, red/orange skirt, chartreuse/green skirt, green/chartreuse skirt, pink
TIED BY EDGEWATER

MASTER JACK FLAT (WHITE)— Edgewater

Hook: Mustad 34007, tandem
Tail: Saddle hackle, white; breast feathers, white; Flashabou, pearl; Krystal Flash, pearl
Body: Foam, white
Eyes: Black on yellow post
Variations: Chartreuse, blue, yellow, black, purple
TIED BY EDGEWATER

MASTER JACK MYLAR (GREEN)— Edgewater

Hook: Mustad 34007, tandem
Tail: Saddle hackle, chartreuse; breast hackle, white; Flashabou, pearl; Krystal Flash, pearl; witch hair, green
Body: Foam; witch tape, green
Eyes: Black on silver
Variations: Light blue, silver, electric blue, chartreuse, pearlescent, translucent, peacock black, electric blue/light blue skirt, silver swirl, light blue/electric blue skirt, red/orange skirt, chartreuse/green skirt, green/chartreuse skirt, pink
TIED BY EDGEWATER

MOFFO CHARTREUSE & YELLOW BIG BOY—Lenny Moffo

Hook: Mustad 34007/3407; Daiichi 2546; Tiemco 811S, tandem
Tail: Fish hair, yellow; Flashabou, pearl
Body: Wool, chartreuse
Wing: Fish hair, yellow, chartreuse; Flashabou, pearl
Eyes: Black on yellow
Variations: Blue & Pink
TIED BY MCKENZIE FLY TACKLE

MYLAR TUBING MINNOW—Pete Parker

Hook: Tiemco 811S; 2/0, 3/0
Thread: 3/0 Dynacord
Wing: Pearl Mylar tubing; top colored with blue or green permanent marker
Gills: Red permanent marker
Glitter Head: Thread covered with hot glue, silver glitter; marker pens or lacquer for top; 5-minute epoxy
Eyes: Decal
TIED BY PETE PARKER

PETE'S ANCHOVIE—Pete Parker

Hook: Tiemco 811S; Eagle Claw D067F; 3/0, 4/0
Thread: 3/0 Dynacord
Wing: Super Hair, white, smoke, lime green, olive, blue, black; Fire Fly, copper, green; Flashabou, peacock
Gills: Red Super Hair
Glitter Head: Thread covered with hot glue, silver glitter; marker pens or lacquer for top; 5-minute epoxy
Eyes: 10mm doll eyes or decal
Markings: Black permanent maker, dots on white wing
TIED BY PETE PARKER

PETE'S CHOVIE—Pete Parker

Hook: Tiemco 800S; 2/0, 3/0
Thrad: 3/0 Dynacord
Wing: Super Hair, white, smoke, chartreuse, olive; Flashabou, peacock
Gills: Red Super Hair, beard style
Glitter Head: Thread covered with hot glue, silver glitter; marker pens or lacquer for top; 5-minute epoxy
Eyes: 7mm plastic

Markings: Black permanent marker, irregular, on white wing
TIED BY PETE PARKER

PETE'S MACKEREL—Pete Parker

Hook: Tiemco 811S; Eagle Claw D067F; 3/0, 4/0
Thread: 3/0 Dynacord
Wing: Super Hair, white, smoke, olive; Flashabou, peacock
Gills: Super Hair, red
Eyes: 8mm doll eyes
Glitter Head: Thread covered with hot glue, silver glitter; marker pens or lacquer for top; 5-minute epoxy
Markings: Black permanent marker, irregular, on back
TIED BY PETE PARKER

PETE'S SLIDER—Pete Parker

Hook: Eagle Claw 66S; 4/0
Thread: 3/0 Dynacord
Tail: Super Hair, chartreuse, olive; Flashabou, peacock
Body: 1/2 inch poly foam caulk saver; Mylar tubing; Soft Body Epoxy
Body HACKLE: Green spike or Cactus Chenille
Eyes: Decal
Glitter Head: Thread covered with hot glue, silver glitter; marker pens or lacquer for top; Soft Body Epoxy
TIED BY PETE PARKER

RON'S BILLFISH FLY (BLUE)— Ron Ayotte

Hook: Mustad 34007/34011; Tiemco 800S/811S, size 3/0 and larger, stinger hook loop optional
Thread: 3/0 monocord or uni-thread
Wing: FisHair, Flashabou, Crystal Hair; select and layer colors to match bait fish being imitated
Topping: Peacock herl
Cheek/Throat: Red calf tail or marabou
Head: Overlay thread with micro tinsel or braided tinsel
Eyes: Large doll eyes, round or oval
Finish: Devcon 5-minute epoxy
TIED BY RON AYOTTE

RON'S BILLFISH FLY (BLUE/GREEN)— Ron Ayotte

Hook: Mustad 34007/34011; Tiemco 800S/811S, size 3/0 and larger, stinger hook loop optional
Thread: 3/0 monocord or uni-thread
Wing: FisHair, Flashabou, Crystal Hair; select and layer colors to match bait fish being imitated
Topping: Peacock herl
Cheek/Throat: Red calf tail or marabou
Head: Overlay thread with micro tinsel or braided tinsel
Eyes: Large doll eyes, round or oval
Finish: Devcon 5-minute epoxy
TIED BY RON AYOTTE

Lance's Offshore Popper
(dorado, green/yellow)

Master Jack Mylar
(green)

Pete's Mackerel

Lance's Offshore Popper
(white/pink)

Moffo Chartreuse & Yellow Big Boy

Pete's Slider

Master Blaster Flat
(white)

Mylar Tubing Minnow

Master Blaster Mylar
(red)

Ron's Billfish Fly
(blue)

Pete's Anchovie

Master Jack Flat
(white)

Pete's Chovie

Ron's Billfish Fly
(blue/green)

RON'S BILLFISH FLY (ORANGE)—
Ron Ayotte
Hook: Mustad 34007/34011; Tiemco 800S/811S, size 3/0 and larger, stinger hook loop optional
Thread: 3/0 monocord or uni-thread
Wing: FisHair, Flashabou, Crystal Hair; select and layer colors to match bait fish being imitated
Topping: Peacock herl
Cheek/Throat: Red calf tail or marabou
Head: Overlay thread with micro tinsel or braided tinsel
Eyes: Large doll eyes, round or oval
Finish: Devcon 5-minute epoxy
TIED BY RON AYOTTE

SAMSON'S BALEO—Jack Samson
Hook: Tandem, behind foam with plastic tube insert
Thread: Black
Tag: White chenille
Tail: Bucktail, white, tan; hackle, white, black, grizzly, dun
Wing: Bucktail, white, tan; hackle, white, black, grizzly, dun; silver Flashabou
Cheeks: White hackle
Head: Epoxy over thread, glitter
Eyes: Painted black on yellow
TIED BY JACK SAMSON

SAMSON'S BONITO—Jack Samson
Hook: Tandem, behind foam with plastic tube insert
Thread: Black
Tag: White chenille
Tail: Silver Flashabou; hackle, white, olive grizzly, dun, light blue
Body: White chenille
Wing: Hackle, white, black, light blue, dun; silver Flashabou; peacock herl; white marabou
Cheeks: White hackle
Gills: Red marabou
Head: Epoxy over thread, glitter
Eyes: Painted black on yellow
TIED BY JACK SAMSON

SAMSON'S DORADO—Jack Samson
Hook: Tandem, behind foam with plastic tube insert
Thread: Black
Tag: White chenille
Tail: Flashabou, gold, light blue; hackle, white, light blue, yellow, black; white marabou
Body: White chenille
Wing: Flashabou, gold, light blue; hackle, white, light blue, yellow, black; white marabou; peacock herl
Cheeks: Golden pheasant tippet
Gills: Red marabou
Head: Epoxy over thread, glitter
TIED BY JACK SAMSON

SAMSON'S GREEN MACKEREL—
Jack Samson
Hook: Tandem, behind foam with plastic tube insert
Thread: Black
Tag: White chenille
Tail: Flashabou, gold, blue; hackle, white, black, grizzly, pale olive grizzly; white marabou
Wing: Flashabou, gold, blue; hackle, white, black, grizzly, pale olive grizzly; white marabou; peacock herl
Cheeks: White hackle
Head: Epoxy over thread, glitter
TIED BY JACK SAMSON

SAMSON'S MULLET—Jack Samson
Hook: Tandem, behind foam with plastic tube insert
Thread: Black
Tag: White chenille
Tail: White marabou; hackle, white, black, grizzly
Body: White chenille
Wing: White marabou; hackle, white, black, grizzly, dun; silver Flashabou
Head: Epoxy over thread, glitter
Eyes: Painted black on yellow
TIED BY JACK SAMSON

SUBSALT BAITFISH TANDEM (WHITE/BLUE)—Bighorn Fly Trading
Hook: Tandem Gamakatsu O'Shaunessey Siwash 3/0-8/0
Tail: Trailer: FisHair, white, blue, clipped to tail shape; white bucktail
Body: Clear Larva Lace over white thread
Wing: Craft fur, white, light blue; FisHair, dark blue; dark blue bucktail; silver Flashabou
Head: Blue pearl braid; epoxy
Eyes: Plastic, oval black on silver
Variations: White/chartreuse
TIED BY BIGHORN FLY TRADING

SUBSALT BAITFISH TANDEM (WHITE/CHARTREUSE)—
Bighorn Fly Trading
Hook: Tandem Gamakatsu O'Shaunessey Siwash 3/0-8/0
Tail: Trailer: FisHair, white, chartreuse, clipped to tail shape; white bucktail
Body: Clear Larva Lace over white thread
Wing: Craft fur, chartreuse; FisHair, chartreuse; chartreuse bucktail; chartreuse pearl Fire Flash
Head: Chartreuse pearl braid; epoxy
Eyes: Adhesive black on silver
Variations: White/blue
TIED BY BIGHORN FLY TRADING

THREE EYED JACK (BLUE/PURPLE)—
C.E. Mullin
Hook: None, tube fly
Thread: Dressmakers with sparkle
Tail: FisHair, blue, purple
Body: Pipet tube; micro centrifuge tube
Head: Tulip Sparkle Paint Writer
Eyes: Three moveable doll eyes, black in white
Variations: Blue, white, orange
TIED BY CASTLE ARMS

THREE EYED JACK (ORANGE)—
C.E. Mullin
Hook: None, tube fly
Thread: Dressmakers with sparkle
Tail: Orange FisHair
Body: Pipet tube; micro centrifuge tube
Head: Tulip Sparkle Paint Writer
Eyes: Three moveable doll eyes, black in white
Variations: Blue, white, blue/purple
TIED BY CASTLE ARMS

THREE EYED JACK (WHITE)—C.E. Mullin
Hook: None, tube fly
Thread: Dressmakers with sparkle
Tail: White FisHair; pearl Krystal Flash; white Sevenstrand luminous skirt
Body: Pipet tube; micro centrifuge tube
Head: Tulip Sparkle Paint Writer
Eyes: Three moveable doll eyes, black in white
Variations: Blue, blue/purple, orange
TIED BY CASTLE ARMS

SALTWATER FLIES

Ron's Billfish Fly (orange)

Three Eyed Jack (orange)

Samson's Green Mackerel

Samson's Baleo

Three Eyed Jack (white)

Samson's Mullet

Samson's Bonito

Subsalt Baitfish Tandem (white/blue)

Subsalt Baitfish Tandem (white/Chartreuse)

Samson's Dorado

Three Eyed Jack (blue/purple)

INSHORE FLIES

GUIDO RAHR

ABEL ANCHOVY—Steve Abel

Hook: Mustad 7692/34007/3407; Daiichi 2546; Tiemco 811S; sizes 1/0-4/0
Thread: Size A black or chartreuse
Body: Silver or pearl Diamond Braid
Collar: White bucktail, FisHair or Polar Hair
Wing: Blue on green on white; bucktail, FisHair or Polar Hair
Topping: Silver, pearl Flashabou; peacock herl
Beard: Red Flashabou, Crystal Hair or Krystal Flash
Eyes: 5 or 6mm paper or doll eyes, black on white
Head: Hot glue (Thermogrip Glue Gun); Jolly Glaze or clear nail polish
Variations: Wahoo Fly or Tarpon Fly
TIED BY STEVE ABEL

ABEL ANCHOVY (WAHOO FLY)—Steve Abel

Hook: Mustad 34011; sizes 3/0-5/0
Thread: Size A chartreuse
Body: Mylar tubing over Krystal Flash
Tail: Krystal Flash, pearl, chartreuse, olive, blue, black; Mylar tubing strands
Beard: Red Flashabou, Crystal Hair or Krystal Flash
Eyes: Large doll eyes, black on white
Head: Hot glue (Thermogrip Glue Gun); Jolly Glaze or clear nail polish
Variations: Tarpon Fly
TIED BY STEVE ABEL

ABEL ANCHOVY (Turrall)—Steve Abel

Hook: Mustad 34007/3407; Daiichi 2546; Tiemco 811S
Thread: Black
Wing: Bucktail, white, chartreuse, blue; peacock herl; pearl Flashabou
Front Hackle: Orange Krystal Flash
Head: Black thread
Eyes: Painted black on white
TIED BY TURRALL

AGENT BONEFISH

Hook: Mustad 34007/3407; Daiichi 2546; Tiemco 811S
Thread: Fluorescent red
Body: Orange chenille
Wing: Orange Fish Hair; grizzly hackle
TIED BY ROGER HEMION/HUNTERS ANGLING SUPPLIES

A.J.'S SAND EEL—A.J. Hand

Hook: Mustad 34011, 34007/3407; Daiichi 2546; Tiemco 811S
Thread: White
Tail: Craft fur, white, lavender, olive, tan; Krystal Flash, pearl
Body: Tail materials; pearl Mylar, epoxy
Eyes: Bead chain painted black
TIED BY MYSTIC BAY FLIES

AL'S STRIPERCEIVER—Al Bovyn

Hook: Mustad 34007/3407; Daiichi 2546; Tiemco 811S
Thread: Chartreuse
Tail: White bucktail; chartreuse hackle; pearl Flashabou; lime Krystal Flash
Body: Pearl glitter tape or diamond braid
Wing: Yellow bucktail
Throat: Red Krystal Flash
Eyes: Adhesive black on silver; epoxy
TIED BY AL BOVYN/AMERICAN ANGLING SUPPLIES

BAITFISH FLY (EMERALD/PEARL)—Dave Whitlock

Hook: Tiemco 811S size 1/0
Thread: White
Wing: Hackle, green grizzly; white marabou; Flashabou, green, pearl
Hackle: Green grizzly; Flashabou, green, pearl
Cheeks: Red Flashabou
Head: Hot glue
Eyes: Plastic black on white
Weedguard: Mono loop
Variations: Blue/pearl, chartreuse/pearl, olive/pearl
TIED BY UMPQUA FEATHER MERCHANTS

BANANA SUNDAY (YELLOW)—Moana

Hook: Tiemco 811S, size 4-6
Thread: Yellow
Tail: Pearl Flashabou
Body: Yellow chenille
Wing: White calf tail; pearl Flashabou
Eyes: Silver bead chain
TIED BY UMPQUA FEATHER MERCHANTS

BARE BLUEFISH (YELLOW)—C. Boyd Pfeiffer

Hook: Eagle Claw 66SS, straightened; Mustad 34011
Thread: Yellow
Tail: Yellow bucktail
Body: none
Variations: White, blue, pink, green, black
TIED BY C. BOYD PFEIFFER

BARKER CRAB—Jeff Barker

Hook: Mustad 34007; Tiemco 800S; size 2
Body: Lamb's wool, creme to light gray
Shell/Legs/Pincers: Thin chamois, light gray or dirt tan; permanent markers
Eyes: Plastic black
Weight: Non-toxic Brite Eyes
TIED BY JEFF BARKER/ANGLERS WORKSHOP

BARR'S CRAB—John Barr

Hook: Tiemco 811S, sizes 4-2/0
Tail: Tan marabou; rainbow Krystal Flash
Body: Deer hair; blue, brown permanent marker; white Plasti-Dip
Legs: Single strand live rubber, white; black permanent marker
Eyes: 30-pound mono; red glass bead

Weight: Lead eyes
TIED BY JOHN BARR

BAYSALT CORBINA CRAB—Bighorn Fly Trading

Hook: Gamakatsu, size 2-4
Thread: White
Tail: White hackle tips
Body: White chenille
Shellback: White sparkle yarn
Body Hackle: White sili legs
Underwing: White sparkle yarn
Eyes: Black plastic bead chain
TIED BY BIGHORN FLY TRADING

BC TOO APTE TOO PLUS—Stu Aapte

Hook: Mustad 34007/3407; Daiichi 2546; Tiemco 811S
Thread: Red
Tail: Yellow rabbit; yellow Crystal Hair
Body: Thread
Body Hackle: Orange fox squirrel tail
Head: Epoxy over thread
Eyes: Painted black on yellow
Weedguard: Anti-foul mono rear loop
TIED BY MCKENZIE FLY TACKLE

BENDBACK (BLUE/WHITE)

Hook: Mustad 34007, size 2/0
Thread: Black
Body: White chenille
Wing: Bucktail, white, blue; blue Crystal Flash; peacock herl; grizzly hackle
TIED BY ELIOT NELSON/ANGLERS WORKSHOP

BENDBACK (CHARTREUSE)

Hook: Mustad 34011, size 2-4/0
Hook option: Tiemco 411S Bendback hook
Body: Pearl Cloissone Braid
Wing: Bucktail, chartreuse; Flashabou, pearl; peacock herl
Head: Thread, fluorescent red, chartreuse
Eyes: Painted, black on yellow
Variations: white, green/white, blue/white, yellow, red/white, red/yellow, orange/yellow, orange/red, purple, and black. Miheve's Bendback Rattler includes a Venom Mfg. rattle bead in body.
TIED BY GREG MIHEVE

BENDBACK (ORANGE/RED)

Hook: Mustad 34011, size 2-4/0
Hook option: Tiemco 411S Bendback hook
Body: Pearl Cloissone Braid
Wing: Bucktail, orange over yellow, yellow Krystal Flash in between
Head: Thread, fluorescent red, yellow
Eyes: Painted, black pupil on yellow
Variations: white, green/white, blue/white, yellow, red/white, red/yellow, orange/yellow, chartreuse, purple, and black. Miheve's Bendback Rattler includes a Venom Mfg. rattle bead in body.
TIED BY GREG MIHEVE

Al's Striperceiver

Baysalt Corbina Crab

Abel Anchovy

BC Too Apte Too Plus

Baitfish Fly
(emerald/pearl)

Abel Anchovy
(wahoo fly)

Banana Sunday
(yellow)

Bendback
(blue/white)

Abel Anchovy

Bare Bluefish
(yellow)

Agent Bonefish

Barker Crab

Bendback
(chartreuse)

A.J.'s Sand Eel

Barr's Crab

Bendback
(orange/red)

BENDBACK (WHITE/GREEN)— Chico Fernandez

Hook: Tiemco 411S Bendback hook, size 2/0
Thread: Black
Body: White chenille
Wing: Bucktail, white, green; grizzly hackle; Flashabou, pearl, silver; peacock herl
Gills: Red thread
Eyes: Painted black on white
Variations: White/blue, yellow
TIED BY UMPQUA FEATHER MERCHANTS/THE FLY SHOP

BIG EYE GHOST— Joe Calcavecchia

Hook: Mustad 34007/3407; Daiichi 2546; Tiemco 811S
Thread: Red
Tail: Grizzly hackle; pearl Krystal Flash
Body: Pearlescent glitter tape or diamond braid
Wing: Gray bucktail; peacock
Bottom Wing: White bucktail
Throat: Red calf tail
Cheeks: Mallard flank feather or silver pheasant breast feather
Eyes: Adhesive, black on silver
TIED BY JOE CALCAVECCHIA/AMERICAN ANGLING SUPPLIES

BIG FISH FLY (WHITE/BLUE)— Chico Fernandez

Hook: Tiemco 811S; size 4/0
Thread: White
Tail: White FisHair
Body: Thread
Wing: FisHair, white, blue; Flashabou, blue, silver
Variations: White/green/blue
TIED BY UMPQUA FEATHER MERCHANTS

BLACK AND BLUE

Hook: Mustad 34007, size 2/0
Thread: Black
Tail: Blue grizzly; blue Fire Flash
Body: Blue Mylar tubing
Front Hackle: Black bucktail
TIED BY ELIOT NELSON/CUSTOM TIED FLIES

BLACK DEATH

Hook: Mustad 34007/3407; Daiichi 2546; Tiemco 811S; sizes 2/0-3/0
Thread: Red
Tail: Black hackle
Body Hackle: Red marabou
Head: Thread under epoxy
Eyes: Painted black on yellow
TIED BY JOE BRANHAM/THE FLY SHOP

BLIND CHARLIE (GOLD)

Hook: Mustad 34007/3407; Daiichi 2546; Tiemco 811S
Thread: White

Tail: Flashabou, pearl
Body: Flat gold tinsel; clear V-rib
Wing: Light variant hackle tips
Variations: Pink, silver
TIED BY THE FLY SHOP

BLIND CHARLIE (PINK)

Hook: Mustad 34007/3407; Daiichi 2546; Tiemco 811S
Thread: White
Tail: Krystal Flash, pink
Body: Krystal Flash, pink; clear mono
Wing: Light variant hackle tips; pink Krystal Flash
Variations: Gold, silver
TIED BY THE FLY SHOP

BLIND CHARLIE (SILVER)

Hook: Mustad 34007/3407; Daiichi 2546; Tiemco 811S
Thread: White
Tail: Krystal Flash, pearl
Body: Flat silver tinsel; clear V-rib
Wing: White hackle tips; pearl Crystal Flash
Variations: Gold, pink
TIED BY THE FLY SHOP

BLONDE, ARGENTINE (TURRALL)— Joe Brooks

Hook: Mustad 34007/3407; Daiichi 2546; Tiemco 811S
Thread: Black
Tail: White bucktail
Body: Silver tinsel
Wing: Blue bucktail; Christmas tree Flashabou
TIED BY TURRALL

BLONDE, IRISH (TURRALL)—Joe Brooks

Hook: Mustad 34007/3407; Daiichi 2546; Tiemco 811S
Thread: Black
Tail: White bucktail
Body: Silver tinsel
Wing: Green bucktail; green Flashabou
TIED BY TURRALL

BLUE RUNNER OFFSHORE FLY— Jon Olch

Hook: Mustad 34007/3407; Daiichi 2546; Tiemco 811S
Thread: Blue
Tail: Streamer Hair, white
Body: Silver braid
Beard: Streamer Hair, blue
Wing: Streamer Hair, blue; silver Flashabou
Eyes: Painted black on yellow
TIED BY JON OLCH

BOB'S SMELT—Bob Nauheim

Hook: Mustad 34007/3407; Daiichi 2546; Tiemco 811S; sizes 1-3/0
Thread: Olive
Tail: White bucktail; white hackle; pearl

pink Flashabou
Body: Silver braid tinsel
Beard: Red hackle
Wing: White bucktail; peacock herl
Cheeks: Wood duck, mallard, or widgeon breast feathers; pearl pink Flashabou
TIED BY BOB NAUHEIM

BOILERMAKER (YELLOW)—Edgewater

Hook: Mustad 34011 1/0, 3/0; Mustad 9082S 2/0
Tail: Bucktail, red; bucktail, yellow; Krystal Flash, pearl
Body: Foam, yellow
Eyes: Black on yellow post
Variations: Black, chartreuse, peppermint, white/red tail, blue, white purple.
TIED BY EDGEWATER

BONE APPETIT—Ellen Reed

Hook: Mustad 34007/3407; Daiichi 2546; Tiemco 811S
Thread: Tan
Tail: Dark brown grizzly; gold Crystal Flash; tan marabou; orange bucktail
Body: Tan Sparkle Chenille
Body Hackle: Dark brown
Wing: Dark brown grizzly hackle; tan marabou
Eyes: Smallest (4/32) lead/bronze
Weedguard: Single strand monofilament
TIED BY ELLEN REED

BONEFISH BUGGER (PINK/WHITE)— Chico Fernandez

Hook: Tiemco 411S size 4
Tail: Grizzly hackle; white marabou
Body: Pink chenille
Body Hackle: Grizzly
Wing: Pink Krystal Flash; black Ultra Hair
Eyes: Nickel-plated lead
Variations: Tan/orange
TIED BY UMPQUA FEATHER MERCHANTS

BONEFISH CLOUSER (CHARTREUSE)— Bob Clouser

Hook: Mustad 34007/3407; Daiichi 2546; Tiemco 811S; sizes 2-6
Wing: Bucktail, chartreuse, white; rainbow Krystal Flash
Eyes: Lead eyes painted black on red
Variations: Pink, tan
AVAILABLE THROUGH THE FLY SHOP

BONEFISH CLOUSER (PINK)— Bob Clouser

Hook: Mustad 34007/3407; Daiichi 2546; Tiemco 811S; sizes 2-6
Wing: Bucktail, pink, white; rainbow Krystal Flash
Eyes: Lead eyes painted black on red
Variations: Pink, tan
AVAILABLE THROUGH THE FLY SHOP

SALTWATER FLIES

Bendback
(white/green)

Blind Charlie
(pink)

Blind Charlie
(silver)

Boilermaker
(yellow)

Big Eye Ghost

Blonde, Argentine

Bone Appetit

Big Fish Fly
(white/blue)

Bonefish Bugger
(pink/white)

Black and Blue

Blonde, Irish

Bonefish Clouser
(chartreuse)

Blue Runner Offshore Fly

Black Death

Blind Charlie
(gold)

Bob's Smelt

Bonefish Clouser
(pink)

BONEFISH CRITTER—Tim Borski

Hook: Mustad 34007 size 1-4
Tail: Eye stalks—burnt mono
Body: Hot orange Crystal Chenille; tan wool; Pantone marker #147-M
Body Hackle: Wide, palmered grizzly or cree or badger
Eyes: Lead, varied
Weed Guard: 15 or 20-pound Mason hard mono
TIED BY TIM BORSKI

BONEFISH CRITTER (PEARL)—Edgewater

Hook: Mustad 34007
Thread: White
Tail: Rubber legs, white
Body: Tubing wrapped, pearl
Eyes: Bead eyes
Variations: Chartreuse, pearl/brown tail, pink.
TIED BY EDGEWATER

BONEFISH JOE—Les Fulcher

Hook: Mustad 3407, size 2-6
Tail: Tan or grizzly hackle
Body: Brown, gray or tan deer hair
Wing: Deer hair
Mouth Parts: White marabou; pink vernille
Head: Dumbbell weight; chenille, variegated, tan, orange
Weedguard: Two single strand mono
TIED BY LES FULCHER

BONEFISH SLIDER—Tim Borski

Hook: Tiemco 811S/411S; sizes 2-4
Tail: Hot orange Krystal Flash; tan craft fur; brown permanent marker (Pantone 147-M)
Body: Natural tan deer hair
Body Hackle: Grizzly, trimmed on bottom
Wing: Natural tan deer hair
Head: Natural tan deer hair; brown permanent marker (Pantone 147-M)
Eyes: Lead eyes painted black on yellow
Weedguard: 15 OR 20-pound hard Mason, single strand
TIED BY UMPQUA FEATHER MERCHANTS/THE FLY SHOP

BONEFISH SOFT Hackle (CHARTREUSE)—Craig Mathews

Hook: Mustad 3407; Daiichi 2546; Tiemco 800S; sizes 4-10
Thread: 3/0 white monocord
Body: Chenille, chartreuse
Wing: Deer hair
Front Hackle: Sharptail grouse
Variations: Tan, white, olive; underwire .020
TIED BY CRAIG MATHEWS/BLUE RIBBON FLIES

BONEFISH SPECIAL—Chico Fernandez

Hook: Mustad 34007/3407; Daiichi 2546; Tiemco 811S; size 4-6

Thread: Black
Tail: Hot orange marabou
Body: Gold tinsel; clear mono
Wing: Grizzly hackle tips; white bucktail or calf tail
TIED BY UMPQUA FEATHER MERCHANTS/THE FLY SHOP

BONEFISH, SURFACE SHRIMP (Turrall)

Hook: Mustad 34007/3407; Daiichi 2546; Tiemco 811S
Thread: White
Body: Tan yarn
Wing: Bucktail, tan and brown; pearl Krystal Flash
Eyes: Painted white on black
TIED BY TURRALL

BONITO DUSTER—Tom Kintz

Hook: Tiemco 811S, size 4
Thread: White size A flat nylon
Tail: White marabou; Flashabou, blue, green, gold
Body: Pearl Mylar braid; 20-pound green mono
Gills: Red permanent marker (Sharpie)
Eyes: Adhesive black on silver
TIED BY TOM KINTZ

BOTTOM FEEDER (LIME/WHITE)—Greg Miheve

Hook: Mustad 34011, hook bent, sizes 4-1/0
Thread: 3/0 monocord, white
Tail: White bucktail, silver Flashabou
Body: Silver tinsel
Gills: Fluorescent red or fire orange chenille or flat waxed nylon
Wing: Bucktail, lime, white; pearl Krystal Flash
Eyes: Nickel-plated lead, painted black
Variations: Peacock/white, green/white, blue/white, orange/yellow, chartreuse, purple/white, brown/orange; peacock herl over any color combination
TIED BY GREG MIHEVE

BOTTOM FEEDER (PEACOCK/WHITE)—Greg Miheve

Hook: Mustad 34011, hook bent, sizes 4-1/0
Thread: 3/0 monocord, white
Tail: White bucktail, silver Flashabou
Body: Silver tinsel
Gills: Fluorescent red or fire orange chenille or flat waxed thread
Wing: Bucktail, white; Flashabou, silver; pea   cock herl
Head: Thread, top painted dark green
Eyes: Nickel-plated lead, painted black
Variations: Lime/white, green/white, blue/white, orange/yellow, chartreuse, purple/white, brown/orange; peacock herl over any color combination
TIED BY GREG MIHEVE

BOUFACE (RED/WHITE)—John Barr

Hook: Tiemco 811S, sizes 4-3/0
Thread: White
Tail: Rabbit strip, white; Flashabou, pearl, red
Body: Thread, white
Collar: Marabou, red
Variations: Yellow, chartreuse, orange, etc.
TIED BY JOHN BARR

BOZO BAIT—Tom Kintz

Hook: Tiemco 811S, size 4/0
Thread: White size A flat nylon
Body: Silver Mylar braid
Wing/Throat: White Bozo Hair
Toppings: Bozo Hair, chartreuse, blue; Flashabou, blue, green, gold
Head: Epoxy
Eyes: 12mm doll eyes black on white
TIED BY TOM KINTZ

BRAIDED BARRACUDA FLY (ORANGE)—Chico Fernandez

Hook: Long shank size 2/0
Thread: Orange
Tail: Braided orange nylon
Head: Epoxy over thread
Eyes: Painted black on white
Variations: White/green, fluorescent green
TIED BY UMPQUA FEATHER MERCHANTS

BRANHAM'S REDFISH SHRIMP—Joe Branham

Hook: Mustad 34011; size 1/0
Thread: Brown
Tail: Brown bucktail; Krystal Flash, black, pearl
Body: Brown chenille
Body Hackle: Brown
Shellback: Brown bucktail; silicone
Eyes: Black plastic
Weight: Lead barbell
Weed Guard: Two single strand mono
TIED BY JOE BRANHAM/THE FLY SHOP

BRANHAM'S TIGHT-LIPPED DARTER (BROWN)—Joe Branham

Hook: Mustad 34007/3407; Daiichi 2546; Tiemco 811S; size 1/0
Thread: Brown
Tail: Brown bucktail;
Body Hackle: Red marabou; brown deer hair
Throat: Red Krystal Flash
Wing: Pearl Krystal Flash; peacock herl
Head: Brown deer hair
Eyes: Doll eyes, moveable, black on white
Lip: Brown deer hair; silicone
Variations: Gray
TIED BY JOE BRANHAM/THE FLY SHOP

SALTWATER FLIES

Bonefish Critter

Bonefish, Surface Shrimp

Bouface
(red/white)

Bonefish Critter
(pearl)

Bozo Bait

Bonefish Joe

Braided Barracuda Fly
(orange)

Bonito Duster

Bonefish Slider

Bottom Feeder
(lime/white)

Branham's Redfish Shrimp

Bonefish Soft Hackle
(chartreuse)

Bonefish Special

Bottom Feeder
(peacock/white)

Branham's Tight-Lipped Darter
(brown)

BRANHAM'S TIGHT-LIPPED DARTER (GRAY)—Joe Branham

Hook: Mustad 34007/3407; Daiichi 2546; Tiemco 811S; size 1/0
Thread: White
Tail: White bucktail;
Body Hackle: Marabou, white, gray
Throat: Red Krystal Flash
Wing: Pearl Krystal Flash; gray bucktail; deer hair; peacock herl
Head: Deer hair, white, gray
Eyes: Doll eyes, moveable, black on white
Lip: White deer hair; silicone
Variations: Brown
TIED BY JOE BRANHAM/THE FLY SHOP

BREAKER BUSTER—John Shewey

Hook: Mustad 34007/3407; Daiichi 2546; Tiemco 811S; size 1/0-1
Thread: Red
Tail: Yellow marabou; orange Krystal Flash
Body Hackle: Red marabou
Collar: Yellow marabou
Eyes: Medium nickel plate lead eyes
Variations: Substitute red Krystal Flash
TIED BY JIM SYNDER

BUCKTAIL BAITFISH—Ron Ayotte

Hook: Mustad 34007/34011/92608, sizes 4/0-6
Wing: Bucktail of one or more colors, white bucktail; Crystal Hair
Head: Overwrap with micro tinsel
Eyes: Prism
Finish: Devcon 5-minute epoxy
TIED BY RON AYOTTE

BUCKTAIL BAITFISH DOUBLE— Ron Ayotte

Hook: Bend Mustad 34011 or 92608 into keel hook, sizes 4/0-6
Wing: Bucktail of one or more colors, white bucktail; Crystal Hair
Head: Overwrap with micro tinsel
Eyes: Prism
Finish: Devcon 5-minute epoxy
TIED BY RON AYOTTE

BUCKTAIL SNOOKER—Ron Ayotte

Hook: Mustad 34007; Tiemco 811S/800S, sizes 4/0-2
Thread: 3/0 green monocord
Tail: Bucktail, blue, green, white; Flashabou or Crystal Hair
Topping: Peacock herl
Throat: Red bucktail or marabou
Head: Overlaid with green micro tinsel
Eyes: Medium doll eyes, black on yellow
TIED BY RON AYOTTE

BUNNY BLENNIE (CHARTREUSE)— John Shewey

Hook: Rubber Worm hook with wire weed guard; sizes 1/0-4/0; Optional: Mustad 34007/3407; Daiichi 2546; Tiemco 811S
Thread: Red
Tail: Rabbit strip, chartreuse

Body Hackle: Rabbit strip, chartreuse
Legs: Rubber legs, chartreuse
Eyes: Lead eyes, painted red on white
Variations: White, orange, yellow; black has white or yellow rabbit strip glued hide-to-hide on tail
TIED BY JIM SYNDER

BUNNY FLY— Mark Lewchik/Gary Steinmiller

Hook: Mustad 34007/3407; Daiichi 2546; Tiemco 811S
Thread: White
Tail: White hackle; pearl Krystal Flash
Body: Rabbit strip
Wing: Pearl Krystal Flash
Eyes: Nickel-plated lead
TIED BY MARK LEWCHIK/RIVERS END TACKLE CO

BURK'S DEEP H2O BONE— Andy Burk

Hook: Mustad 34007/3407; Daiichi 2546; Tiemco 811S; size 2
Tail: Hot orange marabou
Body: Pearl green Flashabou; V-rib, clear
Wing: Marabou, hot orange, brown; cree or variant hackle; pearl Krystal Flash
Eyes: Lead painted black on yellow; epoxy
TIED BY ANDY BURK/THE FLY SHOP

BURSEL CRAB (B.C.)—Joe Bursel

Hook: Mustad 34007/3407; Daiichi 2546; Tiemco 811S
Pincers: Fox squirrel
Body: Deer hair or elk hair
Eyes: Lead
TIED BY JOE BURSEL

BURSEL TRANSLUCENT MINNOW (B.T.M.)—Joe Bursel

Hook: Mustad 34007/3407; Daiichi 2546; Tiemco 811S
Bottom Wing: Polar bear Ultra Hair
Lateral Line: Pearl Krystal Flash
Top Wing: Smoke Ultra Hair
Eyes: Lead
TIED BY JOE BURSEL

CALAMARI (CHARTREUSE)— Bill & Kate Howe

Hook: Long shank 1/0
Thread: Chartreuse
Tail: Bucktail, chartreuse; hackle, chartreuse; sili legs, chartreuse; Fire Fly, green, gold; Lite Brite, chartreuse
Body Hackle: Rabbit fur strip, chartreuse
Front Hackle: Rubber strands, chartreuse
Eyes: Plastic, black on amber
Head: Thread; glitter; epoxy
Variations: Hot Pink, tan, light purple
TIED BY BILL & KATE HOWE/THE FLY SHOP

CALAMARI (HOT PINK)— Bill & Kate Howe

Hook: Long shank 1/0

Thread: Hot pink
Tail: Bucktail, hot pink; hackle, hot pink, white; sili legs, hot pink, white; Flashabou, pink; Lite Brite, pink
Body Hackle: Rabbit fur strip, hot pink
Front Hackle: Rubber strands, hot pink
Eyes: Plastic, black on amber
Head: Thread; glitter; epoxy
Variations: Chartreuse, tan, light purple
TIED BY BILL & KATE HOWE/THE FLY SHOP

CALAMARI (TAN)—Bill & Kate Howe

Hook: Long shank 1/0
Thread: Black
Tail: Bucktail, tan; hackle, furnace; sili legs, tan, red; Fire Flash, copper; Lite Brite, copper
Body Hackle: Rabbit fur strip, tan
Front Hackle: Rubber strands, red, brown
Eyes: Plastic, black on amber
Head: Thread; glitter; epoxy
Variations: Chartreuse, hot pink, light purple
TIED BY BILL & KATE HOWE/THE FLY SHOP

CALAMARI EXPRESS—Art Scheck

Hook: Mustad 3407 or Eagle Claw 254, size 5/0
Thread: 3/0 monocord for rear of fly; Danville flat waxed nylon or Dynacord for deer hair head
Tail: Pearl Krystal Flash
Body: Marabou or craft fur, white, tan, pink, orange
Tentacles: White, grizzly hackle
Collar: Deer hair, white, natural
Eyes: Plastic doll eyes or adhesive prismatic on stainless steel leader wire, epoxy
Head: Deer hair trimmed to arrowhead shape
TIED BY ART SCHECK

CANARD CRAB—Terry Baird

Hook: Gamakatsu, sizes 4-8
Body: Flashabou, pearl
Weight: Nickel-plated lead
Body Hackle:
Wing: Red fox squirrel split wing; calf tail, white, orange
Front Hackle: Red sili legs
Eyes: Black plastic bead chain on stalks
TIED BY TERRY BAIRD/BIGHORN FLY TRADING

CANDY EEL (BROWN)—Bob Popovics

Hook: Mustad 34007/3407; Daiichi 2546; Tiemco 811S; size 1/0
Tail: Ultra Hair, white, brown; saltwater pearl Flashabou
Body: Epoxy over tail materials
Eyes: Adhesive black on silver
Variations: Olive
TIED BY UMPQUA FEATHER MER-CHANTS

SALTWATER FLIES

Branham's Tight-Lipped Darter (gray)

Bunny Fly

Burk's Deep H2O Bone

Bursel Crab (B.C.)

Calamari (tan)

Breaker Buster

Calamari Express

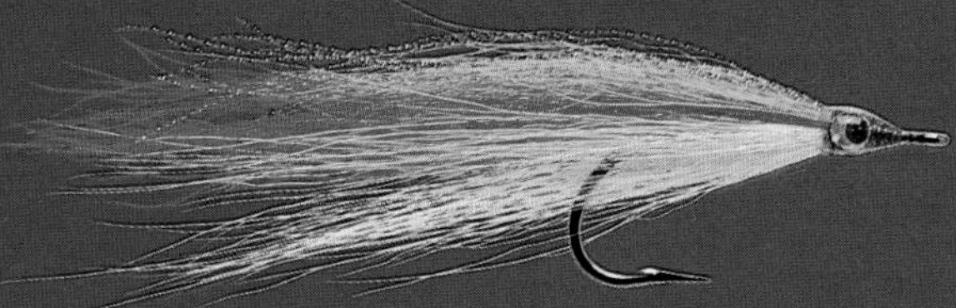

Bucktail Baitfish

Bursel Translucent Minnow (B.T.M.)

Bucktail Baitfish Double

Calamari (chartreuse)

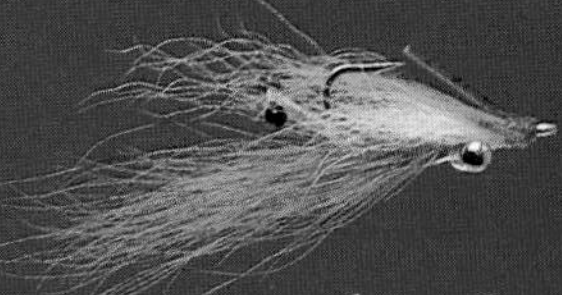

Canard Crab

Bucktail Snooker

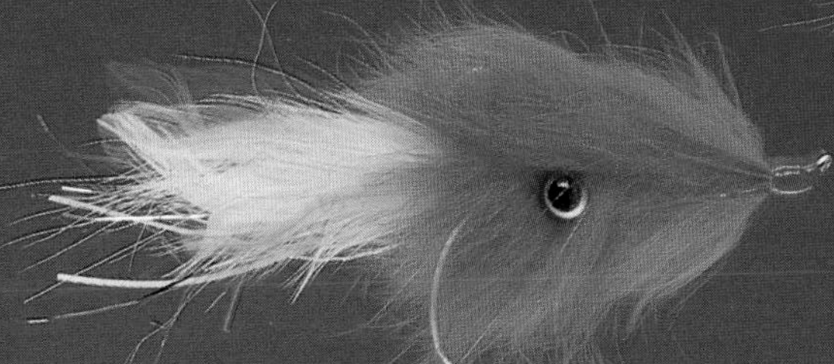

Calamari (hot pink)

Bunny Blennie (chartreuse)

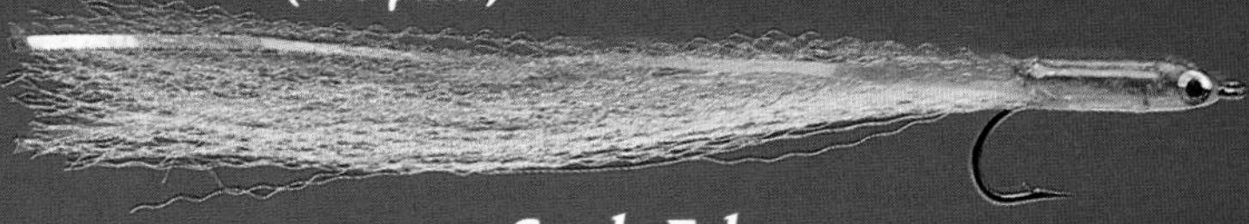

Candy Eel (brown)

CATHERWOOD'S AMERICAN EEL—
Bill Catherwood
Hook: Mustad 34007/3407; Daiichi 2546;
Tiemco 811S
Belly: Olive marabou
Wing: Hackle, black, blue grizzly, olive
drab
Head: Black deer hair
Eyes: Glass, tied in, black on amber
TIED BY BILL CATHERWOOD

CHAPPY FERRY (RED/WHITE)—
Jeremy Ehn
Hook: Mustad 34007/3407; Daiichi 2546;
Tiemco 811S
Tail: White hackle
Body: Deer hair, white, red; epoxy
Body Hackle: White deer hair
Eyes: Adhesive, black on silver
Variations: Chartreuse, optic orange
TIED BY JEREMY EHN/ORVIS TYSONS
CORNER

CHARBLUE REDFISH—Dan Johnson
Hook: Mustad 34007; sizes 1/0-4
Thread: Chartreuse
Body: Estaz, blue-green #30
Wing: Chartreuse marabou; chartreuse
Krystal Flash; blue grizzly
TIED BY DAN JOHNSON/THE FLY FISH-
ERMAN

CHARLIE'S ANGEL (JOHNNY GLENN &
JAIME BOYLE)—Charlie Finnerty
Hook: Mustad 34007, size 2
Thread: White flat waxed nylon
Tail: Continuation of body
Body: Polar bear Super Hair; rainbow
Krystal Flash; green Super Hair;
silicone; pearl Mylar
Gills: Red permanent marker
Eyes: Adhesive, black on silver
TIED BY JOHNNY GLENN/ORVIS NEW
YORK

CHERNOBYL CRAB—Tim Borski
Hook: Mustad 34007; Tiemco 811S; 1/0-2
Tail: Hot orange Krystal Flash; white calf
tail; grizzly hackle
Body: Spun deer hair
Body Hackle: Wide hackle palmered,
grizzly or cree or badger
Eyes: Lead, painted black on yellow on
black
Weed Guard: 15 or 20-pound Mason hard
mono
TIED BY TIM BORSKI/UMPQUA FEATHER
MERCHANTS

CHRIS' ELECTRIC BILL —Chris Mihulka
Hook: Mustad 34007/3407; Eagle Claw
L067M Billy Pate
Thread: Black
Tail: White arctic fox tail
Body: Pearlescent tubing
Wing: Green Icelandic goat; peacock

sword; pearlescent Mylar strips
Head: Epoxy over black thread
Eyes: Black on yellow
TIED BY MCKENZIE FLY TACKLE

CHRIS' GREEN/WHITE
BUNNY NEEDLEFISH—Chris Mihulka
Hook: Mustad 34007/3407; Eagle Claw
L067M Billy Pate
Thread: Chartreuse
Tail: Rabbit strips, white, chartreuse,
glued hide to hide
Body: Epoxy over chartreuse thread
Eyes: Black on yellow
TIED BY MCKENZIE FLY TACKLE

CHRIS' GRAY BIGFISH—Chris Mihulka
Hook: Mustad 92618 size 6/0
Thread: Black
Tail: Gray rabbit strips glued hide to hide
Body: Gray rabbit
Eyes: Black on white doll eyes
Variations: Purple, chartreuse, white,
black.
TIED BY MCKENZIE FLY TACKLE

CHROME SLIDER—Mark Lewchik
Hook: Tiemco 511S
Tail: Bucktail, white, green; silver
Flashabou
Body: Balsa; prismatic tape, green/silver;
shrink tubing
Gills: Painted
Eyes: Adhesive, black on red
TIED BY MARK LEWCHIK/RIVERS END
TACKLE CO

CHUM FLY #1—C. Boyd Pfeiffer
Hook: Mustad 34011
Tail: Cross cut rabbit strip
Body: Pom-Pom or other acrylic yarn ball,
with or without glitter
Variations: Colors that imitate ground
chum
TIED BY C. BOYD PFEIFFER

CHUM FLY #2—C. Boyd Pfeiffer
Hook: Mustad 34011
Tail: Rabbit strip
Body: Pom-Pom or other acrylic yarn ball,
with or without glitter
Wing: Rabbit strip, continuation of tail
Variations: Colors that imitate ground
chum
TIED BY C. BOYD PFEIFFER

CLAM BEFORE THE STORM—
Craig Mathews
Hook: Mustad 3407; Daiichi 2546; Tiemco
800S; sizes 4-8
Thread: 3/0 white monocord
Tail: Pink vernille
Body: Lead wire; white furry foam
Variations: Cream, tan, light olive
TIED BY CRAIG MATHEWS/BLUE RIB-
BON FLIES

CLARET BUMBLE (IRISH SEA TROUT)—
Peter Masters
Hook: Wet fly size 8
Thread: Black
Tail: Golden pheasant tippet
Body: Claret seal fur
Rib: Copper wire
Body Hackle: Claret cock
Front Hackle: Blue jay
TIED BY PETER MASTERS, ENGLAND

CLAYHILL CRAB (MIDNITE BLACK)—
Denton Hill
Hook: Mustad 3407 size 2
Thread: Danville Flymaster 6/0 color to
match
Tail: Krystal Flash, red; marabou, red;
grizzly hackle, red
Body: Clayhill material, black
Eyes: Mono eyes, white or plastic stems,
black on white
Variations: Belize green, black, chocolate,
dace tan, gray
TIED BY LANCE GRAY/RIVERBORN FLY
COMPANY

CLOUSER DEEP MINNOW
(DARRYL STEEL)—Bob Clouster
Hook: Mustad 34007/3407; Daiichi 2546;
Tiemco 811S; sizes 4-6/0
Thread: Matches top colour of wing
Wing: Bucktail, white, pink; pearl Krystal
Flash
Eyes: Nickel-plated lead eyes; prismatic
gold on red
Variations: Chartreuse, orange, green,
blue, black; weedguard, double
strands 40-pound mono
TIED BY DARRYL STEEL, AUSTRALIA

CLOUSER'S DEEP MINNOW (BLACK)—
Bob Clouster
Hook: Mustad 34007/3407; Daiichi 2546;
Tiemco 811S; sizes 6-2/0
Thread: Black
Wing: Bucktail, black; green Krystal Flash
Eyes: Lead eyes painted black on red
Variations: Red/white, chartreuse/white,
chartreuse/yellow, golden shiner,
sculpin, silver shiner
TIED BY UMPQUA FEATHER MER-
CHANTS

CLOUSER'S DEEP MINNOW
(RED/WHITE)—Bob Clouser
Hook: Mustad 34007/3407; Daiichi 2546;
Tiemco 811S; sizes 6-2/0
Thread: White
Wing: Bucktail, white, red; pearl Crystal
Flash; pearl Flashabou
Eyes: Lead eyes painted black on red
Variations: Black, chartreuse/white,
chartreuse/yellow, golden shiner,
sculpin, silver shiner
TIED BY UMPQUA FEATHER MER-
CHANTS

SALTWATER FLIES

Catherwood's American Eel

Chris' Green/White Bunny Needlefish

Claret Bumble
(Irish sea trout)

Chris' Gray Bigfish

Chappy Ferry
(red/white)

Clayhill Crab
(midnight black)

Chrome Slider

Charblue Redfish

Clouser Deep Minnow
(Darryl Steel)

Charlie's Angel

Chum Fly #1

Chernobyl Crab

Chum Fly #2

Clouser Deep Minnow
(black)

Chris' Electric Bill

Clam Before The Storm

Clouser Deep Minnow
(red/white)

CLOUSER MINNOW, BLACK
(Turrall)—Bob Clouser
Hook: Mustad 34007/3407; Daiichi 2546; Tiemco 811S
Thread: Black
Tail: Bucktail, white
Body: Thread, white
Wing: Bucktail, black; Krystal Flash, black
Eyes: Lead eyes painted black on white
TIED BY TURRALL

CLOUSER MINNOW, BLUE (Turrall)—
Bob Clouser
Hook: Mustad 34007/3407; Daiichi 2546; Tiemco 811S
Thread: Black
Tail: Bucktail, white
Body: Thread, white
Wing: Bucktail, blue; Krystal Flash, pearl
Eyes: Lead eyes painted black on white
TIED BY TURRALL

CLOUSER MINNOW, CHARTREUSE
(Turrall)—Bob Clouser
Hook: Mustad 34007/3407; Daiichi 2546; Tiemco 811S
Thread: Black
Tail: Bucktail, white
Body: Thread, white
Wing: Bucktail, chartreuse; Krystal Flash, chartreuse
Eyes: Lead eyes painted black on white on black
TIED BY TURRALL

CLOUSER MINNOW,
CHARTREUSE/WHITE (GREG MIHEVE)—
Bob Clouser
Hook: Mustad 34007/3407; Daiichi 2546; Tiemco 811S; sizes 4-5/0
Thread: Chartreuse
Wing: Bucktail, white, chartreuse; chartreuse Krystal Flash
Gills: Fluorescent red thread
Eyes: Non-toxic, black on yellow
Variations: Tan/white, blue/white, black/white, green/white, red/white, pink/white, orange white
TIED BY GREG MIHEVE

CLOUSER MINNOW, TAN/WHITE
(GREG MIHEVE)—Bob Clouser
Hook: Mustad 34007/3407; Daiichi 2546; Tiemco 811S; sizes 4-5/0
Thread: Tan
Wing: Bucktail, white, tan; pearl Krystal Flash
Gills: Fluorescent red thread
Eyes: Non-toxic, black on red
Variations: Chartreuse/white, blue/white, black/white, green/white, red/white, pink/white, orange white
TIED BY GREG MIHEVE

COBIA DIVER— Randy L. Morgan
Hook: Mustad 34007, size 2/0

Tail Support: 25-pound Mason
Tail: Black rabbit strip
Rear Collar: Black rabbit strip
Front Collar: Red deer hair
Head: Red deer hair
TIED BY RANDY L. MORGAN/THE FLY FISHERMAN

COCKROACH—Chico Fernandez
Hook: Mustad 34007/3407; Daiichi 2546; Tiemco 811S; sizes 3/0-4/0
Thread: Black
Tail: Grizzly hackle
Collar: Tan bucktail
Head: Thread under epoxy
Eyes: Painted black on yellow
TIED BY UMPQUA FEATHER MERCHANTS/THE FLY SHOP

COOK'S CRITTER/VANCE'S GRASS
SHRIMP, TAN (GREG MIHEVE)—
Vance Cook
Hook: Mustad 34007/3407; Daiichi 2546; Tiemco 811S; sizes 2-8
Thread: 3/0 Monocord, tan
Tail: Copper Krystal Flash
Body: Tan chenille or yarn
Body Hackle: Tan
Shellback: Pearl Mylar tubing; may use permanent marker
Beard: Tan FisHair, Fish-Fuz, calf tail or squirrel tail
Eyes: Silver bead chain
Variations: White, pink, olive, brown
TIED BY GREG MIHEVE

COPPER LIZ—Liz Steele
Hook: Mustad 34007/3407; Daiichi 2546; Tiemco 811S
Thread: Brown
Body: Brown Antron; copper Lite Brite
Wing: Brown FisHair; copper Lite Brite; pink grizzly
TIED BY LIZ STEELE/THE FLY FISHERMAN

CRAZY CHARLIE (CHARTREUSE)—
Riverborn Fly Company
Hook: Mustad 3407, sizes 4-8
Thread: Danville Flymaster 6/0 #504 and Flymaster Plus 1/0 #1
Body: Silver Mylar tinsel #10; clear Larva Lace
Wing: Krystal Flash lime green #18; chartreuse calf tail
Eyes: Silver bead chain
Variations: Brown, orange, tan, white, yellow
TIED BY LANCE GRAY/RIVERBORN FLY COMPANY

CRAZY CHARLIE (ORANGE)—
Bob Nauheim
Hook: Mustad 34007/3407; Daiichi 2546; Tiemco 811S
Tail: Silver Flashabou
Body: Larva Lace, clear Swannundaze

over silver Mylar
Wing: Orange kip tail
Eyes: Silver bead chain
Variations: Various colors
TIED BY JACKSON CARDINAL FLIES

CRAZY CHARLIE (PINK)—Bob Nauheim
Hook: Mustad 34007/3407; Daiichi 2546; Tiemco 811S; size 4-8
Thread: White
Tail: Krystal Flash, pink
Body: Krystal Flash, pink; V-rib, clear
Wing: Krystal Flash, pink; grizzly hackle
Eyes: Silver bead chain
Variations: White, tan, yellow, brown
TIED BY THE FLY SHOP

CRAZY CHARLIE (YELLOW)—
Bob Nauheim
Hook: Mustad 34007/3407; Daiichi 2546; Tiemco 811S; size 4-8
Thread: White
Tail: Krystal Flash, yellow
Body: Krystal Flash, yellow; V-rib, clear
Wing: Krystal Flash, yellow; yellow grizzly hackle
Eyes: Silver bead chain
Variations: White, tan, pink, brown
TIED BY THE FLY SHOP

CRAZY RED—Jon Olch
Hook: Mustad 34007/3407; Daiichi 2546; Tiemco 811S
Thread: Red
Tail: White leather
Body: Black chenille
Front Hackle: Marabou, white, red; pearl Flashabou
Eyes: Silver bead chain
TIED BY JON OLCH

CRYSTAL CHARLIE (PEARL)—
Riverborn Fly Company
Hook: Mustad 3407, sizes 4-6
Thread: Danville Flymaster 6/0 white and Flymaster Plus 1/0 white
Body: Pearl Mylar; epoxy
Wing: Pearl Krystal Flash; white calf tail; grizzly
Eyes: Silver bead chain
Variations: Belize green, bonefish orange, chartreuse, root beer, shrimp pink, tan, yellow sunrise
TIED BY LANCE GRAY/RIVERBORN FLY COMPANY

CRYSTAL SHRIMP (ORANGE)
Hook: Mustad 3407, sizes 6-8
Thread: Flymaster orange
Body: Orange Krystal Flash; V-rib
Wing: Orange Krystal Flash; orange grizzly
Variations: Belize green, chartreuse, pearl, root beer, sunrise yellow
TIED BY LANCE GRAY/RIVERBORN FLY COMPANY

SALTWATER FLIES

Clouser Minnow, black (Turrall)

Cockroach

Crazy Charlie (pink)

Clouser Minnow, blue (Turrall)

Cook's Critter/Vance's Grass Shrimp, (tan)

Crazy Charlie (yellow)

Clouser Minnow, chartreuse (Turrall)

Clouser Minnow, chartreuse/white

Copper Liz

Crazy Red

Clouser Minnow, tan/white

Crazy Charlie (chartreuse)

Crystal Charlie (pearl)

Cobia Diver

Crazy Charlie (orange)

Crystal Shrimp (orange)

CUDA CATCHER (YELLOW)—
C. Boyd Pfeiffer

Hook: Eagle Claw 254SS; Mustad 34007/3407; Daiichi 2546; Tiemco 811S

Thread: Yellow

Tail: Kreinik braid, yellow

Body: Thread over braid; fingernail polish, enamel or acrylic paint, epoxy

Variations: Chartreuse, green, red, pink, black, white

TIED BY C. BOYD PFEIFFER

CUDA CATCHER TOO (RED)—
C. Boyd Pfeiffer

Hook: Eagle Claw 254SS; Mustad 34007/3407; Daiichi 2546; Tiemco 811S

Thread: Red

Tail: Red synthetic fibers, Ultra Hair, Super Hair, Dynel, etc.

Body: Thread over braid fore and aft; fingernail polish, enamel or acrylic paint, epoxy

Variations: Chartreuse, green, yellow, pink, black, white

TIED BY C. BOYD PFEIFFER

CUDA FLY—John Barr

Hook: Tiemco 811S, size 3/0; rear, size 2/0

Thread: Chartreuse

Tail: Frayed Mylar tubing

Body: Large Mylar tubing; top, green permanent marker

Eyes: Doll eyes

TIED BY JOHN BARR

CUDA FLY (FLUORESCENT GREEN)

Hook: Mustad 34007/3407; Daiichi 2546; Tiemco 811S; Tandem, size 3/0

Thread: Green

Tail: Frayed fluorescent green Everglow tubing

Body: Fluorescent green Everglow tubing

Throat: Red marabou

Head: Thread under epoxy

Eyes: Painted black on yellow

Variations: Flourescent orange

AVAILABLE THROUGH THE FLY SHOP

CUDA FLY (FLUORESCENT ORANGE)

Hook: Mustad 34007/3407; Daiichi 2546; Tiemco 811S; Tandem, size 3/0

Thread: Orange

Tail: Frayed fluorescent orange Everglow tubing

Body: Fluorescent orange Everglow tubing

Throat: Red marabou

Head: Thread under epoxy

Eyes: Painted black on yellow

Variations: Fluorescent green

AVAILABLE THROUGH THE FLY SHOP

CURCIONE'S BEACH BUG—
Nick Curcione

Hook: Mustad 34011, size 2

Thread: White

Body: Green Krystal Flash; epoxy; red chenille

Wing: Chartreuse grizzly; light green Fish Hair; green Flashabou

Eyes: Lead painted black

TIED BY ORVIS

CURCIONE'S SARDINA—Nick Curcione

Hook: Mustad 34011, size 2/0

Thread: White

Wing: Hackle, white, blue; white Fish Hair; pearl Flashabou; pearl Crystal Flash

Eyes: Plastic, black on red

Head: Epoxy over thread

TIED BY ORVIS

CURCIONE'S TUNA TONIC—
Nick Curcione

Hook: Mustad 34007, size 2/0

Thread: White

Body: Gold Mylar; epoxy

Wing: White marabou; pearl Fly Flashabou; light blue Krystal Flash

Eyes: Plastic, black on red

Head: Epoxy over thread

TIED BY ORVIS

DAN'S SHRIMP—Dan Johnson

Hook: Mustad 34011, size 1/0

Thread: Brown

Tail: Cree hackle

Body: Aunt Lydia's orange yarn; copper wire; Swiss Straw, orange; Estaz, orange

Body Hackle: Speckle legs, pumpkinseed

Wing: Orange Swiss Straw

Eyes: 80-pound monofilament

Variations: Olive

TIED BY DAN JOHNSON/THE FLY FISHERMAN

DAN'S SHRIMP (OLIVE)—Dan Johnson

Hook: Mustad 34011, size 1/0

Thread: Brown

Tail: Olive grizzly hackle

Body: Aunt Lydia's olive yarn; copper wire; Swiss Straw, olive; Estaz, olive

Body Hackle: Speckle legs, pumpkinseed

Wing: Olive Swiss Straw

Eyes: 80-pound monofilament

TIED BY DAN JOHNSON/THE FLY FISHERMAN

DECEIVER, BLACK (TURRALL)—
Lefty Kreh

Hook: Mustad 34007/3407; Daiichi 2546; Tiemco 811S

Thread: Black

Wing: Black hackle; black Krystal Flash

Front Hackle: Black marabou

Eyes: Painted red on yellow

TIED BY TURRALL

DECEIVER, BLACK/WHITE
(GREG MIHEVE)—Lefty Kreh

Hook: Mustad 34007/3407; Daiichi 2546; Tiemco 811S; sizes 2-5/0

Thread: 3/0 Monocord, white

Tail: White saddle hackle; silver Flashabou

Body: Silver tinsel

Underwing: White bucktail

Wing: Black bucktail; purple Flashabou

Gills: Fluorescent red thread

Head: Thread, top painted black

Eyes: Painted black on white

Variations: White, peacock/white, blue/white, green/white, red/white, yellow, red/yellow, and chartreuse. Grizzly saddle hackle on side.

TIED BY GREG MIHEVE

DECEIVER, BLUE (MYSTIC BAY)—
Lefty Kreh

Hook: Mustad 34007/3407; Daiichi 2546; Tiemco 811S

Thread: Black

Tail: Saddle hackle, white; Krystal Flash, blue, pearl

Body: Silver tinsel

Wing: Bucktail, white, blue; peacock herl

Gills: Red paint

Head: Black thread

Eyes: Painted, black on white

Variations: Chartreuse, etc.

TIED BY MYSTIC BAY FLIES

DECEIVER, CHARTREUSE
(MYSTIC BAY)—Lefty Kreh

Hook: Mustad 34007/3407; Daiichi 2546; Tiemco 811S

Thread: Black

Tail: Saddle hackle, white; Krystal Flash, chartreuse, pearl

Body: Silver tinsel

Wing: Bucktail, white, chartreuse; peacock herl

Gills: Red paint

Head: Black thread

Eyes: Painted, black on white

Variations: Blue, etc.

TIED BY MYSTIC BAY FLIES

DECEIVER, CHARTREUSE (TURRALL)—
Lefty Kreh

Hook: Mustad 34007/3407; Daiichi 2546; Tiemco 811S

Thread: Red

Wing: Grizzly and white hackle; pearl Krystal Flash

Front Hackle: Chartreuse marabou

Eyes: Painted black on yellow

TIED BY TURRALL

DECEIVER, COCKROACH (TURRALL)—
Lefty Kreh

Hook: Mustad 34007/3407; Daiichi 2546; Tiemco 811S

Thread: Black

Wing: Grizzly hackle; copper Krystal Flash

Front Hackle: Brown marabou

Eyes: Painted red on yellow

TIED BY TURRALL

SALTWATER FLIES

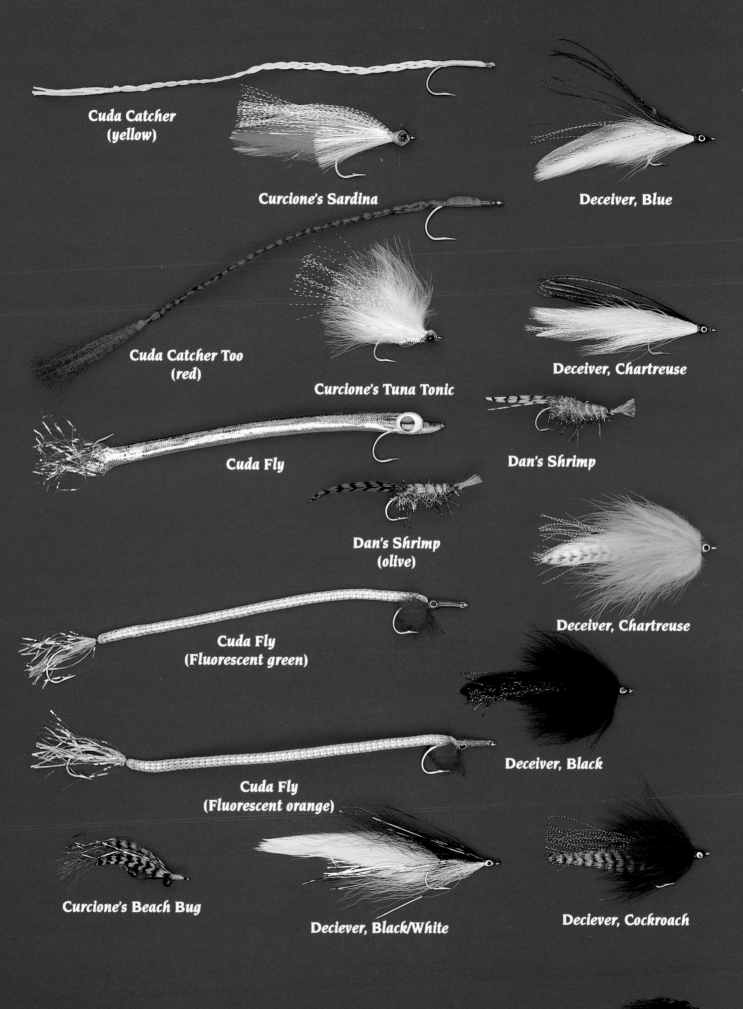

**Cuda Catcher
(yellow)**

Curcione's Sardina

Deceiver, Blue

**Cuda Catcher Too
(red)**

Curcione's Tuna Tonic

Deceiver, Chartreuse

Cuda Fly

Dan's Shrimp

**Dan's Shrimp
(olive)**

**Cuda Fly
(Fluorescent green)**

Deceiver, Chartreuse

Deceiver, Black

**Cuda Fly
(Fluorescent orange)**

Curcione's Beach Bug

Deciever, Black/White

Deciever, Cockroach

DECEIVER, GRIZZLY WHITE (TURRALL)—Lefty Kreh

Hook: Mustad 34007/3407; Daiichi 2546; Tiemco 811S
Thread: Red
Wing: Grizzly and white hackle; pearl Krystal Flash
Front Hackle: White marabou
Eyes: Painted black on yellow
TIED BY TURRALL

DECEIVER, LEFTY'S (RED/WHITE)—Lefty Kreh

Hook: Mustad 34007/3407; Daiichi 2546; Tiemco 811S
Thread: Red
Tail: White hackle
Body: Thread
Collar: White bucktail
Wing: Red bucktail
Eyes: Painted black on white
Variations: Black, cockroach, red/yellow, white, white/blue, white/green, yellow/green
TIED BY UMPQUA FEATHER MERCHANTS

DECEIVER, LEFTY'S (RED/YELLOW)—Lefty Kreh

Hook: Mustad 34007/3407; Daiichi 2546; Tiemco 811S
Thread: Red
Tail: Yellow hackle
Body: Thread
Collar: Yellow bucktail
Wing: Red bucktail
Eyes: Painted black on white
Variations: Black, cockroach, red/white, white, white/blue, white/green, yellow/green
TIED BY UMPQUA FEATHER MERCHANTS

DECEIVER, ORANGE (TURRALL)—Lefty Kreh

Hook: Mustad 34007/3407; Daiichi 2546; Tiemco 811S
Thread: Yellow
Wing: Grizzly and yellow hackle; pearl Krystal Flash
Front Hackle: Hot orange marabou
Eyes: Painted orange on black
TIED BY TURRALL

DECEIVER (WHITE/BLUE)—Riverborn

Hook: Mustad 3407, sizes 4/0-2/0
Thread: Flat waxed white or black, Flymaster 500
Tail: White hackle
Body: Pearl Mylar tubing
Collar: White bucktail
Wing: Pearl Krystal Flash; blue bucktail; blue grizzly; peacock herl
Throat: Red marabou
Head: Black, fluorescent red stripe
Eyes: Painted black/yellow/black
Variations: White/gray, white/green, yellow/green, yellow/red
TIED BY LANCE GRAY/RIVERBORN FLY COMPANY

DECEIVER, WHITE/SILVER (GREG MIHEVE)—Lefty Kreh

Hook: Mustad 34007/3407; Daiichi 2546; Tiemco 811S; sizes 2-5/0
Thread: 3/0 Monocord, white
Tail: White saddle hackle; silver Flashabou
Body: Silver tinsel
Collar: White bucktail
Gills: Fluorescent red thread
Eyes: Painted black on white
Variations: White, peacock/white, blue/white, green/white, red/white, yellow, red/yellow, and chartreuse. Grizzly saddle hackle on side.
TIED BY GREG MIHEVE

DEEP BAITFISH (WEIGHTED, BLUEGILL)—Dave Whitlock

Hook: Tiemco 9394, sizes 2-6
Thread: Yellow
Underwing: Icelandic sheep wool, orange, yellow, red; yellow Krystal Flash
Overwing: Grizzly hackle; Icelandic sheep wool, yellow; yellow Krystal Flash
Eyes: Nickel-plated lead painted black on yellow
Variations: Shad, crappie
TIED BY UMPQUA FEATHER MERCHANTS/THE FLY SHOP

DEEPSALT MINNOW (BLACK)—Bighorn Fly Trading

Hook: Gamakatsu
Thread: Black
Wing: Bucktail, black; pearl Fire Flash
Eyes: Nickel-plated barbell, painted black on red
Variations: Blue, pink
TIED BY BIGHORN FLY TRADING

DEEPSALT MINNOW (BLUE)—Bighorn Fly Trading

Hook: Gamakatsu
Thread: Blue
Wing: Bucktail, blue, white; pearl Fire Flash
Eyes: Nickel-plated barbell, painted black on red
Variations: Black, pink
TIED BY BIGHORN FLY TRADING

DEEPSALT MINNOW (PINK)—Bighorn Fly Trading

Hook: Gamakatsu
Thread: Pink
Wing: Bucktail, pink, white; pearl Fire Flash
Eyes: Nickel-plated barbell, painted black on red
Variations: Black, blue
TIED BY BIGHORN FLY TRADING

DEEP SEA SERPENT (BLACK)—Chris Windram

Hook: Mustad 34007, sizes 4-1/0
Thread: Black nylon
Tail: Rabbit, black

Body: Rabbit, black
Front Hackle: Black
Eyes: Lead, painted black on white
Variations: Chartreuse/white, red/white, red gill/black, red gill/white, white/badger.
TIED BY CHRIS WINDRAM/TIGHT LINES

DEEP SEA SERPENT (CHARTREUSE/WHITE)—Chris Windram

Hook: Mustad 34007, sizes 4-1/0
Thread: Creme nylon
Tail: Rabbit, chartreuse
Body: Rabbit, chartreuse
Front Hackle: White
Eyes: Lead, painted black on white
Variations: Black, red/white, red gill/black, red gill/white, white/badger.
TIED BY CHRIS WINDRAM/TIGHT LINES

DEEP SEA SERPENT (RED GILL/BLACK)—Chris Windram

Hook: Mustad 34007, sizes 4-1/0
Thread: Black nylon
Tail: Rabbit, black
Body: Rabbit, black
Front Hackle: Red, black
Eyes: Lead, painted black on white
Variations: Chartreuse/white, red/white, black, red gill/white, white/badger.
TIED BY CHRIS WINDRAM/TIGHT LINES

DEEP SEA SERPENT (RED GILL/WHITE)—Chris Windram

Hook: Mustad 34007, sizes 4-1/0
Thread: Creme nylon
Tail: Rabbit, white
Body: Rabbit, white
Front Hackle: Red, white
Eyes: Lead, painted white on white
Variations: Chartreuse/white, red/white, white, red gill/black, white/badger.
TIED BY CHRIS WINDRAM/TIGHT LINES

DEEP SEA SERPENT (RED/WHITE)—Chris Windram

Hook: Mustad 34007, sizes 4-1/0
Thread: Creme nylon
Tail: Rabbit, red
Body: Rabbit, red
Front Hackle: White
Eyes: Lead, painted black on white
Variations: Black, chartreuse/white, red gill/black, red gill/white, white/badger.
TIED BY CHRIS WINDRAM/TIGHT LINES

DEEP SEA SERPENT (WHITE/BADGER)—Chris Windram

Hook: Mustad 34007, sizes 4-1/0
Thread: Creme nylon
Tail: Rabbit, white
Body: Rabbit, white
Front Hackle: Badger
Eyes: Lead, painted black on white
Variations: Black, chartreuse/white, white gill/black, white gill/white, red/white.
TIED BY CHRIS WINDRAM/TIGHT LINES

Deceiver, Grizzly White

Deceiver, White/Silver

Deep Sea Serpent
(chartreuse/white)

Deceiver, Lefty's
(red/white)

Deep Baitfish
(weighted, bluegill)

Deep Sea Serpent
(red gill/black)

Deceiver, Lefty's
(red/yellow)

Deepsalt Minnow
(black)

Deep Sea Serpent
(red gill/white)

Deepsalt Minnow
(blue)

Deep Sea Serpent
(red/white)

Deceiver, Orange

Deepsalt Minnow
(pink)

Deceiver
(white/blue)

Deep Sea Serpent
(black)

Deep Sea Serpent
(white/badger)

DEEP SIX—Tony Weaver
Hook: Mustad 34007
Thread: White
Tail: White rabbit
Underbody: Lead wire
Body Hackle: White rabbit
Front Hackle: Chartreuse rabbit
Eyes: Non-toxic, black on yellow
Variations: All white
TIED BY TONY WEAVER

DEEP WATER SQUID—Tom Rosenbauer
Hook: Mustad 34007, size 1/0
Thread: White
Tail: White hackle
Body: White Lite Brite
Front Hackle: White Lite Brite
Eyes: Non-toxic black on white
TIED BY ORVIS

DEEP WATER TARPON (BLACK/GRIZZLY)—Greg Miheve
Hook: Mustad 34007/3407; Daiichi 2546; Tiemco 811S; Homosassa Plated; sizes 2-5/0
Thread: Black
Tail: Hackle, black, grizzly; black bucktail; black Flashabou
Weight: Lead wire
Body: Chenille, black
Body Hackle: Black
Head: Chenille, black
Eyes: Silver bead chain
Variations: Orange/pink
TIED BY GREG MIHEVE

DEEP WATER TARPON (ORANGE/PINK)—Greg Miheve
Hook: Mustad 34007/3407; Daiichi 2546; Tiemco 811S; Homosassa Plated; sizes 2-5/0
Thread: Pink
Tail: Hackle, pink; orange marabou; pearl Flashabou
Weight: Lead wire
Body: Chenille, orange
Body Hackle: Pink
Eyes: Silver bead chain
Variations: Black/grizzly
TIED BY GREG MIHEVE

DEEP WATER WHISTLER (ORANGE/BLACK)—Dan Blanton
Hook: Mustad 34007/3407; Daiichi 2546; Tiemco 811S, sizes 3/0-4/0
Thread: Orange
Tail: Bucktail, black; hackle, black
Body: Thread
Collar: Bucktail, black
Wing: Hackle, black; peacock herl
Front Hackle: Marabou, Orange
Eyes: Silver bead chain
Variations: Red/white, red/yellow, Orange/yellow
TIED BY UMPQUA FEATHER MERCHANTS/THE FLY SHOP

DEEP WATER WHISTLER (RED/WHITE)—Dan Blanton
Hook: Mustad 34007/3407; Daiichi 2546; Tiemco 811S, sizes 3/0-4/0
Thread: Red
Tail: Bucktail, white; hackle, white
Body: Thread
Collar: Bucktail, white
Wing: Hackle, white, grizzly; silver Flashabou; peacock herl
Front Hackle: Marabou, red
Eyes: Silver bead chain
Variations: Orange/black, orange/yellow, red/yellow
TIED BY UMPQUA FEATHER MERCHANTS/THE FLY SHOP

DEL BROWN PERMIT FLY—Del Brown
Hook: Mustad 34007/3407; Daiichi 2546; Tiemco 811S; size 1/0
Thread: Danville's flat waxed nylon chartreuse
Tail: Pearl Flashabou; badger hackle
Body: Antron yarn, brown, tan
Body Hackle: White rubber legs, red tips
Eyes: Nickel-plated lead
TIED BY DEL BROWN/UMPQUA

DINK (CHARTREUSE)—Edgewater
Hook: Mustad 34007
Tail: Marabou, chartreuse; Krystal Flash, pearl
Body: Foam, chartreuse
Eyes: Black on yellow post
Variations: Yellow, white, black, blue peppermint, purple.
TIED BY EDGEWATER

DIVER EEL
Hook: Mustad 34007/3407; Daiichi 2546; Tiemco 811S; size 2
Thread: Black
Tail: Black rabbit strip
Collar: Black deer hair
Head: Black deer hair
Eyes: Plastic black on yellow
Weedguard: Mono loop
TIED BY UMPQUA FEATHER MERCHANTS/THE FLY SHOP

DIXON'S DEVIL WORM—Paul Dixon
Hook: Mustad 34007 size 2
Thread: Black
Tail: Blood red marabou
Body: Rear 3/4 pink Lite Brite; front 1/4 black/green Lite Brite
TIED BY PAUL DIXON/DIXON'S SPORTING LIFE

D.L.'S BARRED STRIPER FLY—D.L. Goddard
Hook: Mustad 34007, size 3/0
Thread: Mono
Wing: White bucktail, black marking pencil; purple bucktail; peacock herl

Head: Mono thread, epoxy
Eyes: #3 1/2 adhesive, black on silver
Variations: Various colors, blue, brown, olive, etc.
TIED BY D.L. GODDARD

D.L.'S BARRED TARPON FLY—D.L. Goddard
Hook: Mustad 34007, size 3/0, 4/0
Wing: White bucktail, black marking pencil; orange bucktail; peacock herl
Head: Pearlescent thread; epoxy
Eyes: #2 1/2 adhesive, black on silver
Variations: Various color combinations.
TIED BY D.L. GODDARD

D.L.'S EPOXY GLASS MINNOW—D.L. Goddard
Hook: Mustad 34007, size 1
Tail: Mylar tubing; black feather
Body: Fine Mylar tubing; epoxy; green glitter
Eyes: #2 adhesive, black on silver
TIED BY D.L. GODDARD

D.L.'S EPOXY SAND EEL—D.L. Goddard
Hook: Mustad 34011, size 4
Tail: Mylar tubing; sand colored feather
Body: Fine Mylar tubing; epoxy
Body Hackle:
Wing: ?
Front Hackle: ?
Eyes: #2 adhesive, black on silver
TIED BY D.L. GODDARD

D.L.'S EPOXY SILVERSIDE—D.L. Goddard
Hook: Mustad 34007, sizes 1-6
Tail: Bucktail, white, brown; root beer Krystal Flash
Body: Bucktail, white, brown; root beer Krystal Flash; epoxy
Head: Mono thread
Eyes: #2 adhesive, black on silver
Variations: Various color combinations
TIED BY D.L. GODDARD

DOLPHIN OFFSHORE FLY—Jon Olch
Hook: Mustad 34007/3407; Daiichi 2546; Tiemco 811S
Thread: Green
Tail: Streamer Hair, gold; gold Krystal Flash
Body: Silver braid
Beard: Streamer Hair, green
Wing: Streamer Hair, green; silver Mylar
Eyes: Painted black on white
TIED BY JON OLCH

Deep Six

Deep Water Whistler
(red/white)

D.L.'s Barred Tarpon Fly

Deep Water Squid

Del Brown Permit Fly

D.L.'s Epoxy Glass Minnow

Deep Water Tarpon
(black/grizzly)

Dink
(chartreuse)

D.L.'s Epoxy Sand Eel

Diver Eel

D.L.'s Epoxy Silverside

Dixon's Devil Worm

Deep Water Tarpon
(orange/pink)

Dolphin Offshore Fly

Deep Water Whistler
(orange/black)

D.L.'s Barred Striper Fly

D'S SALTY MINNOW—
Darrel Sickmon
Hook: Mustad 34007/34011; Tiemco 811S
Thread: White
Tail: Blue dun mini-marabou; pearlescent decorative cord or tubing
Body: Pearl Cactus Chenille; Synthetic Living Fibre, white; pearl Krystal Flash
Gills: Synthetic Living Fibre, red
Wing: Rainbow Krystal Flash; Synthetic Living Fibre, warm gray, iron gray, peacock herl
Head: Thread dyed with markers, coated with 5-minute Epoxy and craft store glitter
Eyes: 4.5mm gold plastic
Variations: Silver Minnow, Baby Bluegill, Baby Rainbow Trout, Yellow/ringed Perch, all-Black.
TIED BY DARREL SICKMON/THE TROUT FISHER

EDGEWATER DIVER (BLACK)—
Edgewater
Hook: Mustad 34011
Tail: Sea hair, black; Flashabou, pearl; Krystal Flash, pearl
Body: Foam, black
Eyes: Nickel-platedd lead eyes or black on yellow post
Variations: White, chartreuse.
TIED BY EDGEWATER

EHN'S JETTIN' SQUID—Jeremy Ehn
Hook: Mustad 34007/3407; Daiichi 2546; Tiemco 811S
Thread: White
Tail: Marabou, black, pink
Body: White chenille
Front Hackle: White
Eyes: Nickel-plated; adhesive, black on silver; epoxy
Variations: White, pink, pink/white; with or without black
TIED BY JEREMY EHN/ORVIS TYSONS CORNER

EHN'S 4-EYED SHRIMP (PINK)—
Jeremy Ehn
Hook: Mustad 34007/3407; Daiichi 2546; Tiemco 811S
Tail: Pink bucktail
Body: Epoxy over thread and marabou
Body Hackle: Pink marabou
Wing: Pink marabou
Beard: White micro fibbets
Eyes: Double nickel plate lead eyes
Variations: Creme, white, green
TIED BY JEREMY EHN/ORVIS TYSONS CORNER

EHN'S SURF-SIDE HARES EAR (PINK)—
Jeremy Ehn
Hook: Mustad 34007/3407; Daiichi 2546; Tiemco 811S

Tail: Pink hackle
Body: Hares ear dubbing
Body Hackle: Pink Estaz
Shellback: Pink hackle
Variations: Creme, white, green
TIED BY JEREMY EHN/ORVIS TYSONS CORNER

ELIOT'S SURF EEL—Eliot Nelson
Hook: Mustad 34007, size 2/0
Thread: Fluorescent red
Tail: Brown grizzly
Body: Fluorescent red thread
Front Hackle: Brown bucktail
TIED BY ELIOT NELSON/CUSTOM TIED FLIES

EPOXY CHARLIE (PINK)—Joe Branham
Hook: Mustad 34007/3407; Daiichi 2546; Tiemco 811S; size 4-8
Thread: Pink
Body: Krystal Flash, pink; epoxy
Wing: Krystal Flash, pink; pink grizzly hackle; calf hair, pink
Eyes: Silver bead chain
Variations: White, tan, yellow, brown
TIED BY UMPQUA FEATHER MERCHANTS/THE FLY SHOP

EPOXY CHARLIE (YELLOW)—
Joe Branham
Hook: Mustad 34007/3407; Daiichi 2546; Tiemco 811S; size 4-8
Thread: Yellow
Body: Krystal Flash, yellow; epoxy
Wing: Krystal Flash, yellow; yellow grizzly hackle; yellow calf tail
Eyes: Silver bead chain
Variations: White, tan, pink, brown
TIED BY UMPQUA FEATHER MERCHANTS/THE FLY SHOP

EPOXY CRAB (ROOT BEER)—
Riverborn Fly Company
Hook: Mustad 3407, sizes 2-6
Thread: Danville Flymaster 6/0 brown and Flymaster Plus 1/0 brown
Tail: Brown marabou; copper Krystal Flash; brown grizzly hackle
Body Hackle: Root beer sili legs
Body: Epoxy, brown
Eyes: Gold bead chain
Variations: Shrimp pink, bonefish orange, chartreuse, Belize green, tan, yellow sunrise
TIED BY LANCE GRAY/RIVERBORN FLY COMPANY

EPOXY DOUGH CRAB—Joe Bursel
Hook: Mustad 34007/3407; Daiichi 2546; Tiemco 811S
Pincers: Rubber band; black permanent marker
Body: Brown epoxy dough; black permanent marker; white epoxy dough

Body Hackle: Live rubber legs; black permanent marker
Eyes: Stems from hobby shop
TIED BY JOE BURSEL

EPOXY FLY, NIX'S (ROOTBEER)—
Jimmy Nix
Hook: Mustad 34007/3407; Daiichi 2546; Tiemco 811S; sizes 4-8
Tail: Grizzly hackle; tan marabou
Body: Epoxy, tan
Eyes: Painted black
Weedguard: Two mono strands
Variations: Clear, pink
TIED BY UMPQUA FEATHER MERCHANTS

EPOXY LICE
Hook: Mustad 34007/3407; Daiichi 2546; Tiemco 811S
Thread: White
Tail: White bucktail; peacock herl; pearl Krystal Flash
Body: Epoxy over tail material, white thread
Eyes: Adhesive, black on silver Mylar
TIED BY HUNTERS ANGLING SUPPLIES

EPOXY MARABOU
(CHARTREUSE/WHITE)—Chris Windram
Hook: MUSTAD 34007, sizes 6-1
Thread: Light olive nylon
Tail: Marabou, chartreuse, white; pearl Krystal Flash
Body: Epoxy over Mylar tubing
Gills: Painted
Eyes: Painted black on white
TIED BY CHRIS WINDRAM/TIGHT LINES

EPOXY PUFF (BELIZE GREEN)—
Riverborn Fly Company
Hook: Mustad 3407, sizes 4-6
Thread: Danville Flymaster 6/0 green and Flymaster Plus 1/0 green
Tail: Olive marabou; green Krystal Flash; olive grizzly hackle
Body: Epoxy, olive
Eyes: Silver bead chain
Variations: Shrimp pink, bonefish orange, chartreuse, root beer, tan, yellow sunrise
TIED BY LANCE GRAY/RIVERBORN FLY COMPANY

EPOXY REDFISH FLY
Hook: Mustad 34007/3407; Daiichi 2546; Tiemco 811S; size 4
Tail: Grizzly hackle; tan marabou
Body: Epoxy
Weedguard: Two single strand mono
Eyes: Black plastic
TIED BY UMPQUA FEATHER MERCHANTS/THE FLY SHOP

D's Salty Minnow

Eliot's Surf Eel

**Epoxy Fly, Nix's
(root beer)**

**Epoxy Charlie
(pink)**

Epoxy Lice

**Edgewater Diver
(black)**

**Epoxy Charlie
(yellow)**

**Epoxy Marabou
(chartreuse/white)**

Ehn's Jettin' Squid

**Epoxy Crab
(root beer)**

**Epoxy Puff
(Belize green)**

**Ehn's 4-Eyed Shrimp
(pink)**

**Ehn's Surf-Side Hares Ear
(pink)**

Epoxy Dough Crab

Epoxy Redfish Fly

EPOXY SAND EEL—Tom Kintz

Hook: Mustad 34011 size 2
Thread: White size A flat nylon
Tail: White marabou; olive Krystal Flash
Body: Pearl Mylar braid; epoxy
Wing: Olive Krystal Flash; olive Ultra Hair
Gills: Red permanent marker (Sharpie)
Eyes: Adhesive black on silver
TIED BY TOM KINTZ

EPOXY SERPENT (BLACK)—Chris Windram

Hook: Mustad 34007, sizes 4-1/0
Thread: Black nylon
Tail: Rabbit, black
Body: Epoxy over black Mylar tubing
Gills: Painted
Eyes: Painted black on white
Variations: Olive
TIED BY CHRIS WINDRAM/TIGHT LINES

EPOXY SERPENT (OLIVE)—Chris Windram

Hook: Mustad 34007, sizes 4-1/0
Thread: Olive nylon
Tail: Rabbit, olive
Body: Epoxy over olive Mylar tubing
Gills: Painted
Eyes: Painted black on white
Variations: Black
TIED BY CHRIS WINDRAM/TIGHT LINES

EPOXY SLAMAROO—Lenny Moffo

Hook: Mustad 34007/3407; Daiichi 2546; Tiemco 811S
Tail: Natural gum rubber; brown permanent marker; tips red or orange, permanent marker
Body: Peacock Krystal Flash; epoxy
Eyes: Glass eyes glued on lead barbell eyes
TIED BY LENNY MOFFO

EPOXY SQUID—Tim Borski

Hook: Mustad 34007; Tiemco 811S; size 1-2/0
Tail: White deer hair; white hackles, hot pink wool; pearl Mylar
Body: Gold Mylar; epoxy
Eyes: Amber glass taxidermy
TIED BY TIM BORSKI

EPOXY SQUIRREL TAIL—Capt Kevin Guerin

Hook: Mustad 34007/3407; Daiichi 2546; Tiemco 811S
Thread: Brown
Body: Epoxy over thread
Wing: Brown hackle; red fox squirrel tail; pearl Flashabou
Eyes: Black plastic bead
WEEDGUARD: Two stands monofilament
TIED BY CAPT KEVIN GUERIN

ERIC'S SAND EEL—Eric Peterson

Hook: Mustad 34011, 34007/3407; Daiichi 2546; Tiemco 811S
Thread: White
Tail: Craft fur, white, lavender, olive, tan; Krystal Flash, pearl
Body: Epoxy over tail materials
Eyes: Painted, black over white
TIED BY MYSTIC BAY FLIES

ESTUARY SHINER—DARK—Al Bovyn

Hook: Mustad 9674B, sizes 2 or 4
Thread: Black
Tail: Furnace or brown hackle
Body: White or creme wool
Rib: Flat silver Mylar tinsel
Wing: Furnace hackle
Throat: Red schlappen
Cheeks: Jungle cock (optional)
Variations: Light version
TIED BY AL BOVYN

ESTUARY SHINER—LIGHT—Al Bovyn

Hook: Mustad 9674B, sizes 2 or 4
Thread: Black
Body: Flat silver Mylar tinsel
Rib: Medium silver oval tinsel
Wing: Silver badger hackle
Throat: Red schlappen
Cheeks: Jungle cock (optional)
Variations: Dark version
TIED BY AL BOVYN

E. T.'S SHRIMP—Ellen Reed

Hook: Mustad 34007/3407; Daiichi 2546; Tiemco 811S
Tail: Peacock sword; peacock Crystal Flash; badger hair
Body: Olive deer hair
Body Hackle: Olive deer hair
Wing: Peacock sword; peacock Krystal Flash
Eyes: Smallest (4/32) lead/bronze
Weedguard: Single strand monofilament
TIED BY ELLEN REED

EVERGLOW SERPENT (CHARTREUSE)—Chris Windram

Hook: Mustad 34007, sizes 4-1/0
Thread: Light olive nylon
Tail: Chartreuse rabbit
Body: Epoxy over chartreuse Everglow tubing
Gills: Painted
Eyes: Painted black on white
Variations: Orange, lime, white
TIED BY CHRIS WINDRAM/TIGHT LINES

EVERGLOW SERPENT (LIME)—Chris Windram

Hook: Mustad 34007, sizes 6-1/0
Thread: Light olive nylon
Tail: Lime rabbit
Body: Epoxy over lime Everglow tubing
Gills: Painted
Eyes: Painted black on white
Variations: Orange, chartreuse, white
TIED BY CHRIS WINDRAM/TIGHT LINES

EVERGLOW SERPENT (ORANGE)—Chris Windram

Hook: Mustad 34007, sizes 4-1/0
Thread: Creme nylon
Tail: Orange rabbit
Body: Epoxy over orange Everglow tubing
Gills: Painted
Eyes: Painted black on white
Variations: Chartreuse, lime, white
TIED BY CHRIS WINDRAM/TIGHT LINES

EVERGLOW SERPENT (WHITE)—Chris Windram

Hook: Mustad 34007, sizes 4-1/0
Thread: Creme nylon
Tail: White rabbit
Body: Epoxy over white Everglow tubing
Gills: Painted
Eyes: Painted black on white
Variations: Chartreuse, lime, orange
TIED BY CHRIS WINDRAM/TIGHT LINES

FAST SINK TARPON FLY—Jon Cave

Hook: Mustad 34007/3407; Daiichi 2546; Tiemco 800S; sizes 2/0-4/0
Thread: Flat waxed nylon
Tail: FisHair; Krystal Flash; large neck hackle
Body: Larva Led under thread
Body Hackle: Large neck hackle
Variations: Various color combinations.
TIED BY JON CAVE

FEATHERBED SHRIMP—Art Scheck

Hook: Mustad 34007 or Daiichi 2546, sizes 2-4
Thread: 6/0 or 8/0 tan
Weight: Heavy lead wire, doubled, under hook shank
Antennae: Orange Krystal Flash
Body: Dubbing, natural and orange rabbit, coarse tan synthetic (shredded Aunt Lydia yarn)
Mouth/Legs: Rabbit fur, natural, orange
Shellback: Hen back feather (mottled tan), Flexament
Rib: 3X tippet material
Legs: Teased out dubbing
Eyes: 30 pound Maxima, bent, burnt ends
Weedguard: 12 or 16 pound test mono
TIED BY ART SCHECK

FEATHER CRAB, NIX'S—Jimmy Nix

Hook: Mustad 34007/3407; Daiichi 2546; Tiemco 811S; sizes 4-6
Thread: Red
Tail: Red Flashabou
Body: Clipped white hackle; Blue/green ringneck pheasant feather
Legs: Rubber bands
Claws: Ringneck pheasant feather
TIED BY UMPQUA FEATHER MERCHANTS

Epoxy Sand Eel

Eric's Sand Eel

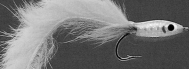

Everglow Serpent (orange)

Epoxy Serpent (black)

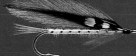

Estuary Shiner—dark

Everglow Serpent (white)

Estuary Shiner—light

Epoxy Serpent (olive)

E.T.'s Shrimp

Fast Sink Tarpon Fly

Epoxy Slamaroo

Everglow Serpent (chartreuse)

Featherbed Shrimp

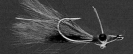

Epoxy Squid

Epoxy Squirrel Tail

Everglow Serpent (lime)

Feather Crab, Nix's

FERGUSON'S GREEN AND SILVER—
Bruce Ferguson

Hook: Mustad 34011, sizes 6-2; Partridge J.S. Sea Streamer; sizes 8-2
Tail: White hair; pearl Crystal Hair
Body: Silver diamond braid rear 2/3; medium fluorescent chartreuse chenille front 1/3
Wing: White hair
Topping: Pearl Crystal Hair
TIED BY BRUCE FERGUSON

FERGUSON'S GREEN AND SILVER—
Bruce Ferguson

Hook: Mustad 34011 or 92608; Tiemco 9394, sizes 1/0-8
Tail: White polar bear or bucktail
Body: Oval or braided silver tinsel rear 2/3; fluorescent green chenille front 1/3
Wing: White polar bear or bucktail
TIED BY RON AYOTTE

FERGUSON'S HERRING FLY—
Bruce Ferguson

Hook: Front, 1/0 Mustad 34007; Rear, size 1 Mustad 92553S; doubled 35 or 48-pound stiff mono
Tail: Silver Krystal Flash
Body: Silver diamond braid
Underwing: White hair
Overwing: Very dark green hair
Topping: Black Krystal Flash
Variations: Overwing color can vary to light gray-green, with gray-green topping
TIED BY BRUCE FERGUSON

FINGER MULLET (WHITE/RED Head)

Hook: Mustad 34011, sizes 1/0-3/0
Thread: White 3/0 Monocord for tail, red Kevlar, head
Tail: White saddle hackle, grizzly saddle hackle, white bucktail, pearlescent Flashabou
Body: White deer hair, red deer hair
Eyes: White round beads, painted black pupil
Variations: White, black/grizzly, yellow, chartreuse, fluorescent pink.
TIED BY GREG MIHEVE

FIXED TUBE POLAR BEAR STREAMER—
Ken Durrant

Hook: Reversed stainless
Thread: White
Body: Flashabou pearl
Wing: Flashabou, pearl, green; polar bear, white, green; peacock herl
Eyes: Painted black on yellow
TIED BY KEN DURRANT, CANADA

FLASHGLASS (GREEN/SILVER)

Hook: Mustad 34011, sizes 2-1/0
Thread: 3/0 Monocord, black
Tail: Flashabou, silver
Body: Flashabou wrapped, silver

Body Wing: Flashabou, silver
Wing: Flashabou, green;
Gills: Fluorescent fire orange flat waxed nylon
Head: Black thread
Variations: Silver, blue/silver, green/silver, blue/green/silver, blue/green/gold, chartreuse. Can substitute pearl for silver; Krystal Flash for Flashabou.
TIED BY GREG MIHEVE

FLASHY LADY—Joe Butorac

Hook: Mustad 92608, sizes 6-2/0
Thread: Transparent sewing thread
Body: None on smaller sizes; pearl Mylar
Wing: Pink bucktail; continuation of Mylar head tubing, unravelled
Head: Pearl Mylar tubing; epoxy
Eyes: Black paint
Variations: Blue, yellow, green, white.
TIED BY JOE BUTORAC

FLAT ILLEGAL—Jim Buckingham

Hook: Mustad 34007/3407, sizes 1-8
Thread: Danville flat waxed nylon
Tail: Pearl Krystal Flash
Body: Poly braid, orange, pearl
Wing: White calf tail; grizzly hackle
Eyes: Machined brass; black nickel plate
Weedguard: 15-pound hard Mason
TIED BY JIM BUCKINGHAM

FLAT ILLEGAL EPOXY—Jim Buckingham

Hook: Mustad 34007/3407, sizes 2-6
Thread: Flat waxed nylon
Tail: Pearl Krystal Flash; grizzly hackle
Body: Poly braid, pearl; epoxy`
Body Hackle: Grizzly
Eyes: Brass, black nickel, medium and small
Weedguard: Optional, 15-pound hard Mason, crimped hinge
TIED BY JIM BUCKINGHAM

FLAT ILLEGAL SHRIMP—
Jim Buckingham

Hook: Mustad 34007/3407, sizes 1-8
Thread: Danville flat waxed nylon
Tail: Pearl Krystal Flash
Body: Poly braid, pearl
Wing: Olive calf tail
Claws: Grizzly hackle, trimmed
Eyes: Machined brass; black nickel plate
Weedguard: 15-pound hard Mason, crimped hinge
TIED BY JIM BUCKINGHAM

FLATS MASTER (CHARTREUSE)—
Mike Wolverton

Hook: Mustad 34007/3407; Daiichi 2546; Tiemco 811S
Thread: Chartreuse
Tail: Chartreuse marabou
Body: Chartreuse thread
Wing: Brown sparkle yarn
Front Hackle: Grizzly
Eyes: Silver bead chain

Variations: White, yellow, pink, orange
TIED BY UMPQUA FEATHER MERCHANTS

FLATS MASTER (PINK)—
Mike Wolverton

Hook: Mustad 34007, sizes 6-2
Thread: Pink
Tail: Marabou, fluorescent pink
Body: Danville flat waxed thread, pink
Wing: Tan craft fur
Front Hackle: Grizzly
Eyes: Small silver bead chain
Variations: Orange, yellow, white, chartreuse
TIED BY MIKE WOLVERTON

FLATSSALT SHRIMP (BLUE)—
Bighorn Fly Trading

Hook: Gamakatsu, sizes 2-4
Thread: Blue
Tail: White sparkle yarn; flat pearl Mylar
Antennae: Pearl Krystal Flash
Shellback: Flat pearl Mylar
Body: Blue thread
Rib: Clear mono
Front: White sparkle yarn
Eyes: Black plastic bead
Variations: Orange
TIED BY BIGHORN FLY TRADING

FLORIDA SHRIMP—Jon Olch

Hook: Mustad 34007/3407; Daiichi 2546; Tiemco 811S
Thread: Pink
Body: Silver braid
Wing: Pink craft fur; grizzly hackle
Front Hackle: Pink grizzly
Eyes: Pink plastic bead chain
TIED BY JON OLCH/UMPQUA FEATHER MERCHANTS

FLUTE FLY (YELLOW)—
Doug Swisher & Bob Marvin

Hook: Mustad 34011
Tail: Bucktail, yellow; Flashabou, pearl
Body: Foam, yellow
Variations: Black, chartreuse, blue, white, purple.
TIED BY EDGEWATER

FOOLS GOLD—Jon Cave

Hook: Mustad 3407; Daiichi 2546; Tiemco 800S; sizes 1-2/0
Thread: Yellow flat waxed nylon
Body: Yellow-gold Crystal Chenille
Wing: Yellow polar bear, bucktail or kip tail; yellow-orange Flashabou; gold Krystal Flash
Cheeks: Golden pheasant crest feathers
TIED BY JON CAVE

FRANKEE-BELLE—
Frankee Albright/Belle Mathers

Hook: Mustad 34007/3407; Daiichi 2546; Tiemco 811S
Body: White chenille
Wing: Tan bucktail; variant hackle
TIED BY JACKSON CARDINAL FLIES

SALTWATER FLIES

Ferguson's Green and Silver

Ferguson's Green and Silver

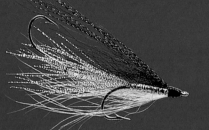

Ferguson's Herring Fly

Finger Mullet
(white/red head)

Fixed Tube Polar Bear Streamer

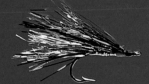

Flashglass
(green/silver)

Flashy Lady

Flat Illegal

Flat Illegal Epoxy

Flat Illegal Shrimp

Flats Master
(chartreuse)

Flats Master
(pink)

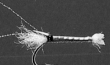

Flatssalt Shrimp
(blue)

Florida Shrimp

Flute Fly
(yellow)

Fools Gold

Frankee-Belle

FROG NOBBLER, BLACK (Turrall)

Hook: Mustad 34007/3407; Daiichi 2546; Tiemco 811S
Thread: Black
Tail: Marabou, black
Body: Chenille, chartreuse and black
Rib: Silver tinsel
Body Hackle: Black
Eyes: Silver bead chain
TIED BY TURRALL

FROG NOBBLER, ORANGE (Turrall)

Hook: Mustad 34007/3407; Daiichi 2546; Tiemco 811S
Thread: Black
Tail: Marabou, hot orange
Body: Chenille, hot orange
Rib: Silver tinsel
Body Hackle: Hot orange
Eyes: Silver bead chain
TIED BY TURRALL

FROG NOBBLER, PINK (Turrall)

Hook: Mustad 34007/3407; Daiichi 2546; Tiemco 811S
Thread: Black
Tail: Marabou, hot pink
Body: Chenille, hot pink
Rib: Silver tinsel
Body Hackle: Hot pink
Eyes: Silver bead chain
TIED BY TURRALL

FROG NOBBLER, WHITE (Turrall)

Hook: Mustad 34007/3407; Daiichi 2546; Tiemco 811S
Thread: Black
Tail: Marabou, white
Body: Chenille, white
Rib: Silver tinsel
Body Hackle: White
Eyes: Silver bead chain
TIED BY TURRALL

FULL TAIL DEEP MINNOW—Terry Baird

Hook: Gamakatsu
Thread: Green
Tail: FisHair, green, tied and trimmed
Body: Flashabou Mylar
Underwing: FisHair, chartreuse
Wing: Chartreuse bucktail; FisHair, green; wide pearl Mylar
Front Hackle:
Eyes: Lead barbell
TIED BY TERRY BAIRD/BIGHORN FLY TRADING

FUZZY CRAB—John Kumiski

Hook: Mustad 34007/3407; Daiichi 2546; Tiemco 811S
Thread: Black
Tail: Brown kip tail; grizzly hackle clipped
Body: Brown Furry Foam
Body Hackle: Grizzly
Eyes: Lead barbell
TIED BY JOHN KUMISKI

GARTSIDE FLOATING MINNOW— Jack Gartside

Hook: Eagle Claw 254N; Mustad 34007/34011; sizes 4-3/0
Thread: 6/0 white
Tail: White marabou
Underbody: White closed cell foam (Orvis Fly Foam or GurglerFoam) 1/8" thick
Body: 1/2" silver Corsair tubing; thread line left white; top section colored olive/black
Eyes: Painted, black on yellow
Variations: Colors and tail materials, such as Glimmer material; thread/lateral line colored black
TIED BY JACK GARTSIDE

GARTSIDE SAND EEL—Jack Gartside

Hook: Mustad 34007/34011; Daiichi 2546; Partridge CS52; sizes 6-1/0
Thread: 6/0 white
Tail/insert: Pearl Glimmer or Flashabou
Body: 1/4" white or silver/white Corsair tubing; or 1/2" silver slendered down to 1/3"; thread line left white or colored black or brown
Eyes: Painted, black on yellow
Variations: Back colors: olive, brown/olive, blue, gray. Tail & insert: marabou, fox, mallard flank, peacock herl, rubber bands, strips of leather.
TIED BY JACK GARTSIDE

GENERAL EZ (YELLOW)— C. Boyd Pfeiffer

Hook: Eagle Claw 66SS, straightened; Mustad 34011
Thread: Yellow
Tail: none
Body: none
Collar: Yellow bucktail
Variations: White, black, blue, green, pink
TIED BY C. BOYD PFEIFFER

GHOSTBUSTER (BROWN)—Jon Olch

Hook: Mustad 34007/3407; Daiichi 2546; Tiemco 811S
Thread: Brown
Tail: Brown leather;
Body: Brown rabbit strip; brown marabou
Body Hackle: Brown rabbit
Wing: Grizzly hackle
Eyes: Silver bead chain
TIED BY JON OLCH

GLASS MINNOW—Chico Fernandez

Hook: Mustad 34007/3407; Daiichi 2546; Tiemco 811S; size 1/0
Thread: White
Body: Silver tinsel under mono
Wing: White Ocean Hair; silver Flashabou
Gills: Red thread
Eyes: Painted black on yellow
Variations: White/brown, white/green
TIED BY UMPQUA FEATHER MER-CHANTS

GLASS MINNOW (BLUE/GREEN/WHITE)

Hook: Mustad 34011, sizes 2-1/0
Thread: 3/0 Monocord, white
Body: Monofilament over silver tinsel
Gills: Fluorescent fire orange thread
Wing: Calf tail, blue, green, white; blue Flashabou or green, silver, pearl
Head: Top painted black
Eyes: Painted black on white
Variations: White, blue/white, green/white, blue/green/yellow, chartreuse.
TIED BY GREG MIHEVE

GLAUCOUS YELLOW SCREAMER— Al Allard

Hook: Mustad 34007/34011/36980; Tiemco 7999, sizes 2/0-8
Thread: Monocord, yellow or black
Tail: Red hackle tips
Body: Fluorescent yellow chenille
Rib: Wide silver tinsel
Wing: White polar bear or bucktail; red Flashabou
Flank: Fibers from dark tips of flight feathers from Glaucous gull; substitute dark turkey
Head: Thread lacquered or epoxy
TIED BY RON AYOTTE

GNARLY CHARLIE—Terry Baird

Hook: Gamakatsu
Thread: White
Body: Mylar Flashabou
Body Hackle: Chartreuse sili legs
Wing: White calf tail
Eyes: Nickel-plated lead
Variations: Various colors
TIED BY TERRY BAIRD/BIGHORN FLY TRADING

GOLD/BROWN SHRIMP— Chico Fernandez

Hook: Mustad 34007/3407; Daiichi 2546; Tiemco 811S; sizes 4-6
Thread: Black
Body: Golden brown dubbing
Wing: Brown variant hackle; brown bucktail
TIED BY UMPQUA FEATHER MER-CHANTS

GOLD LIZZIE—Liz Steele

Hook: Mustad 34007; sizes 4-1/0
Thread: Brown
Tail: Red floating yarn
Body: .020 lead wire; gold tinsel yarn
Wing: Brown bucktail; brown marabou; gold Flashabou
Variations: Lime, tin, copper
TIED BY LIZ STEELE/THE FLY FISHER-MAN

SALTWATER FLIES

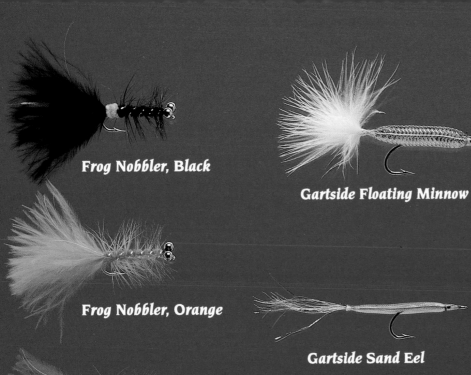

Frog Nobbler, Black

Gartside Floating Minnow

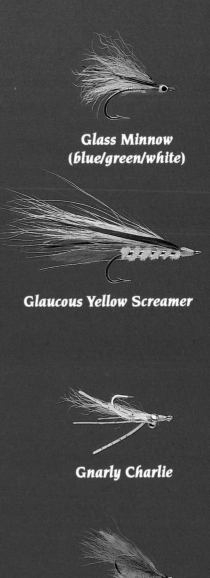

Glass Minnow (blue/green/white)

Frog Nobbler, Orange

Gartside Sand Eel

Glaucous Yellow Screamer

Frog Nobbler, Pink

General EZ (yellow)

Gnarly Charlie

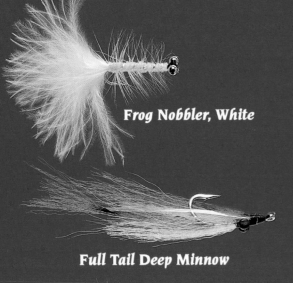

Frog Nobbler, White

Ghostbuster (brown)

Gold/Brown Shrimp

Full Tail Deep Minnow

Fuzzy Crab

Glass Minnow

Gold Lizzie

GOODY GOODY APTE TOO PLUS— Stu Apte

Hook: Mustad 34007/3407; Daiichi 2546; Tiemco 811S
Thread: Red
Tail: Purple rabbit; pearl Crystal Hair
Body: Thread
Body Hackle: Gray fox squirrel tail
Head: Epoxy over thread
Eyes: Painted black on yellow
Weedguard: Anti-foul mono rear loop
TIED BY MCKENZIE FLY TACKLE

GREEN LANTERN—Jon Olch

Hook: Mustad 34007/3407; Daiichi 2546; Tiemco 811S
Thread: White
Tail: Streamer Hair, white
Body: Gold braid
Beard: White bucktail
Wing: Green, chartreuse bucktail; Flashabou, gold, pearl
Eyes: Painted black on yellow
TIED BY JON OLCH

GREG'S CRAB (SPOTTED TAN)— Greg Miheve

Hook: Mustad 34007/3407; Daiichi 2546; Tiemco 811S
Thread: 3/0 Monocord, white or match body color
Tail: Cree hackle tips; pearl Flashabou
Weight: Lead eyes
Body: Deer hair; plumber's lead tape over leg butts; white epoxy over tape; brown permanent marker
Body Hackle: Knotted rubber band legs, 4 on one side, 2 large claws on other
Eyes: Black flower stamens; HAN coating
Variations: Tan, brown, black, olive
TIED BY GREG MIHEVE

GREG'S FLATS FLY (BANDED PINK)— Greg Miheve

Hook: Mustad 34007/3407; Daiichi 2546; Tiemco 811S; sizes 2-6
Thread: 3/0 Monocord, pink
Tail: Calf tail, pink; Krystal Flash, pink
Underbody: Wide pearl tinsel
Body: 3/0 monocord, banded, pink; clear V-rib, tapered
Body Hackle: Hackle, pink, tapered larger at hook eye
Eyes: Bead chain or lead eyes
Variations: Banded tan, brown, orange, or LiveHart in white, yellow or chartreuse
TIED BY GREG MIHEVE

GREG'S FLATS FLY (BANDED TAN)— Greg Miheve

Hook: Mustad 34007/3407; Daiichi 2546; Tiemco 811S; sizes 2-6
Thread: 3/0 Monocord, tan
Tail: Calf tail, tan; Krystal Flash, tan
Underbody: Wide pearl tinsel
Body: 3/0 monocord, banded, tan; clear V-rib, tapered

Body Hackle: Hackle, tan, tapered larger at hook eye
Eyes: Bead chain or lead eyes
Variations: Banded pink, brown, orange, or LiveHart in white, yellow or chartreuse
TIED BY GREG MIHEVE

GREG'S FLATS FLY (LIVEHART/CHARTREUSE)— Greg Miheve

Hook: Mustad 34007/3407; Daiichi 2546; Tiemco 811S; sizes 2-6
Thread: 3/0 Monocord, chartreuse
Tail: Calf tail, chartreuse; Krystal Flash, chartreuse
Underbody: Wide pearl tinsel
Body: 3/0 monocord, banded, chartreuse; clear V-rib
Body Hackle: Hackle, chartreuse, tapered larger at hook eye
LiveHart: Thread, fluorescent tan or fire orange
Eyes: Bead chain or lead eyes
Variations: Banded tan, tan, brown, orange, or LiveHart in white, yellow
TIED BY GREG MIHEVE

GREG'S SQUID (BARRED OLIVE)— Greg Miheve

Hook: Mustad 34007/3407; Daiichi 2546; Tiemco 811S; sizes 1/0-5/0
Thread: 3/0 Monocord, color to match body
Tail: Marabou, olive; hackle, olive grizzly, (six—2 to 6", two—5 to 10"); Flashabou, olive
Body: Tapered fat chenille, barred olive, or Sparkle chenille
Eyes: Plastic bead painted black on olive, or lead eyes
Variations: White, tan, purple, pink, orange, yellow
TIED BY GREG MIHEVE

GREG'S TINY SHINY SHRIMP (BANDED CHARTREUSE)—Greg Miheve

Hook: Mustad 34007/3407; Daiichi 2546; Tiemco 811S; sizes 8-12
Thread: White 3/0 Monocord
Tail: Krystal Flash, chartreuse
Body: Wide pearl Flashabou; chartreuse thread bands; V-rib over
Body Hackle: Chartreuse, palmered, clipped top and sides
Head: Black thread
Variations: Pearl, tan, pink, olive, gray
TIED BY GREG MIHEVE

GREG'S TINY SHINY SHRIMP (BANDED PINK)—Greg Miheve

Hook: Mustad 34007/3407; Daiichi 2546; Tiemco 811S; sizes 8-12
Thread: White 3/0 Monocord
Tail: Krystal Flash, pink
Body: Wide pearl Flashabou; pink thread bands; V-rib over

Body Hackle: Pink, palmered, clipped top and sides
Head: Black thread
Variations: Pearl, tan, chartreuse, olive, gray
TIED BY GREG MIHEVE

GREG'S TINY SHINY SHRIMP (BANDED TAN)—Greg Miheve

Hook: Mustad 34007/3407; Daiichi 2546; Tiemco 811S; sizes 8-12
Thread: White 3/0 Monocord
Tail: Krystal Flash, tan
Body: Wide pearl Flashabou; tan thread bands; V-rib over
Body Hackle: Tan, palmered, clipped top and sides
Head: Black thread
Variations: Pearl, pink, chartreuse, olive, gray
TIED BY GREG MIHEVE

GUERIN SNOOK SLAYER— Capt Kevin Guerin

Hook: Mustad 34007/3407; Daiichi 2546; Tiemco 811S
Tail: White streamer hair; pearl Crystal Flash; grizzly hackle
Body: White wool
Body Hackle: Grizzly
Eyes: Doll eyes, black on white
TIED BY CAPT KEVIN GUERIN

HAIR Wing CRAZY CHARLIE— Bob Nauheim

Hook: Mustad 34007/3407; Daiichi 2546; Tiemco 811S; sizes 2-6
Thread: White
Tail: Silver Flashabou
Body: Silver tinsel; mono
Wing: Fine creme hair; optional silver Flashabou
Eyes: Silver bead chain
TIED BY BOB NAUHEIM

HARDBODY SHINER

Hook: Mustad 34007/3407; Daiichi 2546; Tiemco 811S
Thread: White
Tail: Craft fur, olive, white; Krystal Flash, black; Flashabou, silver
Body: Lead wire; Krystal Flash, pearl; tail material under epoxy
Eyes: Painted, black over white
Gills: Red marking pen
TIED BY MYSTIC BAY FLIES

HARE EEL

Hook: Mustad 34007/3407; Daiichi 2546; Tiemco 811S, size 2
Thread: Black
Tail: Rabbit fur strip, black
Body: Rabbit fur strip, black
Eyes: Plastic black on yellow
Weedguard: Mono loop
TIED BY UMPQUA FEATHER MER-CHANTS/THE FLY SHOP

Goody Goody Apte Too Plus

**Greg's Flats Fly
(livehart/chartreuse)**

**Greg's Tiny Shiny Shrimp
(banded Tan)**

Green Lantern

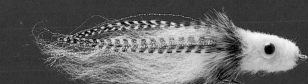

Guerin Snook Slayer

**Greg's Squid
(barred olive)**

Hair Wing Crazy Charlie

**Greg's Crab
(spotted tan)**

**Greg's Tiny Shiny Shrimp
(banded chartreuse)**

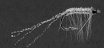

Hardbody Shiner

**Greg's Flat Fly
(banded pink)**

**Greg's Tiny Shiny Shrimp
(banded pink)**

**Greg's Flats Fly
(banded tan)**

Hare Eel

HERMIT CRAB BITTERS (THREE COLORED HERMIT)— Craig Mathews

Hook: Tears of the Keys blanks; Mustad 3407; Daiichi 2546; Tiemco 800S; sizes 4-10
Thread: 3/0 white monocord
Body: Epoxy, amber
Body Hackle: Spandex rubber legs, blue; water proof marker, red, dark blue
Wing: Deer hair
Eyes: Gold bead chain
Variations: Smooth Clawed (olive green with brown mottling; Red and Bar Eyed (cream with red mottling); Green Striped (cream or light olive with green and brown mottling)
TIED BY CRAIG MATHEWS/BLUE RIBBON FLIES

HIETIE

Hook: Tiemco 800S, size 2/0
Thread: White
Tail: White bucktail; pearl Krystal Flash
Body: Thread under epoxy
Wing: Bucktail, white, blue; Krystal Flash, pearl, blue
Eyes: Adhesive, black on gold
TIED BY ED MITCHELL

HONEY LAMB—Ellen Reed

Hook: Mustad 34007/3407; Daiichi 2546; Tiemco 811S
Thread: Rust
Tail: Golden pheasant tippet
Body: Pink chenille
Body Hackle: Grizzly
Wing: Lamb's wool; gold Krystal Flash
Front Hackle: Lamb's wool
Eyes: Smallest (4/32) lead/bronze
Weedguard: Single strand monofilament
TIED BY ELLEN REED

THE HORROR—Chico Fernandez

Hook: Mustad 34007/3407; Daiichi 2546; Tiemco 811S; sizes 4-6
Body: Yellow chenille
Wing: Tan variant hackle; tan bucktail
TIED BY UMPQUA FEATHER MERCHANTS

HUFF BACKCOUNTRY FLY—Steve Huff

Hook: Mustad 34007, size 2/0
Thread: Chartreuse
Tail: White rabbit strip; pearl Crystal Flash
Body: Spun deer hair, natural, red
Body Hackle: Tan marabou; natural deer hair
TIED BY ORVIS

HUFF'S BALLYHOO TARPON FLY— Steve Huff

Hook: Mustad 34007, size 3/0
Thread: Chartreuse
Tail: Yellow bucktail; yellow Fish Hair; yellow Krystal Flash

Body: Chenille, chartreuse, fluorescent red
Eyes: Black plastic bead
TIED BY ORVIS

HUFF'S JOE-TO-GO BONEFISH FLY— Steve Huff

Hook: Mustad 34007, size 2
Thread: Chartreuse
Tail: Grizzly hackle; peacock herl
Body: Brown Crystal Chenille
Front Hackle: Grizzly
Eyes: Plastic bead, black
WEEDGUARD: Two stands monofilament
TIED BY ORVIS

HUFF'S WHITE LIGHTNING—Steve Huff

Hook: Mustad 3407SS, size 3/0; Mustad 34007, size 4/0
Thread: Chartreuse
Tail: Hackle, grizzly, chartreuse; Flashabou, pearl
Body: Thread
Body Hackle: Yellow marabou
TIED BY FLORIDA KEYS SCHOOL & OUTFITTERS

IMPROVED OMNIBUS (GREG TOMPKINS)—Lendall Hunton

Hook: Size 2-8, long shank
Thread: Black
Tail: Marabou, red, yellow, white
Body: Peacock herl
Rib: Silver Mylar
Wing: Arctic fox tail; pearl or white Fire Fly
Front Hackle: Schlappen, red, yellow
TIED BY GREG TOMPKINS/CLEARWATER ANGLER

INDIAN RIVER REDFISH—Dan Johnson

Hook: Mustad 34007; sizes 3/0-2
Thread: Chartreuse
Tail: Hackle, yellow, chartreuse; pearl Flashabou
Body Hackle: Hackle, yellow, chartreuse
Eyes: Lead barbell, 1/36, 1/50, painted black on white
TIED BY DAN JOHNSON/THE FLY FISHERMAN

INTERCEPTOR—Randall Kaufmann

Hook: Mustad 34007/3407; Daiichi 2546; Tiemco 811S; sizes 4-8
Thread: Pink
Tail: Krystal Flash, red, pearl
Body: Pearl Mylar braid
Wing: Krystal Flash, red, pearl
Eyes: Nickel-plated lead painted black/yellow/pink
TIED BY UMPQUA FEATHER MERCHANTS

JABBERWOK—Jeremy Ehn

Hook: Mustad 34007/3407; Daiichi 2546; Tiemco 811S
Thread: White
Tail: White hackle; pearl Krystal Flash

Body: Pearl Estaz
Body Hackle: White
Eyes: Black non-toxic
TIED BY JEREMY EHN/ORVIS TYSONS CORNER

JACK'S FAVORITE BLACK CHUGGER— Capt Lenny Moffo

Hook: Mustad 34007/3407; Daiichi 2546; Tiemco 811S
Tail: Black hackle; black streamer hair; black Krystal Flash; grizzly hackle
Body Hackle: Black rabbit
Head: Black chenille
Eyes: Silver bead chain
Variations: Purple
TIED BY MCKENZIE FLY TACKLE

JERICO'S SHRIMP—Jeremy Ehn

Hook: 2x-long bent
Tail: Pink bucktail
Body: Pearl Krystal Flash; pink hackle trimmed; epoxy
Body Hackle: Pink
Eyes: Black non-toxic; adhesive, black on silver; epoxy
TIED BY JEREMY EHN/ORVIS TYSONS CORNER

JIM BUCK BALLYHO (ORANGE)— Jim Buckingham

Hook: Mustad 34011, sizes 2-5/0
Thread: Flat waxed nylon
Tail: Frayed pearl Mylar tubing; FisHair, orange, red
Throat: White bucktail
Body: Epoxy over thread, red/black/red
Eyes: Adhesive black on yellow
Variations: Blue, chartreuse
TIED BY JIM BUCKINGHAM/MCKENZIE FLY TACKLE

JIM BUCK SQUID (CHARTREUSE)— Jim Buckingham

Hook: Mustad 34011, sizes 1/0-5/0
Thread: Flat waxed nylon, chartreuse
Tail: Pearl Krystal Flash; white marabou; chartreuse hackle
Body: .015 lead wire; chartreuse chenille
Eyes: Glass, black on clear
Variations: Green, white, hot pink, pink/white
TIED BY JIM BUCKINGHAM/MCKENZIE FLY TACKLE

JIM BUCK SQUID (PINK/WHITE)— Jim Buckingham

Hook: Mustad 34011, sizes 1/0-5/0
Thread: Flat waxed nylon, pink
Tail: Pearl Krystal Flash; white marabou; pink hackle
Body: .015 lead wire; white chenille
Eyes: Glass, black on clear
Variations: Green, white, hot pink, chartreuse
TIED BY JIM BUCKINGHAM/MCKENZIE FLY TACKLE

SALTWATER FLIES

Hermit Crab Bitters
(three colored hermit)

Huff's Joe-To-Go Bonefish Fly

Jack's Favorite Black Chugger

Hietie

Huff's White Lightning

Jerico's Shrimp

Honey Lamb

Jim Buck Ballyho
(orange)

The Horror

Improved Omnibus

Jim Buck Squid
(chartreuse)

Huff Backcountry Fly

Indian River Redfish

Interceptor

Jim Buck Squid
(pink/white)

Huff's Ballyhoo Tarpon Fly

Jabberwok

JOE'S CLOUSERCEIVER (WHITE)— Joe Calcavecchia

Hook: Mustad 34007/3407; Daiichi 2546; Tiemco 811S
Thread: Red
Tail: White hackle; pearl Krystal Flash
Body: Pearlescent glitter tape or diamond braid
Collar: White bucktail
Topping: Peacock herl
Throat: Red calf tail
Eyes: Plated lead
TIED BY JOE CALCAVECCHIA/AMERICAN ANGLING SUPPLIES

JOHNNY'S GOTCHA—Johnny Glenn

Hook: Mustad 34007, sizes 2-8
Thread: Fluorescent orange flat waxed nylon
Tail: Pearl braided Mylar
Body: Pearl glitter braid
Wing: Golden yellow Fly Fur; rainbow Krystal Flash
Eyes: Bead chain painted black or lead dumbbell
TIED BY JOHNNY GLENN/MANHATTAN CUSTOM TACKLE

JOHNNY'S NEEDLEFISH—Johnny Glenn

Hook: Size 2/0 trailing size 4 long shank
Tail: Chartreuse FisHair; chartreuse Krystal Flash
Rear Body: 1/4" Corsair
Collar: Chartreuse Glo-Bug yarn
Body/Head: Chartreuse thread; hot orange thread; epoxy
Eyes: Plastic doll eyes
TIED BY JOHNNY GLENN

JON'S BLUE SCREAMER—Jon Wallace

Hook: Mustad 34011, size 2
Thread: 3/0 monocord
Underwing: White Thompson's Polar Hair, Fish Hair, or Streamer Hair
Body: Blue Diamond Braid
Wing: Grizzly hackle; Krystal Flash, silver, blue, peacock, black
Head: Blue Diamond Braid; epoxy
Eyes: Medium lead eyes, painted black on yellow
Variations: See Chartreuse, Red Screamers
TIED BY JON WALLACE/MCKENZIE FLY TACKLE

JON'S CHARTREUSE SCREAMER— Jon Wallace

Hook: Mustad 34011, size 2; Mustad 34007, size 2/0
Thread: 3/0 monocord
Underwing: White Thompson's Polar Hair, Fish Hair, or Streamer Hair
Body: Chartreuse Diamond Braid
Wing: Grizzly hackle; Krystal Flash, pearl, green, black
Head: Chartreuse Diamond Braid; epoxy
Eyes: Medium lead eyes, painted black on yellow
Variations: See Blue, Red Screamers
TIED BY JON WALLACE/MCKENZIE FLY TACKLE

JON'S RED SCREAMER— Jon Wallace

Hook: Mustad 34011, size 2
Thread: 3/0 monocord
Underwing: Red Thompson's Polar Hair, Fish Hair, or Streamer Hair
Body: Red Diamond Braid
Wing: Red hackle; Krystal Flash, pearl, red, black
Head: Red Diamond Braid; epoxy
Eyes: Medium lead eyes, painted black on red
Variations: See Blue, Chartreuse Screamers
TIED BY JON WALLACE/MCKENZIE FLY TACKLE

JUNKYARD DOG—Bill Billadue

Hook: Mustad 9175 size 3/0
Thread: White
Tail: Orange kip tail; hackle, orange, yellow, grizzly
Body: Thread
Collar: Orange kip tail
TIED BY BOB NAUHEIM

KEEL EEL—Bob Popovics

Hook: Long shank; Tiemco 411S; size 1/0
Thread: White
Tail: Ultra Hair, white, smoke
Body: Pearl Flashabou; tail material; epoxy
Eyes: Adhesive black on gold
TIED BY UMPQUA FEATHER MERCHANTS/THE FLY SHOP

KELP CRAB

Hook: Mustad 34007/3407; Daiichi 2546; Tiemco 811S; size 2
Thread: Chartreuse
Body: Epoxy, chartreuse
Body Hackle: Chartreuse rubber legs
Claws: Chartreuse calf tail
Eyes: Black plastic
AVAILABLE THROUGH THE FLY SHOP

KELP POPPER (UMPQUA SWIMMING FROG, ORANGE)—Dave Whitlock

Hook: Tiemco 8089, nickel; size 2-6
Tail: Green and orange grizzly, orange hackle; orange Krystal Flash
Body: Deer hair, green, yellow, black
Collar: Orange hackle; body deer hair
Eyes: Plastic black on white
Weedguard: Mono loop
UMPQUA FEATHER MERCHANTS/THE FLY SHOP

KEVIN'S SNOOK FLY— Capt Kevin Guerin

Hook: Mustad 34007, size 1/0
Tail: Hackle, white, yellow; gold Flashabou
Body: Yellow chenille
Body Hackle: Brown
Front Hackle: Deer hair
Head: Deer hair
Weedguard: Single strand wire
TIED BY FLORIDA KEYS SCHOOL & OUTFITTERS

KEYS TARPON STREAMER— TRADITIONAL

Hook: Mustad 3407SS, sizes 3/0; Mustad 34007, size 4/0
Thread: Orange
Tail: Grizzly hackle, brown, orange; pearl Krystal Flash
Body: Thread
Body Hackle: Grizzly hackle, brown, orange
TIED BY FLORIDA KEYS SCHOOL & OUTFITTERS

K.G. SNOOK WHISTLER— Capt Kevin Guerin

Hook: Mustad 34007/3407; Daiichi 2546; Tiemco 811S
Thread: Red
Tail: Gold Krystal Flash; hackle, grizzly, yellow
Body: Epoxy over red thread
Body Hackle: Marabou, yellow, red
Eyes: Gold bead chain
Weedguard: Single strand monofilament
TIED BY CAPT KEVIN GUERIN

KIRK'S RATTLE ROUSER (CHARTREUSE)—Jon Cave

Hook: Mustad 34007, size 1
Thread: Chartreuse
Tail: Silver Mylar tubing
Body: Rattle; red thread; silver Mylar tubing; epoxy
Wing: Chartreuse bucktail; silver Flashabou; green Krystal Flash
Eyes: Painted black on orange
Variations: Pink, olive
TIED BY ORVIS

KRAFT FUR SHRIMP—Tim Borski

Hook: Mustad 34007; Tiemco 811S; 4-1/0
Tail: Tan craft fur #1872; Pantone marker #147-M; hot orange Krystal Flash
Body: White thread
Body Hackle: Wide palmered hackle, grizzly or badger, clipped on top
Eyes: Lead eyes painted black on yellow
Weedguard: 15 or 20-pound Mason hard mono
TIED BY TIM BORSKI

Joe's Clouserceiver
(white)

Jon's Red Screamer

Kevin's Snook Fly

Johnny's Gotcha

Junkyard Dog

Keys Tarpon Streamer

Johnny's Needlefish

K.G. Snook Whistler

Keel Eel

Jon's Blue Screamer

Kelp Crab

Kirk's Rattle Rouser
(chartreuse)

Jon's Chartreuse Screamer

Kelp Popper
(umpqua swimming frog, orange)

Kraft Fur Shrimp

KRYSTAL FISH—Joe Butorac

Hook: Mustad 34007, sizes 4-3/0; trailing loop of 40 pound mono for optional second hook
Thread: Transparent sewing thread
Wing: Yellow bucktail; Krystal Flash, pearl, peacock, pink
Head: Thread, continuation of Krystal Flash; epoxy
Eyes: Black paint
Variations: Krystal Flash wing can be blue, green, black, brown, pink.
TIED BY JOE BUTORAC

LABRAXUS—David Woodhouse

Hook: Straight eye, long shank, stainless steel
Thread: Chartreuse
Body: Green Mylar tubing
Lower Wing: Bucktail, white; pearl Crystal Flash
Top Wing: Bucktail, blue, purple; pearl Krystal Flash
Head: Thread under epoxy
Eyes: Moveable doll eyes, black on white
Variations: Black on green on yellow wing
TIED BY DAVID WOODHOUSE, ENGLAND

LABRAXUS (TRASER LIGHT)—David Woodhouse

Hook: Straight eye, long shank, stainless steel
Thread: Chartreuse
Body: Green Mylar tubing
Wing: Bucktail, green, black; pearl Crystal Flash
Head: Thread under epoxy
Eyes: Moveable doll eyes, black on white
Traser Light: Blue
Variations: Various fly colors. Traser lights available in blue, red, green, white, yellow, in sizes from .030" to 1" diameter and larger; self activated, continuous cold-light source. (See Traser Lights in SOURCES chapter)
TIED BY DAVID WOODHOUSE, ENGLAND

LANCE'S CRYSTAL POPPER (WHITE/BLUE)—Lance Gray

Hook: Mustad 9028S, size 2/0
Tail: Frayed pearl Mylar tinsel
Body: Pearl Mylar tinsel over foam, blue over white; epoxy face
Eyes: Painted black on yellow on black
Variations: White/black, white/green, white/red, yellow/black, yellow/green, yellow/red
TIED BY LANCE GRAY/RIVERBORN FLY COMPANY

LANCE'S CRYSTAL POPPER JR. (YELLOW/GREEN)—Lance Gray

Hook: Mustad 34011, size 2/0
Tail: Frayed pearl Mylar tinsel
Body: Pearl Mylar tinsel over foam, green

over yellow; epoxy face
Eyes: Painted black on yellow on black
Variations: White/black, white/green, white/red, yellow/black, white/blue, yellow/red
TIED BY LANCE GRAY/RIVERBORN FLY COMPANY

LANCE'S S.S. MINNOW ANCHOVY—Lance Gray

Hook: Mustad 34407, sizes 2/0-1/0
Thread: Flat waxed white or Flymaster black
Tail: White Super Hair
Body: Pearl Krystal Flash; V-rib
Wing: Krystal Flash, pearl, blue; Super Hair, green, light blue; peacock herl
Throat: Red Krystal Flash
Head: Hot glue
Eyes: Plastic black on white
TIED BY LANCE GRAY/RIVERBORN FLY COMPANY

LEFTY'S DECEIVER (BLUE/WHITE)—Lefty Kreh

Hook: Mustad 34007, size 2/0
Thread: White
Tail: White hackle; blue Fire Flash
Body: Blue Mylar tubing
Front Hackle: Blue bucktail
TIED BY ELIOT NELSON/NORTHWEST TIES

LEFTY'S DECEIVER (BLUE/WHITE)—Lefty Kreh

Hook: Mustad 34007/3407; Daiichi 2546; Tiemco 811S; sizes 3/0
Thread: Black
Tail: White hackle; pearl Krystal Flash
Body: Silver braid;
Collar: White bucktail
Wing: Bucktail, blue; grizzly hackle; pearl Krystal Flash; peacock herl
Eyes: Painted black on yellow
Variations: White, green/white, red/white, yellow, etc.
AVAILABLE THROUGH THE FLY SHOP

LEFTY'S DECEIVER (CHARTREUSE)—Lefty Kreh

Hook: Mustad 34007/3407; Daiichi 2546; Tiemco 811S; sizes 2-6/0
Thread: Matches top colour of wing (chartreuse)
Tail: Hackle, grizzly, white; pearl Krystal Flash
Body: Lead wire under thread
Collar: Bucktail, white
Wing: Bucktail, chartreuse; pearl Krystal Flash
Eyes: Prismatic, red on gold
Variations: Lead eyes; wire weedguard; top colors blue, pink, orange, black, red
TIED BY DARRYL STEEL, AUSTRALIA

LEFTY'S DECEIVER (GREEN/WHITE)—Lefty Kreh

Hook: Mustad 34007/3407; Daiichi 2546; Tiemco 811S; sizes 3/0
Thread: Black
Tail: White hackle; pearl Krystal Flash
Body: Silver braid;
Collar: White bucktail
Wing: Bucktail, green; grizzly hackle; pearl Krystal Flash; peacock herl
Eyes: Painted black on yellow
Variations: White, blue/white, red/white, yellow, etc.
AVAILABLE THROUGH THE FLY SHOP

LEFTY'S DECEIVER (GREEN/YELLOW)—Lefty Kreh

Hook: Mustad 34007, size 2/0
Thread: Chartreuse
Tail: Yellow hackle; gold Krystal Flash
Body: Gold Mylar tubing
Front Hackle: Chartreuse bucktail
TIED BY ELIOT NELSON/NORTHWEST TIES

LEFTY'S DECEIVER (OLIVE)—Lefty Kreh

Hook: Mustad 34007/3407; Daiichi 2546; Tiemco 811S
Thread: Red
Tail: Olive grizzly hackle; peacock Crystal Flash
Body: Silver tinsel
Wing: Peacock herl
Front Hackle: White bucktail
Throat: Red Krystal Flash
TIED BY JIM SYNDER

LEFTY'S DECEIVER (PINK)—Lefty Kreh

Hook: Mustad 34007/3407; Daiichi 2546; Tiemco 811S; sizes 2-6/0
Thread: Matches top colour of wing (pink)
Tail: Hackle, grizzly, white; pearl Krystal Flash
Body: Lead wire under thread
Collar: Bucktail, white
Wing: Bucktail, pink; pearl Krystal Flash
Eyes: Prismatic, red on gold
Variations: Lead eyes; wire weedguard; top colors blue, chartreuse, orange, black, red
TIED BY DARRYL STEEL, AUSTRALIA

LEFTY'S DECEIVER (RED/WHITE)—Lefty Kreh

Hook: Mustad 34007/3407; Daiichi 2546; Tiemco 811S; sizes 3/0
Thread: Black
Tail: White hackle; pearl Krystal Flash
Body: Silver braid;
Collar: White bucktail
Wing: Bucktail, red; grizzly hackle; pearl Krystal Flash; peacock herl
Eyes: Painted black on yellow
Variations: White, blue/white, red/white, yellow, etc.
AVAILABLE THROUGH THE FLY SHOP

SALTWATER FLIES

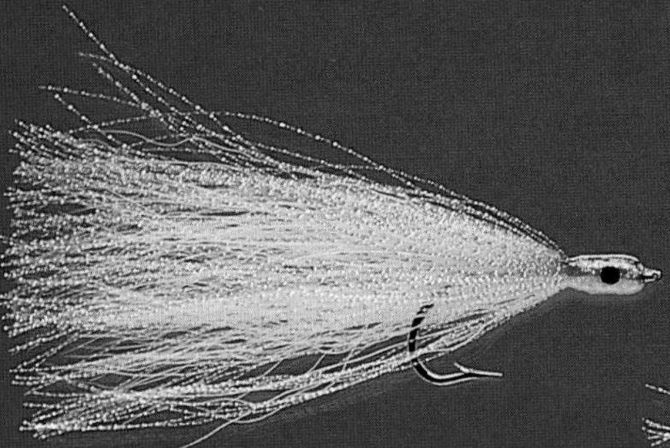

Krystal Fish

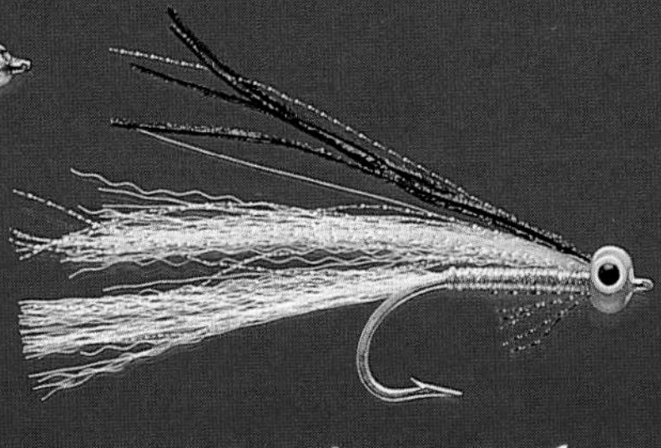

Lance's S.S. Minnow Anchovy

Lefty's Deceiver
(green/white)

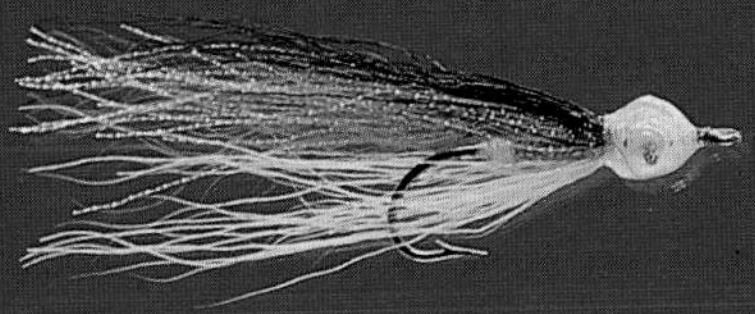

Labraxus

Lefty's Deceiver
(blue/white)

Lefty's Deceiver
(green/yellow)

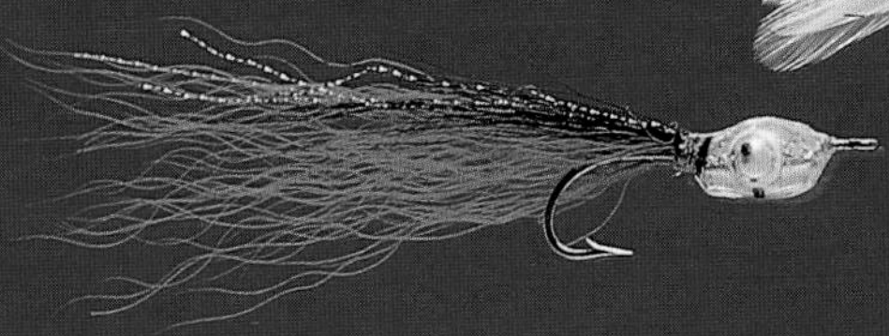

Labraxus
(traser light)

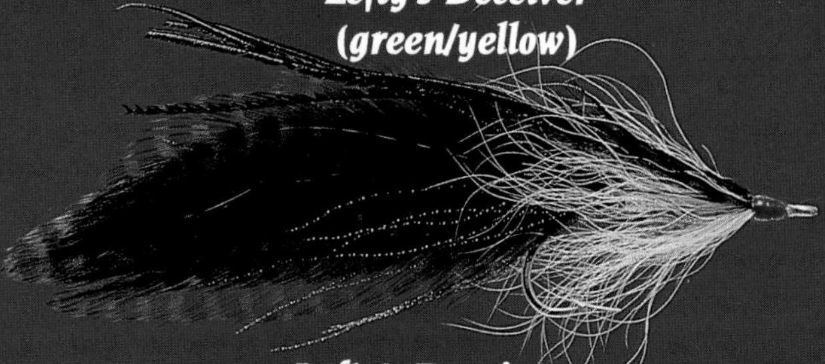

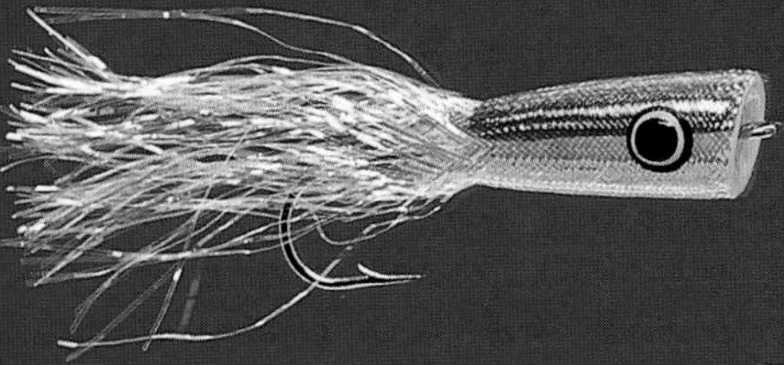

Lance's Crystal Popper
(white/blue)

Lefty's Deceiver
(olive)

Lefty's Deceiver
(blue/white)

Lefty's Deceiver
(pink)

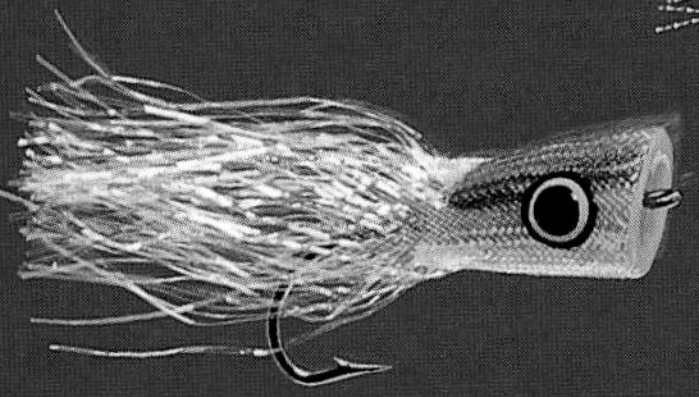

Lance's Crystal Popper Jr.
(yellow/green)

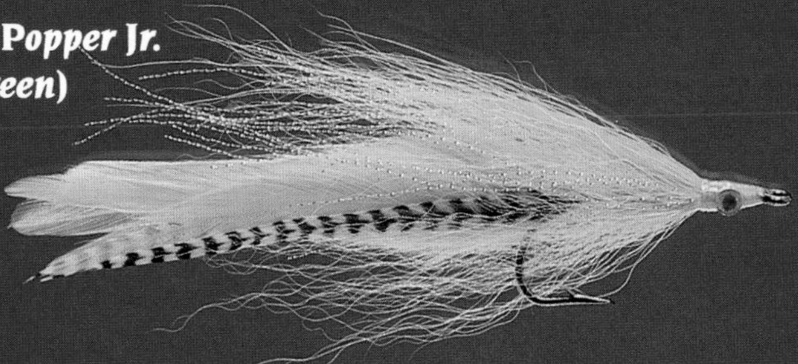

Lefty's Deceiver
(chartreuse)

Lefty's Deceiver
(red/white)

LENNY'S CHARTREUSE BARRACUDA SPECIAL—Capt Lenny Moffo

Hook: Mustad 34007/3407; Daiichi 2546; Tiemco 811S
Tail: Saddle hackle, chartreuse; Crystal Flash, yellow
Body: Epoxy over yellow Krystal Flash
Body Hackle: Saddle hackle, chartreuse
Eyes: Black on orange
TIED BY MCKENZIE FLY TACKLE

LENNY'S CHARTREUSE COCKROACH—Capt Lenny Moffo

Hook: Mustad 34007/3407; Daiichi 2546; Tiemco 811S
Thread: Chartreuse
Tail: Grizzly hackle; pearl Krystal Flash
Body Hackle: Bucktail back
Head: Epoxy over thread
Eyes: Painted black on orange
Variations: Red
TIED BY MCKENZIE FLY TACKLE

LENNY'S CHUGGER—Lenny Moffo

Hook: Mustad 34007/3407, size 3/0-4/0
Tail: Pearl Flashabou; hackle, grizzly, white
Body Hackle: White rabbit strip
Head: White chenille
Eyes: Silver bead chain
TIED BY LENNY MOFFO/MCKENZIE FLY TACKLE

LENNY'S CRUSTACEAN—Capt Lenny Moffo

Hook: Mustad 34007/3407; Daiichi 2546; Tiemco 811S
Tail: Marabou, tan, brown; pearl Crystal Flash; badger hackle
Body: Tan dubbing
Body Hackle: Round white rubber legs
Eyes: Glass, black on amber
TIED BY MCKENZIE FLY TACKLE

LENNY'S WHITE SEA BUNNY—Capt Lenny Moffo

Hook: Mustad 34007/3407; Daiichi 2546; Tiemco 811S
Tail: White rabbit; pearl Krystal Flash
Body Hackle: White rabbit
Head: Thread; pearl Mylar; epoxy
Eyes: Glass, black on amber
TIED BY MCKENZIE FLY TACKLE

LIGHT-LINE CLOUSER (JEREMY EHN)—Bob Clouser

Hook: Mustad 34007/3407; Daiichi 2546; Tiemco 811S
Thread: White
Wing: Bucktail, white, chartreuse; Pearl Krystal Flash
Eyes: Chrome lead eyes
TIED BY JEREMY EHN/ORVIS TYSONS CORNER

LIME LIZZIE—Liz Stelle

Hook: Mustad 34007; sizes 4-1/0
Thread: Chartreuse
Tail: Red floating yarn
Body: .020 lead wire; gold tinsel yarn
Wing: Chartreuse bucktail; chartreuse marabou; gold Flashabou
Variations: Copper, tin, gold
TIED BY LIZ STEELE/THE FLY FISHERMAN

LUREFLASH FLEXI-SHRIMP (RED)—Eric Thompson

Hook: Salmon double, sizes 10-2
Thread: Red
Antennae: Stripped red feather stem; red Krystal Flash
Mouth: Red bucktail
Body: Crystal Chenille, red
Shellback: Bodyflex, red
Front Hackle: Clipped red bucktail
Eyes: Black plastic
Variations: Green
TIED BY ERIC THOMPSON, ENGLAND/CARRILON UK

MAJOR BUNKER—Tom Kintz

Hook: Tiemco 811S, size 4/0
Thread: White size A flat nylon
Tail: Cream or white hackle
Rear Collar: Gray bucktail; brown Streamer Hair; pearl Flashabou
Underbody: .032" lead wire
Body: Pearl Mylar braid
Front Collar: Gray bucktail; Streamer Hair, brown, black; pearl Flashabou
Head: Epoxy
Eyes: 12mm doll eyes black on white
TIED BY TOM KINTZ/UMPQUA FEATHER MERCHANTS

MAJOR HERRING—Tom Kintz

Hook: Tiemco 811S, size 4/0
Thread: White size A flat nylon
Tail: Cream or white hackle
Rear Collar: Gray bucktail; blue Streamer Hair; pearl Flashabou
Underbody: .032" lead wire
Body: Pearl Mylar braid
Front Collar: Gray bucktail; Streamer Hair, blue; pearl Flashabou
Head: Epoxy
Eyes: 12mm doll eyes black on white
TIED BY TOM KINTZ

MANGROVE GHOST—Tim Borski

Hook: Mustad 34007; Tiemco 811S; 1-1/0
Thread: White
Tail: White hackle; pearl Mylar
Body: Gold Mylar; epoxy
Body Hackle: White schlappen
Eyes: Burnt mono
Weedguard: 15 or 20-pound Mason hard mono
TIED BY TIM BORSKI

MARABOU BULLETHEAD—Jack Gartside

Hook: Mustad 34007/3406/34011; Daiichi J196; Partridge CS52; sizes 4-1/0
Thread: 6/0 chartreuse
Underbody: .030 lead wire
Body: 1/2" gold or silver Corsair tubing; thread line colored red
Wing: Marabou, chartreuse, white
Eyes: Painted, black on yellow
Variations: Colors and wing materials, such as Glimmer material or rabbit strip
TIED BY JACK GARTSIDE

MARABOU SHRIMP, KAUFMANN'S (TAN)—Randall Kaufmann

Hook: Mustad 34007/3407; Daiichi 2546; Tiemco 811S; sizes 4-6
Thread: Tan
Body: Copper Krystal Flash
Wing: Tan marabou; tan grizzly; copper Krystal Flash
Front Hackle:
Eyes: Nickel-plated lead painted black on tan
Variations: White, pink, yellow, pearl
TIED BY UMPQUA FEATHER MERCHANTS

MARADEATH—Mark Allen

Hook: Mustad 34011
Thread: Black
Tail: Black saddle hackle; red bucktail;
Body: Black marabou
Eyes: Painted black on red
Head: Epoxy over thread
TIED BY MARK ALLEN/HUNTERS ANGLING SUPPLIES

MARK'S BABY BUNKER—Mark Lewchik

Hook: Mustad 34007/3407; Daiichi 2546; Tiemco 811S
Tail: Craft fur/Fly Fur, purple; pearl Krystal Flash
Body: Pearl Flashabou
Beard: Craft fur/Fly Fur, white;
Wing: Craft fur/Fly Fur, purple, white; permanent marker, blue, black; pearl Krystal Flash
Eyes: Solid plastic, black on yellow
TIED BY MARK LEWCHIK/RIVERS END TACKLE CO

Lenny's Chartreuse
Barracuda Special

Light-Line Clouser

Mangrove Ghost

Lenny's Chartreuse Cockroach

Lime Lizzie

Lureflash Flexi-Shrimp
(red)

Marabou Bullethead

Lenny's Chuggar

Major Bunker

Marabou Shrimp,
Kaufmann's (tan)

Lenny's Crustacean

Maradeath

Major Herring

Lenny's White Sea Bunny

Mark's Baby Bunker

MARK'S BLACK DECEIVER
(MARK LEWCHIK)—Lefty Kreh
Hook: Mustad 34007/3407; Daiichi 2546; Tiemco 811S
Thread: Black
Tail: Black hackle; black Krystal Flash
Body: Black Flashabou
Collar: Black bucktail
Wing: Black Krystal Flash
Gills: Red Flashabou
Eyes: Adhesive, black on silver; epoxy
Variations: Black marabou weighted, black/white, fluorescent yellow, red/yellow
TIED BY MARK LEWCHIK/RIVERS END TACKLE CO

MARK'S BLACK MARABOU WEIGHTED
DECEIVER (MARK LEWCHIK)—LEFTY KREH
Hook: Mustad 34007/3407; Daiichi 2546; Tiemco 811S
Thread: Black
Tail: Black hackle; black Krystal Flash
Body: Black Flashabou
Collar: Black marabou
Wing: Black Krystal Flash
Gills: Red Flashabou
Eyes: Nickel-plated lead; adhesive, black on silver; epoxy
Variations: Black, black/white, fluorescent yellow, red/yellow
TIED BY MARK LEWCHIK/RIVERS END TACKLE CO

MARK'S BLACK/WHITE DECEIVER
(MARK LEWCHIK)—Lefty Kreh
Hook: Mustad 34007/3407; Daiichi 2546; Tiemco 811S
Thread: White
Tail: White hackle; pearl Krystal Flash
Body: Pearl Flashabou
Collar: White bucktail
Wing: Black bucktail; Krystal Flash black, pearl
Gills: Red Flashabou
Eyes: Adhesive, black on silver; epoxy
Variations: Black, black marabou weighted, fluorescent yellow, red/yellow
TIED BY MARK LEWCHIK/RIVERS END TACKLE CO

MARK'S FLUORESCENT YELLOW
DECEIVER (MARK LEWCHIK)—
Lefty Kreh
Hook: Mustad 34007/3407; Daiichi 2546; Tiemco 811S
Thread: Fluorescent yellow
Tail: Fluorescent yellow hackle; pearl Krystal Flash
Body: Chartreuse braid
Collar: Fluorescent yellow bucktail
Wing: Yellow Krystal Flash; peacock herl
Gills: Red Flashabou
Eyes: Adhesive, black on silver; epoxy

Variations: Black, black marabou weighted, black/white, red/yellow
TIED BY MARK LEWCHIK/RIVERS END TACKLE CO

MARK'S HERRING DECEIVER, BLUE
(MARK LEWCHIK)—Lefty Kreh
Hook: Mustad 34007/3407; Daiichi 2546; Tiemco 811S
Thread: White
Tail: White hackle; pearl Krystal Flash
Body: Pearl Mylar
Collar: White bucktail
Wing: Light blue bucktail; Krystal Flash, pearl, blue
Gills: Red Flashabou
Eyes: Adhesive black on silver; epoxy
Variations: Weighted; Peacock
TIED BY MARK LEWCHIK/RIVERS END TACKLE CO

MARK'S HERRING DECEIVER, BLUE
WEIGHTED (MARK LEWCHIK)—
Lefty Kreh
Hook: Mustad 34007/3407; Daiichi 2546; Tiemco 811S
Thread: White
Tail: White hackle; pearl Krystal Flash
Body: Pearl Mylar
Collar: White bucktail
Wing: Light blue bucktail; Krystal Flash, pearl, blue
Gills: Red Flashabou
Eyes: Nickel-plated barbell
Variations: Weighted; Peacock
TIED BY MARK LEWCHIK/RIVERS END TACKLE CO

MARK'S HERRING DECEIVER, PEACOCK
(MARK LEWCHIK)—Lefty Kreh
Hook: Mustad 34007/3407; Daiichi 2546; Tiemco 811S
Thread: White
Tail: White hackle; pearl Krystal Flash
Body: Pearl Mylar
Collar: White bucktail
Wing: Peacock; Krystal Flash, pearl
Gills: Red Flashabou
Eyes: Adhesive black on silver; epoxy
Variations: Blue
TIED BY MARK LEWCHIK/RIVERS END TACKLE CO

MARK'S OFFSHORE MACKEREL
DECEIVER (MARK LEWCHIK)—
Lefty Kreh
Hook: Mustad 34007/3407; Daiichi 2546; Tiemco 811S
Tail: Hackle, yellow, grizzly; gold Flashabou
Body: Gold braid
Collar: Yellow bucktail
Wing: Green bucktail; green Krystal Flash; gold Flashabou; peacock
Gills: Red Flashabou
Eyes: Adhesive black on gold; epoxy
TIED BY MARK LEWCHIK/RIVERS END TACKLE CO

MARK'S RED/YELLOW DECEIVER
(MARK LEWCHIK)—Lefty Kreh
Hook: Mustad 34007/3407; Daiichi 2546; Tiemco 811S
Thread: Red
Tail: Yellow hackle; yellow Krystal Flash
Body: Red thread
Collar: Yellow bucktail
Wing: Red bucktail; yellow Krystal Flash; pearl Flashabou
Gills: Red Flashabou
Eyes: Adhesive, black on yellow; epoxy
Variations: Black, black marabou weighted, fluorescent yellow, red/yellow
TIED BY MARK LEWCHIK/RIVERS END TACKLE CO

MARK'S WORM HATCH FLY—
Mark Lewchik
Hook: Mustad 34007/3407; Daiichi 2546; Tiemco 811S
Tail: Pink marabou, brown permanent marker
Body: Pink chenille, brown permanent marker
Body Hackle: Brown
Variations: Foam strip body
TIED BY MARK LEWCHIK/RIVERS END TACKLE CO

MARTHA'S VINEYARD SQUID FLY—
Jamie Boyle
Hook: Mustad 34011, size 3/0
Thread: White
Tail: White hackle
Body: Silicone over pearl Flashabou
Eyes: Adhesive black on pearl
TIED BY ORVIS

MASTER'S GET YOU (BLACK)—
Peter Masters
Hook: Mchaffy/Masters Wet Fly size 10
Thread: Black Kevlar
Tail: Golden pheasant tippet
Tag: Silver tinsel
Rib: Silver tinsel
Body: Black floss
Wing: Black hair
Front Hackle: Black
Variations: Blue
TIED BY PETER MASTERS, ENGLAND

MASTER'S GET YOU (BLUE)—
Peter Masters
Hook: Mchaffy/Masters Wet Fly size 10
Thread: Black Kevlar
Tail: Golden pheasant tippet
Tag: Silver tinsel
Rib: Silver tinsel
Body: Black floss
Wing: Gray squirrel
Front Hackle: Blue
Variations: Black
TIED BY PETER MASTERS, ENGLAND

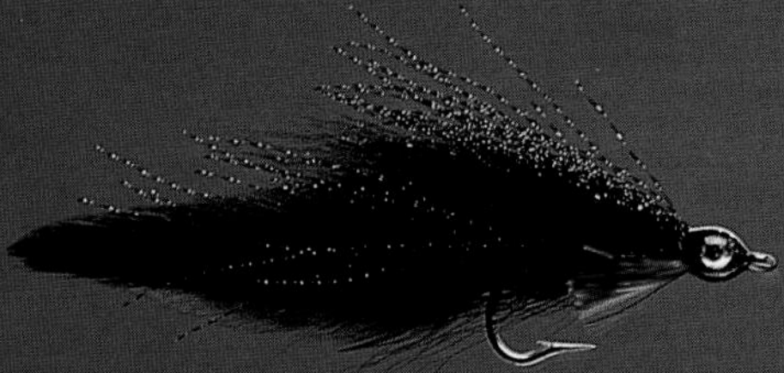

Mark's Black Deceiver

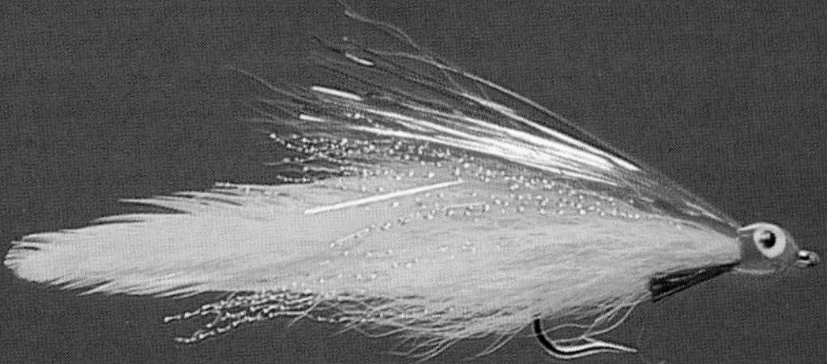

Mark's Red/Yellow Deceiver,

Mark's Herring Deceiver, Blue

Mark's Worm Hatch Fly

Mark's Black Marabou Weighted Deceiver

Mark's Herring Deceiver, Blue Weighted

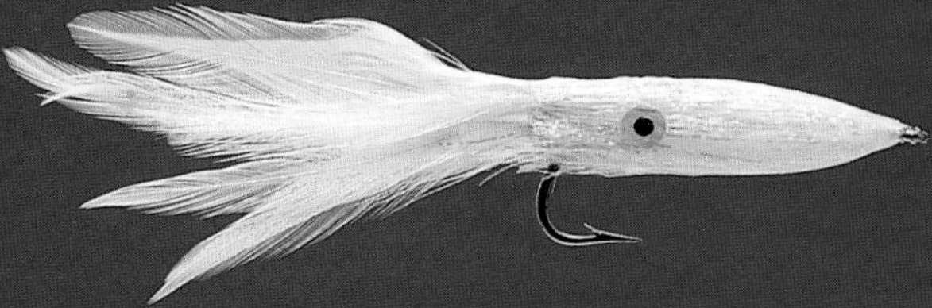

Martha's Vineyard Squid Fly

Mark's Black/White Deceiver

Mark's Herring Deceiver, Peacock

Master's Get You (Black)

Mark's Fluorescent Yellow Deceiver

Mark's Offshore Mackerel Deceiver,

Master's Get You (Blue)

MAXIMUM DECEIVER (BLACK)—
Chris Windram

Hook: Mustad 34007, sizes 3/0-5/0
Thread: Black nylon
Tail: Black hackle
Body: Silver Mylar
Wing: Black hackle; gold Krystal Flash; peacock herl
Head: Black thread
Gills: Red thread
Eyes: Painted black on white
TIED BY CHRIS WINDRAM/TIGHT LINES

MAX'S CHARLIE—Max Poper

Hook: Mustad 34007/3407; Daiichi 2546; Tiemco 811S; sizes 2-6
Thread: Olive
Body: Pearlescent green Krystal Flash
Wing: Pearlescent green Krystal Flash
Eyes: Silver bead chain
TIED BY BOB NAUHEIM

MC CRAB—George Anderson

Hook: Mustad 34007/3407; Daiichi 2546; Tiemco 811S; size 2-1/0
Tail: Tan marabou; tan hackle tips; pearl Krystal Flash
Body: Tan deer hair; black permanent marker; white epoxy belly
Body Hackle: Tan rubber legs and claws; black permanent marker
Eyes: Black plastic
Weight: Lead eyes painted brown
TIED BY UMPQUA FEATHER MER-CHANTS/THE FLY SHOP

MCVAY'S GOTCHA—Jim Mcvay

Hook: Mustad 34007/3407; Daiichi 2546; Tiemco 811S; size 2
Thread: Pink
Tail: Unravelled pearl Mylar tubing
Body: Pearl Mylar tubing
Wing: Tan or blonde craft fur
Eyes: Silver bead chain
AVAILABLE THROUGH THE FLY SHOP

MERCER'S HOT BONEFISH—
Mike Mercer

Hook: Mustad 34007/3407; Daiichi 2546; Tiemco 811S; size 4-6
Thread: Chartreuse
Tail: Chartreuse marabou; chartreuse Krystal Flash; Stretch Floss
Body: Crystal Chenille, chartreuse, orange;
Front Hackle: Yellow grizzly
Eyes: Silver bead chain
TIED BY MIKE MERCER/THE FLY SHOP

MERCER'S SHARKBAIT—Mike Mercer

Hook: Mustad 34007/3407; Daiichi 2546; Tiemco 811S; size 3/0
Tail: Red Ultra Hair; fluorescent red rabbit strip
Body: Fluorescent red dubbing; red Crystal Chenille
Body Hackle: Red grizzly

Head: Thread, black, red; epoxy
TIED BY MIKE MERCER/THE FLY SHOP

MERCER'S TRANSPARENT BONEFISH WORM—Mike Mercer

Hook: Mustad 34007/3407; Daiichi 2546; Tiemco 811S; size 4-6
Body: Pearl Krystal Flash; V-rib, clear
Wing: Craft fur; Stretch Floss
Head: Yellow Krystal Flash; epoxy; silver bead
TIED BY MIKE MERCER/THE FLY SHOP

MIHULKA BLACK/PURPLE SLIMEEL—
Chris Mihulka

Hook: Mustad 34011
Thread: Black
Tail: Hedron Supreme Hair, black, purple
Body: Epoxy over thread
Eyes: Black over yellow
TIED BY MCKENZIE FLY TACKLE

MIHULKA GREEN 49'ER—
Chris Mihulka

Hook: Mustad 36890 Accu-Point
Thread: Black
Body: Pearl Krystal Flash
Wing: Lite Brite, green, olive
Throat: Lime green Lite Brite
Head: Black thread; sparkle nail polish
Variations: See Rainbow; gold/bronze
TIED BY MCKENZIE FLY TACKLE

MIHULKA GRAY BUNNY SQUID—
Chris Mihulka

Hook: Mustad 34007/3407; Eagle Claw L067M Pate
Tail: Pink poly yarn; gray bunny strips
Body: Wool, gray
Eyes: Black on yellow
TIED BY MCKENZIE FLY TACKLE

MIHULKA OLIVE SAND EEL—
Chris Mihulka

Hook: Mustad 34007; Eagle Claw L067M Billy Pate
Tail: Extended pearlescent Mylar tubing
Body: Pearlescent Mylar tubing
Wing: Hedron Supreme Hair, chartreuse, black; Krystal Flash, black
Head: Kreinik caddis green medium braid; epoxy
Eyes: Black on yellow
TIED BY MCKENZIE FLY TACKLE

MIHULKA PRYZM MINNOW—
Chris Mihulka

Hook: Mustad 34011
Tail: Marabou, white; Krystal Flash, pearl
Body: Fishscale epoxy
Eyes: Black on yellow
Weedguard: 15-pound hard Mason
TIED BY MCKENZIE FLY TACKLE

MIHULKA PRYZM POGIE—
Chris Mihulka

Hook: Mustad 34011
Tail: Marabou, gray; Krystal Flash, black

Body: Fishscale epoxy
Eyes: Black on yellow
Weedguard: 15-pound hard Mason
TIED BY MCKENZIE FLY TACKLE

MIHULKA PRYZM SHAD—
Chris Mihulka

Hook: Mustad 34011
Tail: Marabou, white; Krystal Flash, pearl
Body: Fishscale epoxy
Eyes: Black on yellow
Weedguard: 15-pound hard Mason
TIED BY MCKENZIE FLY TACKLE

MIHULKA RAINBOW 49'ER—
Chris Mihulka

Hook: Mustad 36890 Accu-Point
Thread: Black
Body: Pearl Krystal Flash
Wing: Lite Brite, salmon, rainbow
Throat: Pearl Lite Brite
Head: Black thread; sparkle nail polish
Variations: See Green; gold/bronze
TIED BY MCKENZIE FLY TACKLE

MIHULKA SCALE C-SPOON—
Chris Mihulka

Hook: Mustad 34007
Tail: Brown nylon; grizzly hackle
Body: Scale; epoxy
Eyes: Adhesive black on yellow
TIED BY MCKENZIE FLY TACKLE

MIHULKA VIOLET FLASHY FREDDIE—
Chris Mihulka

Hook: Mustad 34007
Body: Pearl Mylar
Wing: Hedron Supreme Hair, white, violet; Krystal Flash, purple, black
Head: Purple braid
Eyes: Adhesive black on yellow
TIED BY MCKENZIE FLY TACKLE

MIHULKA VIOLET/PINK LITTLEFISH—
Chris Mihulka

Hook: Mustad 34007/3407; Eagle Claw L067M Pate
Tail: Fish Hair, white, pink, violet
Body: Epoxy over Fish Hair
Eyes: Painted black on yellow
TIED BY MCKENZIE FLY TACKLE

MINI-EEL (GRAY)—C. Boyd Pfeiffer

Hook: Mustad 34011/34007/3407; Daiichi 2546; Tiemco 811S
Tail: Synthetic wing material, Bestway Super Hair, Thompson Ultra Hair, Touch of Glitz tassel, Fire Fly, Krystal Flash, etc.
Body: Plastic straw over wing material; clear PDI dip
Variations: Straw colors and diameters; add glitter to body while dip dries; dark top, light colored belly as small fish imitation, dark blue/light blue; dark permanent marker on light colored top
TIED BY C. BOYD PFEIFFER

Maximum Deceiver
(black)

Mercer's Transparent
Bonefish Worm

Mihulka Pryzm Shad

Max's Charlie

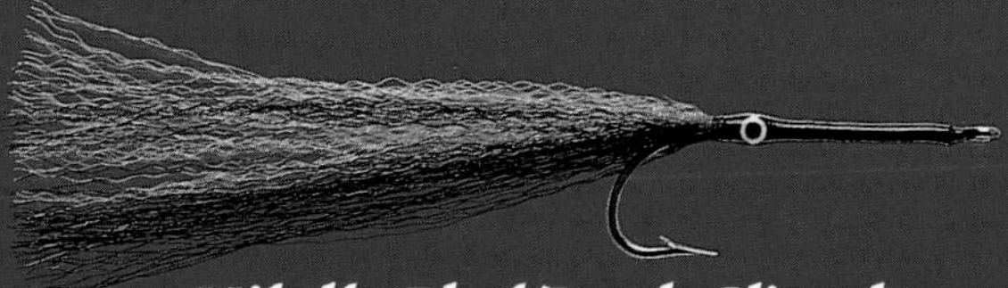

Mihulka Black/Purple Slimeel

Mihulka Rainbow 49'er

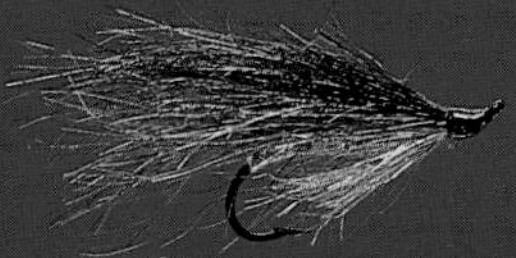

Mihulka Green 49'er

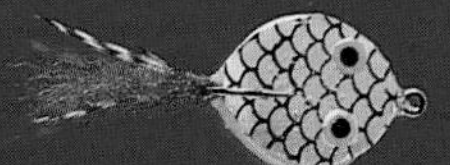

Mihulka Scale C-Spoon

Mc Crab

Mihulka Gray Bunny Squid

Mihulka Violet Flashy Freddie

Mcvay's Gotcha

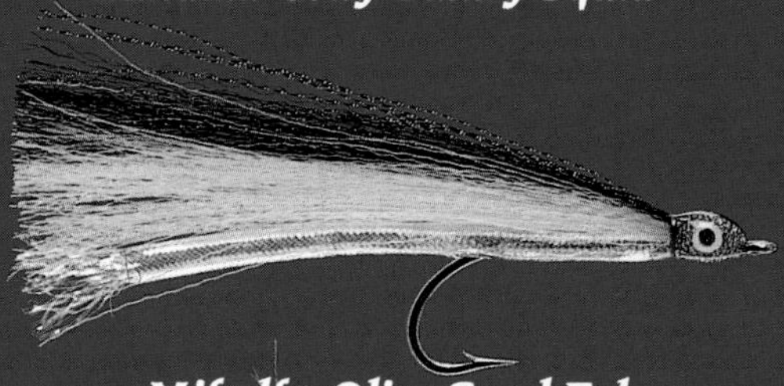

Mihulka Olive Sand Eel

Mercer's Hot Bonefish

Mihulka Pryzm
Minnow

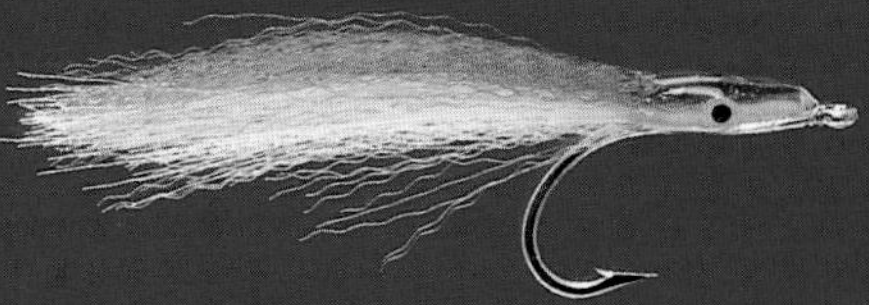

Mihulka Violet/Pink Littlefish

Mercer's Sharkbait

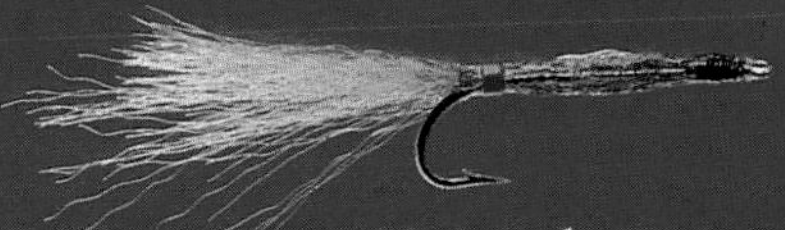

Mini-Eel
(gray)

Mihulka Pryzm Pogie

MINI PUFF (PINK)

Hook: Mustad 34007/3407; Daiichi 2546;
Tiemco 811S; size 4
Wing: Grizzly hackle; tan calf tail
Head: Fluorescent pink chenille
Eyes: Silver bead chain
Variations: Tan/orange
AVAILABLE THROUGH THE FLY SHOP

MINNEEL, WHITE—Greg Miheve

Hook: Mustad 34011, sizes 4-1/0
Thread: Flat waxed nylon, white
Tail: White bucktail; pearl Krystal Flash;
peacock herl
Body: Pearl Flashabou; clear
Swannundaze or V-rib over tail
materials
Gills: Fluorescent red thread
Head: Black thread
Variations: Chartreuse, blue, purple,
yellow, green, black
TIED BY GREG MIHEVE

MOFFO BROWN FLEEING CRAB—
Capt Lenny Moffo

Hook: Mustad 34007/3407; Daiichi 2546;
Tiemco 811S
Thread: 3/0
Tail: Natural gum rubber; brown
permanent marker; tips red or
orange, permanent marker
Body: Brown Aunt Lydia's yarn
Eyes: Plated lead eyes
TIED BY LENNY MOFFO/MCKENZIE FLY
TACKLE

MOFFO BROWN-RIBBED BONEFISH
FLY—Capt Lenny Moffo

Hook: Mustad 34007/3407; Daiichi 2546;
Tiemco 811S
Thread: Brown
Body: Monofilament over pearl Mylar
Wing: Red fox squirrel tail
Eyes: Silver bead chain
Variations: Rainbow-ribbed
TIED BY MCKENZIE FLY TACKLE

MOFFO CHARTREUSE BENDBACK
MINNOW—Capt Lenny Moffo

Hook: Mustad 34007/3407; Daiichi 2546;
Tiemco 811S
Body: Monofilament; gold tinsel
Wing: Bucktail, yellow, green; gold/silver
Mylar; grizzly hackle
Eyes: Painted black on orange
Head: Epoxy over thread
Variations: Black
TIED BY MCKENZIE FLY TACKLE

MOFFO DARK MOHAIR SHRIMP—
Capt Lenny Moffo

Hook: Mustad 34007/3407; Daiichi 2546;
Tiemco 811S
Thread: Black
Body: Dark mohair
Wing: Brown kip tail

Eyes: Silver bead chain
Variations: Light
TIED BY MCKENZIE FLY TACKLE

MOFFO GRAY AND BROWN TARPON
TOY—Capt Lenny Moffo

Hook: Mustad 34007/3407; Daiichi 2546;
Tiemco 811S
Thread: Fluorescent red
Tail: Furnace hackle; pearl Krystal Flash
Body Hackle: Gray rabbit
Head: Thread; epoxy
Eyes: Painted black on yellow
Variations: Gray and purple
TIED BY MCKENZIE FLY TACKLE

MOFFO GREEN ANTRON CRAB—
Capt Lenny Moffo

Hook: Mustad 34007/3407; Daiichi 2546;
Tiemco 811S
Thread: Green
Tail: White marabou; pearl Krystal Flash
Body: Tan Antron
Body Hackle: Rubber legs, gray with red
Eyes: Nickel-plated lead
TIED BY MCKENZIE FLY TACKLE

MOFFO LIGHT FAT-HEAD PERMIT FLY—
Capt Lenny Moffo

Hook: Mustad 34007/3407; Daiichi 2546;
Tiemco 811S
Tail: Tan marabou; pearl Krystal Flash;
grizzly hackle
Body: Pearl Mylar; epoxy
Head: Pearl Mylar; epoxy
Eyes: Glass; black in amber
Variations: Dark
TIED BY MCKENZIE FLY TACKLE

MOFFO OPTIC ORANGE
'CUDA SCOOTA—Capt Lenny Moffo

Hook: Mustad 34007/3407; Daiichi 2546;
Tiemco 811S
Thread: Hot orange
Body: Hot orange thread
Wing: Fish hair, hot orange; Flashabou,
pearl; Krystal Flash, orange
Head: Epoxy over thread
Eyes: Plastic bead
TIED BY MCKENZIE FLY TACKLE

MOFFO ORANGE FAT-BOTTOM BONE-
FISH FLY—Capt Lenny Moffo

Hook: Mustad 34007/3407; Daiichi 2546;
Tiemco 811S
Thread: Black
Tail: Fluorescent orange wool
Body: Gray chenille
Wing: White kip tail; pearl Krystal Flash
Eyes: Silver bead chain
TIED BY MCKENZIE FLY TACKLE

MOFFO PINK BUCKSHOT BONEFISH
FLY—Capt Lenny Moffo

Hook: Mustad 34007/3407; Daiichi 2546;
Tiemco 811S

Tail: Marabou, white; grizzly hackle;
Krystal Flash, pink
Body: Epoxy over pink Krystal Flash
Eyes: Buckshot
TIED BY MCKENZIE FLY TACKLE

MOFFO PURPLE SEA PUP—
Capt Lenny Moffo

Hook: Mustad 34007/3407; Daiichi 2546;
Tiemco 811S
Tail: Purple rabbit; purple Crystal Hair
Body: Purple wool
Body Hackle: Purple rabbit
Eyes: Glass, black on yellow
Variations: Orange
TIED BY MCKENZIE FLY TACKLE

MOFFO TARPON SHRIMP—
Capt Lenny Moffo

Hook: Mustad 34007/3407; Daiichi 2546;
Tiemco 811S
Thread: Pink
Tail: Pink marabou; hackle, pink, grizzly;
pearl Krystal Flash
Body: Tan chenille
Body Hackle: Tan hackle
Eyes: Pink plastic beads
TIED BY MCKENZIE FLY TACKLE

MOFFO WHITE ANTRON GHOST CRAB

Hook: Mustad 34007/3407; Daiichi 2546;
Tiemco 811S
Tail: Marabou, white; grizzly hackle;
Krystal Flash, pearl
Body: Antron yarn
Legs: Rubber with red tips
Eyes: Nickel-platedd lead
Variations: Green, gray, orange.
TIED BY MCKENZIE FLY TACKLE

MONTAGUE BLUE MYSTERY
MINNOW—Jack Montague

Hook: Mustad 34007/3407; Daiichi 2546;
Tiemco 811S
Tail: Fish Hair, white, blue; blue Crystal
Flash
Body: Epoxy over Mylar strip, blue Crystal
Flash
Weedguard: Mono loop
Eyes: Adhesive, black on red
Variations: Green
TIED BY MCKENZIE FLY TACKLE

MONTAGUE CHARTREUSE FLAT
BELLY—Jack Montague

Hook: Mustad 34007/3407; Daiichi 2546;
Tiemco 811S
Thread: Black
Tail: Pearl Mylar tubing ends
Body: Pearl Mylar tubing squashed flat;
epoxy
Wing: Chartreuse marabou; Mylar; copper
Krystal Flash; grizzly hackle
Variations: Red/yellow
TIED BY MCKENZIE FLY TACKLE

**Mini Puff
(pink)**

Moffo Gray and Brown Tarpon Toy

Moffo Purple Sea Pup

Minneel, White

Moffo Green Antron Crab

Moffo Tarpon Shrimp

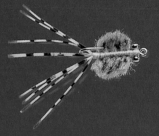

Moffo Brown Fleeing Crab

Moffo Light Fat-Head Permit Fly

Moffo White Antron Ghost Crab

**Moffo Brown-Ribbed
Bonefish Fly**

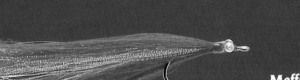

Moffo Optic Orange 'Cuda Scoota

Montague Blue Mystery Minnow

Moffo Chartreuse Bendback Minnow

**Moffo Orange Fat-Bottom
Bonefish Fly**

Montague Chartreuse Flat Belly

Moffo Dark Mohair Shrimp

Moffo Pink Buckshot Bonefish Fly

MONTAGUE DARK BROWN EPOXY BONEFISH FLY—Jack Montague

Hook: Mustad 34007/3407; Daiichi 2546; Tiemco 811S
Tail: Brown nylon; grizzly hackle
Body: Epoxy painted brown over white
Eyes: Painted black on red
Variations: Light brown
TIED BY MCKENZIE FLY TACKLE

MONTAGUE DARK RATTLE CRAB—Jack Montague

Hook: Mustad 34007/3407; Daiichi 2546; Tiemco 811S
Body: Epoxy, dark brown over white
Body Hackle: Philoplume and stem
Front Hackle: Ringneck pheasant breast feathers
Eyes: Black
TIED BY MCKENZIE FLY TACKLE

MONTAGUE FUZZY SHRIMP—Jack Montague

Hook: Mustad 34007/3407; Daiichi 2546; Tiemco 811S
Thread: White
Body: Dark gray marabou
Wing: White nylon
Front Feelers: White nylon
Eyes: Silver bead chain
TIED BY MCKENZIE FLY TACKLE

MONTAGUE LIGHT BROWN EPOXY PERMIT FLY—Jack Montague

Hook: Mustad 34007/3407; Daiichi 2546; Tiemco 811S
Tail: Ringneck pheasant breast feathers; brown nylon
Body: Epoxy, light brown over white
Eyes: Black on red
TIED BY MCKENZIE FLY TACKLE

MONTAGUE NEEDLEFISH—Jack Montague

Hook: Mustad 34007/3407; Daiichi 2546; Tiemco 811S
Tail: Deer hair; badger hackle; white wool; green Fish Hair; peacock herl; green Krystal Flash; Mylar strips
Body: Epoxy, painted olive over white
Eyes: Painted black on white
Weedguard: Single wire strand
TIED BY MCKENZIE FLY TACKLE

MONTAGUE PINK SUPER CHARLIE—Jack Montague

Hook: Mustad 34007/3407; Daiichi 2546; Tiemco 811S
Thread: Black
Body: Epoxy
Wing: Pink nylon; grizzly hackle; pink Krystal Flash
Eyes: Silver bead chain
TIED BY MCKENZIE FLY TACKLE

MONTAGUE SQUID—Jack Montague

Hook: Mustad 34007/3407; Daiichi 2546; Tiemco 811S
Tail: Deer hair; tan hackle; tan marabou
Body: Epoxy, tan
Eyes: Adhesive, black on silver
TIED BY MCKENZIE FLY TACKLE

MORNING STAR—Ed Mitchell

Hook: Daiichi 2546, size 1/0
Thread: Pink
Tail: Pink bucktail; rainbow Krystal Flash; peacock herl
Body: Pearl Crystal braid; peacock herl or synthetic hair topping
Rib: Copper wire
Eyes: Non-toxic, black on yellow; or bead chain or lead
TIED BY ED MITCHELL

MOTHER OF EPOXY

Hook: Mustad 34007/3407; Daiichi 2546; Tiemco 811S
Tail: Tan marabou; badger hackle
Body: Epoxy, tan
Weedguard: Monofilament, two strands
Eyes: Black
Variations: Without weedguard; cream, chartreuse, pink
TIED BY JERRY MARTIN/HUNTERS ANGLING SUPPLIES

M.O.E. (MOTHER OF EPOXY, PINK)—Riverborn Fly Company

Hook: Mustad 3407, sizes 2-8
Thread: Danville Flymaster 6/0 pink and Flymaster Plus 1/0 pink
Tail: Pink marabou; pearl Krystal Flash; grizzly hackle
Body: Epoxy, pink
Body Hackle: Grizzly
Eyes: Silver bead chain
Variations: Belize green, bonefish orange, chartreuse, root beer, tan, yellow sunrise
TIED BY LANCE GRAY/RIVERBORN FLY COMPANY

MRS NELSON (SMALL)—Bill Nelson

Hook: Tandem, first hook Mustad 34007 clipped just ahead of bend, 25-pound mono loop, reversed short shank Mustad 92553, sizes 1-1/0
Wing: Polar Hair or 24 denier FisHair, white, pink, purple; Krystal Flash, pearl, pink, purple
Head: Epoxy
Eyes: Adhesive black on yellow
TIED BY BILL NELSON/MCKENZIE FLY TACKLE

MRS NELSON (MEDIUM)—Bill Nelson

Hook: Tandem, first hook Mustad 34007 clipped just ahead of bend, 25-pound mono loop, reversed short shank Mustad 92553, sizes 1-1/0
Wing: Polar Hair or 24 denier FisHair, white, pink, purple; Krystal Flash, pearl, pink, purple
Head: Epoxy
Eyes: Adhesive black on yellow
TIED BY BILL NELSON/MCKENZIE FLY TACKLE

MRS NELSON (LARGE)—Bill Nelson

Hook: Tandem, first hook Mustad 34007 clipped just ahead of bend, 25-pound mono loop, reversed short shank Mustad 92553, sizes 1-1/0
Wing: Polar Hair or 24 denier FisHair, white, pink, purple; Krystal Flash, pearl, pink, purple
Head: Epoxy
Eyes: Adhesive black on yellow
TIED BY BILL NELSON/MCKENZIE FLY TACKLE

MUDDLED DECEIVER, BLACK (Turrall)

Hook: Mustad 34007/3407; Daiichi 2546; Tiemco 811S
Wing: Black hackle; black Krystal Flash
Front Hackle: Deer hair, black
Head: Deer hair, black
TIED BY TURRALL

MUDDLED DECEIVER, NATURAL (Turrall)

Hook: Mustad 34007/3407; Daiichi 2546; Tiemco 811S
Wing: White hackle; pearl Krystal Flash
Front Hackle: Deer hair
Head: Deer hair
TIED BY TURRALL

MUDDLED DECEIVER, WHITE (Turrall)

Hook: Mustad 34007/3407; Daiichi 2546; Tiemco 811S
Wing: White and grizzly hackle; pearl Krystal Flash
Front Hackle: Deer hair, white
Head: Deer hair, white
TIED BY TURRALL

MULLIN SQUID—Chris Mullin

Hook: Mustad 34007/3407; Daiichi 2546; Tiemco 811S
Thread: Dressmaker
Tail: Sevenstrand luminous skirt; white hackle, black spots permanent marker; Krystal Flash, pearl
Body: Tulip Sparkle Paint Writer
Eyes: Moveable doll eyes, black in white
Variations: White, pink
TIED BY CHRIS MULLIN/CASTLE ARMS

NATURAL SQUID—Tom Kintz

Hook: Mustad 34011 size 2/0
Thread: Tan size A flat nylon
Tail: Mottled creme hackle; pearl Flashabou
Rear Collar: Tan elk hair
Underbody: .032 lead wire
Body: Pearl or gold Mylar braid
Front Collar: Gold Krystal Flash; tan elk hair
Eyes: Plastic, black on yellow or gold
TIED BY TOM KINTZ

Montague Dark Brown
Epoxy Bonefish Fly

Montague Rattle Crab

Montague Fuzzy Shrimp

Montague Light Brown Epoxy
Permit Fly

Montague Needlefish

Montague Pink
Super Charlie

Montague Squid

Morning Star

Mother of Epoxy

M.O.E.
(Mother of
Epoxy, pink)

Mrs Nelson
(small)

Mrs Nelson
(medium)

Mrs Nelson
(large)

Muddled Deceiver, Black

Muddled Deceiver, Natural

Muddled Deceiver, White

Mullin Squid

Natural Squid

NEEDLEFISH—Tony Weaver

Hook: Tiemco 5263
Thread: White
Tail: Pearl Mylar tubing
Body: Pearl Mylar tubing
Wing: Bucktail, white, blue; pearl Crystal Flash
Lower Wing: White bucktail
Eyes: Adhesive, black on pearl; epoxy
TIED BY TONY WEAVER

NELSON ANCHOVY—Bill Nelson

Hook: Tandem, first hook Mustad 34007 clipped just ahead of bend, 25-pound mono loop, reversed short shank Mustad 92553, sizes 1-1/0
Wing: Polar Hair or 24 denier FisHair, white, pink, green, turquoise; Crystal Flash, pearl, pink
Head: Epoxy
Eyes: Adhesive black on yellow
TIED BY BILL NELSON/MCKENZIE FLY TACKLE

NELSON BAITFISH—Bill Nelson

Hook: Tandem, first hook Mustad 34007 clipped just ahead of bend, 25-pound mono loop, reversed short shank Mustad 92553, sizes 1-1/0
Thread: White
Wing: White Polar Hair or 24 denier FisHair; pearl Krystal Flash
Front Hackle: Red Polar Hair or 24 denier FisHair
Head: Epoxy
Eyes: Adhesive black on red
TIED BY BILL NELSON/MCKENZIE FLY TACKLE

NELSON'S BEACH FLY—Bill Nelson

Hook: Mustad 34007/3407; Daiichi 2546; Tiemco 811S
Wing: Polar Hair or 24 denier FisHair, white, orange, blue; Krystal Flash, pearl, orange; purple Lite Brite
Head: Epoxy
Eyes: Adhesive black on yellow
TIED BY BILL NELSON

NELSON CRAB SPAWN—Bill Nelson

Hook: Tandem, first hook Mustad 34007 clipped just ahead of bend, 25-pound mono loop, reversed short shank Mustad 92553, sizes 1-1/0
Wing: Polar Hair or 24 denier FisHair, white, orange; Krystal Flash, pearl, orange
Head: Epoxy
Eyes: Adhesive red on black
TIED BY BILL NELSON/MCKENZIE FLY TACKLE

NELSON FRY—Bill Nelson

Hook: Mustad 34007/3407; Daiichi 2546; Tiemco 811S
Thread: White
Tail: White bucktail; Krystal Flash, pearl, pink
Body: Thread
Eyes: Painted black
TIED BY BILL NELSON

NELSON NEEDLEFISH—Bill Nelson

Hook: Tandem, first hook Mustad 34007 clipped just ahead of bend, 25-pound mono loop, reversed short shank Mustad 92553, sizes 1-1/0
Wing: Polar Hair or 24 denier FisHair, white, pink, green, black; Crystal Flash, pearl, pink, green, black
Head: Epoxy
Eyes: Adhesive black on yellow
TIED BY BILL NELSON/MCKENZIE FLY TACKLE

NELSON SHRIMP SPAWN—Bill Nelson

Hook: Tandem, first hook Mustad 34007 clipped just ahead of bend, 25-pound mono loop, reversed short shank Mustad 92553, sizes 1-1/0
Wing: Polar Hair or 24 denier FisHair, white, green, pink; Krystal Flash, pearl, green, pink
Head: Epoxy
Eyes: Adhesive black on yellow
TIED BY BILL NELSON/MCKENZIE FLY TACKLE

NINE MILE BANK EPOXY (BROWN)—Jim Buckingham

Hook: Mustad 34007/3407, sizes 2-6
Thread: Flat waxed nylon
Tail: Pearl Krystal Flash; brown marabou; furnace hackle
Body: Poly braid, pearl; epoxy
Body Hackle: Furnace
Eyes: Plastic dumb bell
Weedguard: Optional, 15-pound hard Mason, crimped hinge
TIED BY JIM BUCKINGHAM

NOISY NEEDLEFISH—Jon Cave

Hook: Mustad 34011, size 1/0
Thread: Chartreuse
Tail: Chartreuse hackle; peacock herl
Body: Thread over rattle capsule; epoxy
Underbelly: White bucktail; pearl Crystal Flash
Cheeks: Golden Pheasant metallic green neck feathers
Eyes: 5mm doll eyes
TIED BY JON CAVE

OLCH'S MOTIVATOR (PEARL)—Jon Olch

Hook: Mustad 34007/3407; Daiichi 2546; Tiemco 811S
Thread: White
Tail: Tan craft fur; brown variant hackle
Body: Pearl Flashabou; silicone
Eyes: Silver bead chain
TIED BY JON OLCH/UMPQUA FEATHER MERCHANTS

OLCH'S NEEDLEFISH—Jon Olch

Hook: Mustad 34007/3407; Daiichi 2546; Tiemco 811S; tandem
Thread: Chartreuse
Body: Yarn, fluorescent red, chartreuse
Wing: Streamer Hair, white, chartreuse, green
Head: Silicone over thread
Eyes: Doll eyes
TIED BY JON OLCH/UMPQUA FEATHER MERCHANTS

OLCH'S TARPON GLO (GREEN)—Jon Olch

Hook: Mustad 34007/3407; Daiichi 2546; Tiemco 811S
Thread: Chartreuse
Tail: Blue FisHair; hackle, green, grizzly, olive grizzly
Body: Thread under epoxy
Collar: Green, grizzly
Gills: Painted red
Eyes: Painted black on yellow
Variations: Grizzly, orange, yellow
TIED BY JON OLCH/UMPQUA FEATHER MERCHANTS

OLCH'S TARPON GLO (GRIZZLY)—Jon Olch

Hook: Mustad 34007/3407; Daiichi 2546; Tiemco 811S
Thread: Fluorescent red
Tail: Brown bucktail; hackle, grizzly, orange grizzly
Body: Thread under epoxy
Collar: Grizzly, orange grizzly
Head: Chartreuse thread; epoxy
Beak: Fluorescent red thread; epoxy
Eyes: Painted yellow on black
Variations: Green, orange, yellow
TIED BY JON OLCH/UMPQUA FEATHER MERCHANTS

OLCH'S TARPON GLO (ORANGE)—Jon Olch

Hook: Mustad 34007/3407; Daiichi 2546; Tiemco 811S
Thread: Orange
Tail: Red fox squirrel tail; hackle, orange, badger
Body: Thread under epoxy
Collar: Orange, badger
Eyes: Painted black on yellow
Variations: Green, grizzly, yellow
TIED BY JON OLCH/UMPQUA FEATHER MERCHANTS

OLCH'S TARPON GLO (YELLOW)—Jon Olch

Hook: Mustad 34007/3407; Daiichi 2546; Tiemco 811S
Thread: Yellow
Tail: Teal; hackle, orange, yellow
Body: Thread under epoxy
Collar: Orange, yellow
Eyes: Painted black on red
Variations: Green, grizzly, orange
TIED BY JON OLCH/UMPQUA FEATHER MERCHANTS

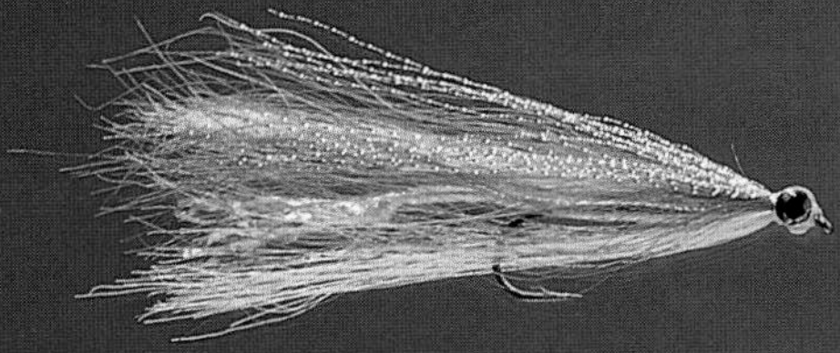

Needlefish

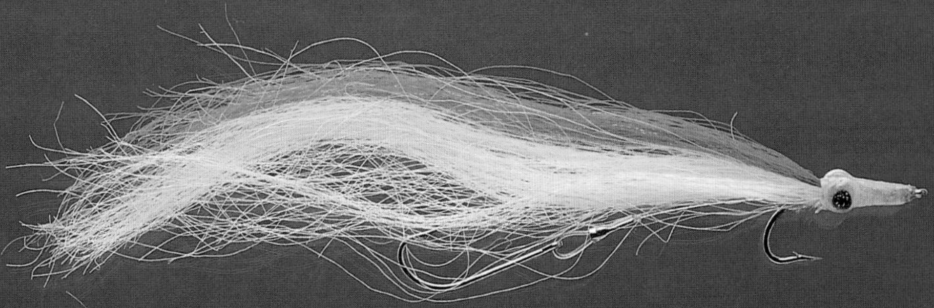

Olch's Needlefish

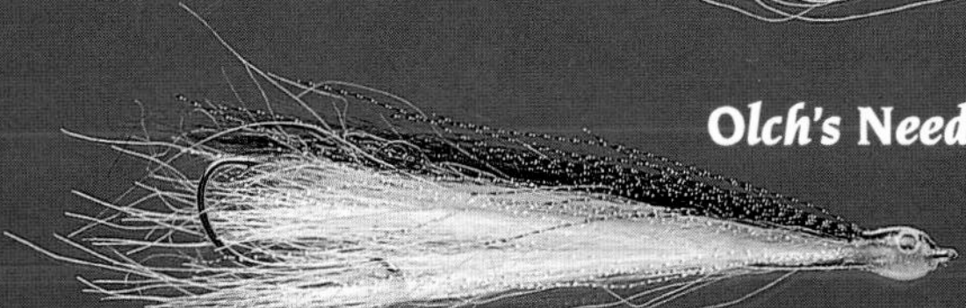

Nelson Needlefish

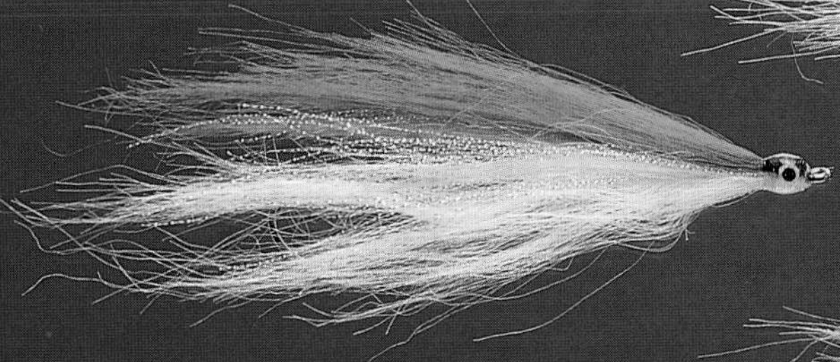

Nelson Anchovy

Olch's Tarpon Glo
(green)

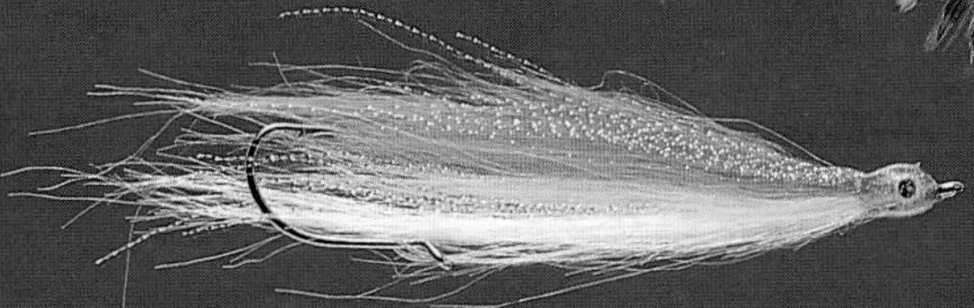

Nelson Shrimp Spawn

Nelson Baitfish

Olch's Tarpon Glo
(grizzly)

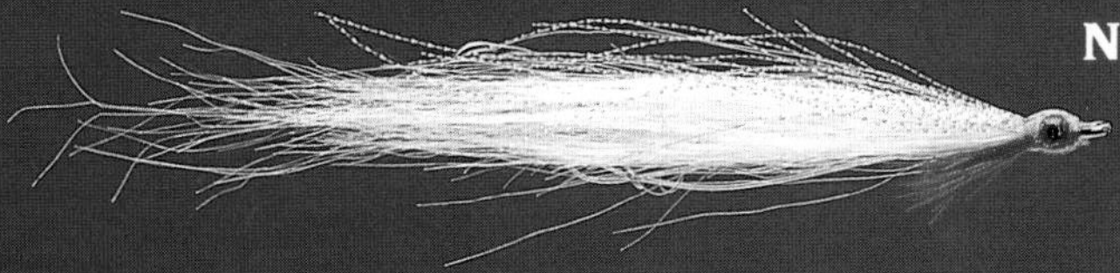

Nine Mile Bank Epoxy
(brown)

Nelson's Beach Fly

Olch's Tarpon Glo
(orange)

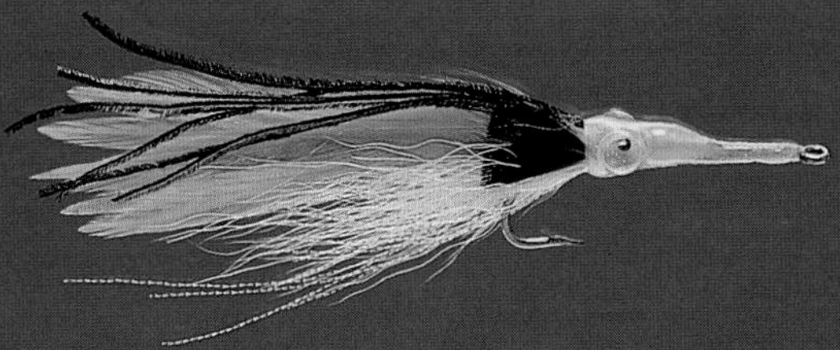

Noisy Needlefish

Nelson's Crab Spawn

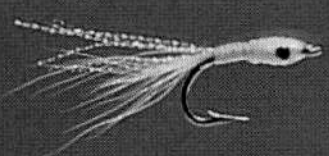

Nelson Fry

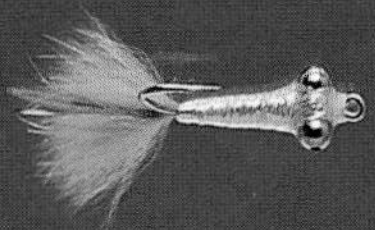

Olch's Motivator
(pearl)

Olch's Tarpon Glo
(yellow)

OPAI MANTIS SHRIMP (ORANGE)—
Bighorn Fly Trading
Hook: Gamakatsu, sizes 8-10
Thread: Orange
Tail: Brown craft fur
Body: Orange yarn; dark mono ribbing
Shellback: Pearlescent sheeting
Legs: Orange Krystal Flash; stiff mono
Antennae: Orange grizzly hackle clipped
Eyes: Mono burnt, painted black
Variations: White
TIED BY BIGHORN FLY TRADING

ORANGE BUTT TARPON FLY—
Tim Borski
Hook: Mustad 34007; 2/0
Thread: Black
Tail: Kraft fur #1872; Pantone marker
#147-M; hot orange Krystal Flash
Body: Fluorescent orange chenille
Front Hackle: Gray fox or gray squirrel
TIED BY TIM BORSKI

THE ORIGINAL
STU APTE TARPON FLY—Stu Apte
Hook: Mustad 34007/3407; Daiichi 2546;
Tiemco 811S
Thread: Red
Tail: Orange and red hackle
Body: Red thread
Body Hackle: Orange and red hackle
TIED BY MCKENZIE FLY TACKLE

OUTLINER CRAB—Terry Baird
Hook: Gamakatsu
Tail: Orange calf tail
Weight: Lead barbell
Body: Flashabou Mylar
Body Hackle:
Wing: White calftail; white FisHair;
orange calf tail
Front Hackle:
Eyes: Black plastic bead chain
TIED BY TERRY BAIRD/BIGHORN FLY
TRADING

PAGE'S PEARLY BAIT—Page Rogers
Hook: Mustad 34011
Thread: Danville flat waxed nylon, white
Tail: White marabou
Body: Pearl Mylar tubing; epoxy
Eyes: Witchcraft 2 EY, black on yellow
TIED BY PAGE ROGERS/UMPQUA
FEATHER MERCHANTS

PAGE'S SAND EEL (BLACK/PEARL)—
Page Rogers
Hook: Mustad 34011; Eagle Claw 066SS
Thread: Danville flat waxed nylon, white
Tail: Fly Fur: Polar White, black; salt-n-
pepper Flashabou
Body: Pearl Mylar tubing; permanent
marker, black on top; epoxy
Gills: Painted, Testors gloss red
Eyes: Witchcraft 2 EY, black on yellow
Variations: Brown/pearl, olive/pearl
TIED BY PAGE ROGERS/UMPQUA
FEATHER MERCHANTS

PAGE'S SAND EEL (BROWN/PEARL)—
Page Rogers
Hook: Mustad 34011; Eagle Claw 066SS
Thread: Danville flat waxed nylon, white
Tail: Fly Fur: Polar White, light pink,
auburn; pink pearlescent Fly Flash;
silver Flashabou
Body: Pearl Mylar tubing; permanent
marker, light pink on sides, dark
brown on top; epoxy
Gills: Painted, Testors gloss red
Eyes: Witchcraft 2 EY, black on silver
Variations: Olive/pearl, black/pearl
TIED BY PAGE ROGERS/UMPQUA
FEATHER MERCHANTS

PAGE'S SAND EEL (OLIVE/PEARL)—
Page Rogers
Hook: Mustad 34011; Eagle Claw 066SS
Thread: Danville flat waxed nylon, white
Tail: Polar White Fly Fur; Fluorescent
Day-Glo chartreuse FisHair; lime
pearlescent Fly Flash; silver
Flashabou; Moss Green Fly Fur
Body: Pearl Mylar tubing; permanent
marker, light green on sides, dark
green on top; epoxy
Gills: Painted, Testors gloss red
Eyes: Witchcraft 2 EY, black on silver
Variations: Brown/pearl, black/pearl
TIED BY PAGE ROGERS/UMPQUA
FEATHER MERCHANTS

PARAURCHIN—Terry Baird
Hook: Mustad 34007/3407; Daiichi 2546;
Tiemco 811S
Thread: Chartreuse
Body: Thread
Body Hackle: Guinea, dark, monofilament
post
Eyes: Lead barbell
TIED BY ROGER LEE/BIGHORN FLY
TRADING

PEACOCK SWORD DECEIVER—
Lenny Moffo
Hook: Mustad 34011, size 1/0-4/0
Tail: Frayed Mylar tubing ends
Body: Mylar tubing, various colors
Wing: Bucktail, white, pink, purple; pearl
Krystal Flash; peacock sword
Head: Black 3/0 flat waxed thread; epoxy
Eyes: Adhesive, black on yellow
TIED BY LENNY MOFFO

PENCIL POPPER (BLACK/SILVER)
Hook: Long shank size 2/0
Tail: White hackle
Body: Foam, black, silver
Body Hackle: White
Eyes: Painted black on yellow
Variations: fluorescent pink/silver
AVAILABLE THROUGH THE FLY SHOP

PENCIL POPPER (BLUE)—Edgewater
Hook: Mustad 33669CT 1/0; Mustad 9082S
2/0
Tail: Marabou, white; Flashabou, pearl
Body: Foam, blue
Eyes: Black on yellow post
Variations: Black, chartreuse, yellow,
white, purple.
TIED BY EDGEWATER

PENCIL POPPER
(FLUORESCENT PINK/SILVER)
Hook: Long shank size 2/0
Tail: White hackle
Body: Foam, fluorescent pink, silver
Body Hackle: White
Eyes: Painted black on yellow
Variations: Black/silver
AVAILABLE THROUGH THE FLY SHOP

PETE'S BELIZE CRAB—Pete Parker
Hook: Mustad 34007; Tiemco 811S;
size 2-4
Thread: Kevlar or Dyna Cord
Body: Green deer hair
Legs: Rubber legs, knotted, or pipe
cleaners; black permanent marker
Claws: Green saddle hackle
Mouth: Afterfeather or filoplume,
pheasant rump feather
Eyes: Imitation flower stamens; epoxy
TIED BY PETE PARKER

PETE'S EPOXY CRAB—Pete Parker
Hook: Tiemco 811S, size 4
Thread: None
Body: Ribbon epoxy; 5-minute epoxy
Legs: Silicone, yellow; black permanent
marker
Eyes: Imitation flower stamens; epoxy
TIED BY PETE PARKER

PETE'S SAND EEL—Peter Masters
Hook: Partridge Macaffey wet fly size 6
Thread: Black Kevlar
Tail: none
Tag: Fluorescent red floss
Rib: Fine silver wire
Body: Fluorescent white floss
Wing: Purple, mauve hair; pearl Crystal
Flash
Eyes: Black painted on white
TIED BY PETER MASTERS, ENGLAND

PETRIE'S SHRIMP—Mark Petrie
Hook: Mustad 34011, size 2
Antennae: Black rubber
Tail: Tan marabou; gold sparkle yarn
Body: Tan Furry Foam over medium Ice
Chenille, orange
Eyes: Burnt 100-pound mono
Weedguard: Mono loop
Variations: Can vary colors as needed.
TIED BY MARK PETRIE/SALTWATER SPE-
CIALTIES

SALTWATER FLIES

Opai Mantis Shrimp (orange)

Page's Sand Eel (brown/pearl)

Pencil Popper (blue)

Orange Butt Tarpon Fly

Page's Sand Eel (olive/pearl)

Pencil Popper (flourescent pink/silver)

The Original Stu Apte Tarpon Fly

Paraurchin

Pete's Belize Crab

Outliner Crab

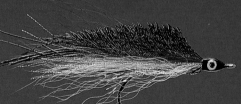

Peacock Sword Deceiver

Pete's Epoxy Crab

Page's Pearly Bait

Pete's Sand Eel

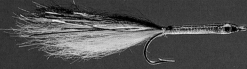

Page's Sand Eel (black/pearl)

Pencil Popper (black/silver)

Petrie's shrimp

PINK PANTHER—Turrall

Hook: Mustad 34007/3407; Daiichi 2546; Tiemco 811S
Tail: Black hackle
Body Hackle: Pink marabou
Wing: Pearl Krystal Flash
Front Hackle: Black deer hair
Head: Black deer hair
TIED BY TURRALL

PINK SANDS, KAUFMANN'S—Randall Kaufmann

Hook: Mustad 34007/3407; Daiichi 2546; Tiemco 811S; sizes 4-8
Thread: Pink
Body: Pink Krystal Flash
Wing: Pink craft fur; white hackle tips; pink Krystal Flash
Front Hackle:
Eyes: Nickel-plated lead painted black/white/pink
Variations: White, pink, yellow, pearl
TIED BY UMPQUA FEATHER MERCHANTS

PISTOL/SNAPPING SHRIMP (OLIVE)—Craig Mathews

Hook: Mustad 3407; Daiichi 2546; Tiemco 800S, sizes 6-10
Thread: 3/0 white monocord
Tail: Rabbit hair, olive; Krystal Flash, olive; golden pheasant tippet
Body: Zelon, olive
Body Hackle: Grizzly hackle, clipped
Head: Orange Antron
Eyes: Gold bead chain
Variations: White, brown, purple, gray/grizzly
TIED BY CRAIG MATHEWS/BLUE RIBBON FLIES

POLAR AIRE SEA MINNOW (ANCHOVIE)—Bill Black

Hook: Mustad 34007/3407; Daiichi 2546; Tiemco 811S
Thread: White
Tail: Mono loop; pearl Lite Brite; Polar Aire, polar white, smoke, green
Eyes: Plastic black on amber
Variations: Herring, Spearing
TIED BY BILL BLACK/SPIRIT RIVER, INC

POLAR AIRE SEA MINNOW (HERRING)—Bill Black

Hook: Mustad 34007/3407; Daiichi 2546; Tiemco 811S
Thread: White
Tail: Mono loop; pearl Lite Brite; pearl Magnum Lite Brite; Polar Aire, polar white, blue
Eyes: Plastic black on white
Variations: Anchovie, Spearing
TIED BY BILL BLACK/SPIRIT RIVER, INC

POLAR AIRE SEA MINNOW (SPEARING)—Bill Black

Hook: Mustad 34007/3407; Daiichi 2546; Tiemco 811S
Thread: White
Tail: Mono loop; pearl Lite Brite; pearl Magnum Lite Brite; Polar Aire, polar white, smoke, yellow
Eyes: Plastic black on white
Variations: Anchovie, Herring
TIED BY BILL BLACK/SPIRIT RIVER, INC

POLAR BEAR MINNOW—Ken Durrant

Hook: Extra long shank
Thread: Black
Tail: Red polar bear
Body: Pearl tubing
Wing: Polar bear, white, red, purple; dark blue Fly Flash; peacock herl
Front Hackle: Red polar bear
Eyes: Painted black on white
TIED BY KEN DURRANT, CANADA

POP'S BONEFISH BITTERS (AMBER)—Craig Mathews

Hook: Tears of the Keys blanks; Mustad 3407; Daiichi 2546; Tiemco 800S; sizes 6-10
Thread: 6/0 amber
Body: Epoxy, amber
Body Hackle: Sili rubber legs, amber
Wing: Zelon, amber
Front Hackle: Deer hair
Eyes: Gold bead chain
Variations: Olive, bright green, white, orange
TIED BY CRAIG MATHEWS/BLUE RIBBON FLIES

POP'S BONEFISH BITTERS (BRIGHT GREEN)—Craig Mathews

Hook: Tears of the Keys blanks; Mustad 3407; Daiichi 2546; Tiemco 811S; sizes 6-10
Thread: 6/0 bright green
Body: Epoxy, bright green
Body Hackle: Sili rubber legs, bright green
Wing: Zelon, bright green
Front Hackle: Deer hair
Eyes: Silver bead chain
Variations: Olive, amber, white, orange
TIED BY CRAIG MATHEWS/BLUE RIBBON FLIES

POP'S BONEFISH BITTERS (OLIVE)—Craig Mathews

Hook: Tears of the Keys blanks; Mustad 3407; Daiichi 2546; Tiemco 811S; sizes 6-10
Thread: 6/0 olive
Body: Epoxy, olive
Body Hackle: Sili rubber legs, olive
Wing: Zelon, olive
Front Hackle: Deer hair
Eyes: Gold bead chain
Variations: Amber, bright green, white, orange
TIED BY CRAIG MATHEWS/BLUE RIBBON FLIES

POP'S BONEFISH BITTERS (ORANGE)—Craig Mathews

Hook: Tears of the Keys blanks; Mustad 3407; Daiichi 2546; Tiemco 811S; sizes 6-10
Thread: 6/0 orange
Body: Epoxy, orange
Body Hackle: Sili rubber legs, orange
Wing: Zelon, orange
Front Hackle: Deer hair
Eyes: Gold bead chain
Variations: Olive, bright green, white, amber
TIED BY CRAIG MATHEWS/BLUE RIBBON FLIES

POP'S BONEFISH BITTERS (WHITE)—Craig Mathews

Hook: Tears of the Keys blanks; Mustad 3407; Daiichi 2546; Tiemco 811S; sizes 6-10
Thread: 6/0 white
Body: Epoxy, white
Body Hackle: Sili rubber legs, white
Wing: Zelon, white
Front Hackle: Deer hair
Eyes: Silver bead chain
Variations: Olive, bright green, amber, orange
TIED BY CRAIG MATHEWS/BLUE RIBBON FLIES

PRAWN PATTERN—Darryl Steel

Hook: Mustad 34007/3407; Daiichi 2546; Tiemco 811S
Thread: White
Tail: Fox or possum hair; Firetail; wood duck feather fibers
Shellback: Gray raffia
Body: Gray raffia
Body Hackle: Grizzly
Eyes: Stem eyes, pink
Variations: Lead wire; wire loop weedguard. Tied in black and pink, with thread to match.
TIED BY DARRYL STEEL, AUSTRALIA

PRETTY DOG, YELLOW—Turrall

Hook: Mustad 34007/3407; Daiichi 2546; Tiemco 811S
Thread: Black
Tail: Marabou, yellow; pearl Flashabou
Body: Gold tinsel
Front Hackle: Orange
Eyes: Painted black on white
Variations: Black, red/white, orange, white.
TIED BY TURRALL

PURPLE PASSION—Frank Steele

Hook: Mustad 34007; sizes 2-2/0
Thread: Gray
Body: Pearl tinsel yarn; weighted
Wing: Bucktail, white, gray, lavender; pearl Krystal Flash; grizzly hackle; peacock herl
TIED BY FRANK STEELE/THE FLY FISHERMAN

Pink Panther

**Polar Aire Sea Minnow
(Spearing)**

**Pop's Bonefish Bitters
(orange)**

Pink Sands, Kaufmann's

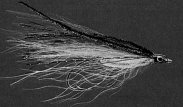

Polar Bear Minnow

**Pop's Bonefish Bitters
(white)**

**Pistol/Snapping Shrimp
(olive)**

Prawn Pattern

**Pop's Bonefish Bitters
(amber)**

**Polar Aire Sea Minnow
(anchovie)**

**Pop's Bonefish Bitters
(bright green)**

Pretty Dog, Yellow

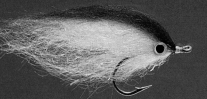

**Polar Aire Sea Minnow
(herring)**

**Pop's Bonefish Bitters
(olive)**

Purple Passion

PURPLE POON TARPON—
Capt Kevin Guerin
Hook: Mustad 34007/3407; Daiichi 2546;
   Tiemco 811S
Thread: Red
Tail: Purple hackle; red Krystal Flash
Body: Red thread under epoxy
Body Hackle: Red marabou
TIED BY CAPT KEVIN GUERIN

PURPLE TARPON
Hook: Mustad 34007/3407; Daiichi 2546;
   Tiemco 811S; size 3/0
Thread: Black
Tail: Purple hackle; purple Flashabou
Rear Hackle: Purple
Head: Thread under epoxy
Eyes: Painted black on yellow
TIED BY JOE BRANHAM/THE FLY SHOP

RABBITSTRIP DIVER (RED/WHITE)—
Larry Dahlberg
Hook: Mustad 34007/3407; Daiichi 2546;
   Tiemco 811S; size 1/0
Tail: White rabbit strip; red Flashabou
Collar: Red deer hair
Head: Deer hair, white, red
Eyes: Plastic black on yellow
Variations: Mullet/sucker, rust/orange
TIED BY UMPQUA FEATHER MER-
CHANTS

RADFORD'S WAGGLER—Steve Radford
Hook: Mustad 34007 size 4
Thread: White
Tail: Pearl Delta Lure
Body: Pearl Delta Lure
Wing: Black squirrel hair; pearl Crystal
   Hair; dark green Flashabou
Front Hackle: Red rabbit fur
Head: Fluorescent light green Antron
TIED BY STEVE PARTON/SPARTON FISH-
ING TACKLE, ENGLAND

RAGHEAD CRAB—Jan Isley
Hook: Mustad 34007/3407; Daiichi 2546;
   Tiemco 811S; size 2-8
Thread: Chartreuse
Tail: Tan marabou; tan hackle; pearl
   Krystal Flash
Body: Tan yarn; glue
Body Hackle: White rubber legs
Eyes: Nickel-plated lead
AVAILABLE THROUGH THE FLY SHOP

RAGHEAD CRAB—
Riverborn Fly Company
Hook: Mustad 3407, sizes 1/0-6
Thread: Flymaster chartreuse
Tail: Tan marabou; rootbeer Krystal
   Flash; furnace hackle
Body: Tan sparkle yarn
Body Hackle: Round white rubber legs
Eyes: Nickel-plated lead eyes
Variations: Brown, olive
TIED BY LANCE GRAY/RIVERBORN FLY
COMPANY

RAINBOW RUNNER OFFSHORE FLY—
Jon Olch
Hook: Mustad 34007/3407; Daiichi 2546;
   Tiemco 811S
Thread: Red
Tail: Streamer Hair, chartreuse, white
Body: Silver braid
Beard: Pink bucktail
Wing: Green bucktail; silver Mylar
Eyes: Painted black on white
TIED BY JON OLCH

RALPH'S HACKLED EPOXY
BONEFISH FLY—Ralph Woodbine
Hook: Mustad 34007, size 6
Thread: 6/0 prewaxed white
Tail: Tan marabou
Body: White yarn; pearl braid; brown
   marking pen; epoxy
Body Hackle: Cree; Zap-A-Gap; Zap-A-
   Gap kicker
Eyes: Medium bead chain painted black
TIED BY RALPH WOODBINE

RALPH'S NYLON CUDA FLY—
Ralph Woodbine
Hook: Mustad 34007, size 2
Thread: 6/0 prewaxed white
Tail: White nylon filaments, 5-inches
   long; pearl Flashabou
Body: White yarn; pearl braid; epoxy
Eyes: Black on yellow painted or decal
Variations: White, green and blue tail or
   all green.
TIED BY RALPH WOODBINE

RAT TAIL (CHARTREUSE)—Steve Shiba
Hook: Mustad 34007/3407; Daiichi 2546;
   Tiemco 811S
Tail: Rat tail, chartreuse
Body: Foam, chartreuse
Eyes: Black on yellow post or nickel
   plated lead eyes
Variations: Black, white, purple,
   black/purple tail, black/raspberry tail.
TIED BY EDGEWATER

RATTLE N POP (WHITE)—Edgewater
Hook: Mustad 34011 3/0; Mustad 9082S
   2/0
Tail: Bucktail, white; Krystal Flash, pearl
Body: Foam, white
Eyes: Black on yellow post
Variations: Black, chartreuse, peppermint,
   white/red tail, yellow, purple.
TIED BY EDGEWATER

RATTLIN' MINNOW—Jon Cave
Hook: Mustad 34011, size 1/0
Thread: Black
Tail: Strands of pearl Mylar tubing
Body: Pearl Mylar tubing over rattle
   capsule and adhesive backed
   aluminum or lead
Wing: Bucktail, black, white; pearl Crystal
   Flash

Gills: Red Flashabou
Eyes: Painted black on yellow or adhesive
TIED BY JON CAVE

RATTLIN' MULLET—Jon Cave
Hook: Mustad 34011
Thread: White
Tail: Bucktail, white, brown; pearl Crystal
   Flash; rattle capsule
Body: Deer hair, natural, brown, white,
   red
Eyes: 7mm doll eyes
TIED BY JON CAVE

RATTLIN' ROGUE 2 (JOHN KUMISKI)—
Tom Jindra
Hook: Mustad 34007/3407; Daiichi 2546;
   Tiemco 811S
Thread: Black
Tail: Frayed silver Mylar tubing
Body: Silver Mylar tubing over rattle
   capsule
Wing: Bucktail, white, green; pearl Crystal
   Flash
Head: Chartreuse chenille
Eyes: Nickel-plated lead
TIED BY JOHN KUMISKI

REDFISH CANDY—Dan Johnson
Hook: Mustad 34007; sizes 2/0-2
Tail: Chartreuse hackle; pearl Flashabou
Body: Pink Estaz
Body Hackle: Chartreuse
Eyes: Lead barbell, 1/36, 1/50, painted
   black on white
TIED BY DAN JOHNSON/THE FLY FISH-
ERMAN

REDFISH FLY—Jon Olch
Hook: Mustad 34007/3407; Daiichi 2546;
   Tiemco 811S
Thread: Fluorescent pink
Tail: White hackle; silver Flashabou
Body: Thread under epoxy
Body Hackle: Marabou, white, red
TIED BY JON OLCH/UMPQUA FEATHER
MERCHANTS

REDFISH MURKY HABIT
(FLASH/GREEN)—Bighorn Fly Trading
Hook: Gamakatsu, size 2-4
Thread: Green
Tail: Hackle, grizzly, white, brown; pearl
   Krystal Flash
Antennae: Pearl Krystal Flash
Tag: Chartreuse chenille
Body: Chartreuse pearl braid
Rear Wing: White calf tail
Body Hackle: Clipped grizzly
Eyes: Black plastic bead chain
Weedguard: Single strand mono at hook
   eye
Variations: Red/white, flash/orange
TIED BY BIGHORN FLY TRADING

SALTWATER FLIES

Purple Poon Tarpon

Rainbow Runner Offshore Fly

Ralph's Hackled Epoxy Bonefish Fly

Rattlin' Mullet

Purple Tarpon

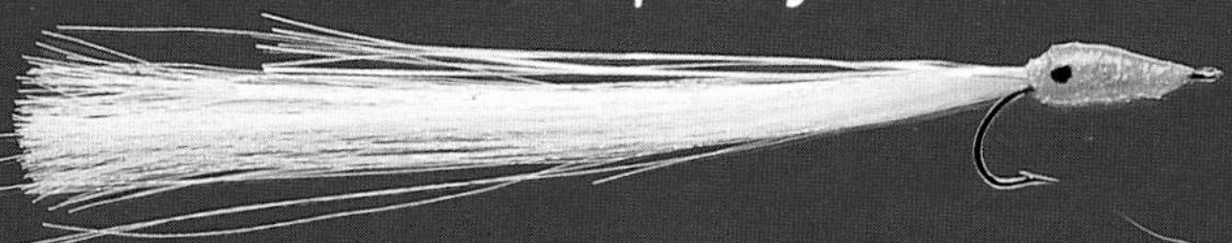

Ralph's Nylon Cuda Fly

Rabbitstrip Diver (red/white)

Rattlin' Rogue 2 (John Kumiski)

Rat Tail (chartreuse)

Redfish Candy

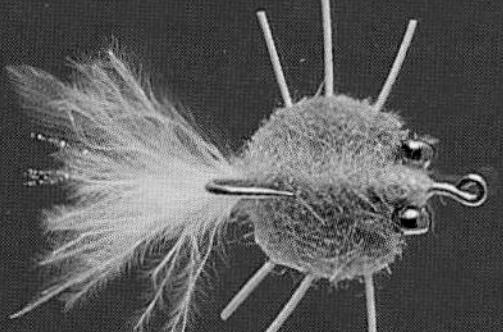

Radford's Waggler

Raghead Crab

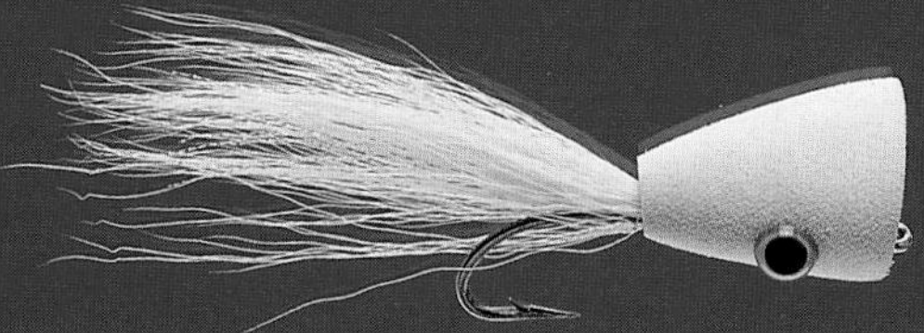

Rattle N Pop (white)

Redfish Fly

Raghead Crab

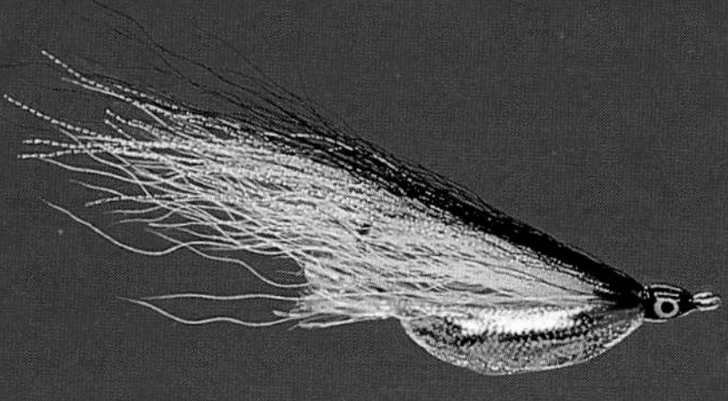

Rattlin' Minnow

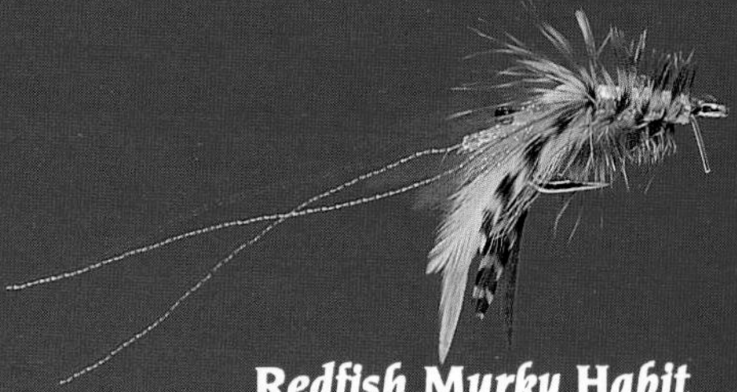

Redfish Murky Habit (flash/green)

REDFISH MURKY HABIT (FLASH/ORANGE)—Bighorn Fly Trading

Hook: Gamakatsu, size 2-4
Thread: Orange
Tail: Hackle, grizzly, white, brown; pearl Krystal Flash
Antennae: Pearl Krystal Flash
Tag: Chartreuse chenille
Body: Orange pearl braid
Rear Wing: White calf tail
Body Hackle: Clipped grizzly
Eyes: Black plastic bead chain
Weedguard: Single strand mono at hook eye
Variations: Red/white, flash/green
TIED BY BIGHORN FLY TRADING

REDFISH MURKY HABIT (RED/WHITE)—Bighorn Fly Trading

Hook: Gamakatsu, size 2-4
Thread: White
Tail: Hackle, grizzly, white, brown; pearl Krystal Flash
Antennae: Pearl Krystal Flash
Tag: Chartreuse chenille
Rear Wing: White calf tail
Body: White chenille
Body Hackle: Clipped red
Eyes: Black plastic bead chain
Weedguard: Single strand mono at hook eye
Variations: Flash/orange, flash/green
TIED BY BIGHORN FLY TRADING

RED WHITE TARPON

Hook: Mustad 34007/3407; Daiichi 2546; Tiemco 811S; size 3/0
Thread: Red
Tail: White hackle
Rear Hackle: Red
Head: Thread under epoxy
Eyes: Painted black on yellow
TIED BY JOE BRANHAM/THE FLY SHOP

REEF DEMON (WHOLLY MACKEREL)—Tom Kintz

Hook: Tiemco 811S, size 4/0
Thread: White size A flat nylon
Tail: Hackle, chartreuse, blue, grizzly; pearl Flashabou
Underbody: .032" lead wire
Body: Pearl Mylar braid
Collar: White bucktail; pearl Flashabou
Topping: Chartreuse bucktail; black permanent marker (Sharpie)
Head: Epoxy
Eyes: 9mm plastic, black on silver
TIED BY TOM KINTZ

REEFSALT SQUID (WHITE)—Bighorn Fly Trading

Hook: Gamakatsu, size 2-4
Thread: White
Tail: Hackle, silver badger, white; white marabou; pink Krystal Flash
Body: White vernille
Side Wing: White FisHair
Wing: White Polar Hair

Eyes: Plastic, black on yellow
Variations: Light blue
TIED BY BIGHORN FLY TRADING

RIO CHICO CRYSTAL

Hook: Mustad 34007/3407; Daiichi 2546; Tiemco 811S; size 1/0
Thread: White
Underwing: Pearl Krystal Flash
Overwing: Red Krystal Flash
Head: Wing material under epoxy
Eyes: Adhesive black on silver
TIED BY JOE BRANHAM/THE FLY SHOP

ROADKILL—Mark Petrie

Hook: Mustad 34007, size 4
Tail: Grizzly hackle; Krystal Flash, red, gold
Body Hackle: Grizzly hackle
TIED BY MARK PETRIE/SALTWATER SPE-CIALTIES

ROCKFISH CHARLEY (CHARTREUSE)

Hook: Mustad 34007/3407; Daiichi 2546; Tiemco 811S; size 2
Thread: Chartreuse
Tail: Pearl Krystal Flash
Body: Chartreuse Krystal Flash; epoxy
Wing: Chartreuse rabbit strip; Pearl Krystal Flash
Eyes: Nickel-plated lead
Variations: Red
AVAILABLE THROUGH THE FLY SHOP

ROCKFISH CHARLEY (RED)

Hook: Mustad 34007/3407; Daiichi 2546; Tiemco 811S; size 2
Thread: Fluorescent pink
Tail: Pearl Krystal Flash
Body: Pink Krystal Flash; epoxy
Wing: Fluorescent pink rabbit strip; Pearl Krystal Flash
Eyes: Nickel-plated lead
Variations: Chartreuse
AVAILABLE THROUGH THE FLY SHOP

ROCKFISH DECEIVER

Hook: Mustad 34007/3407; Daiichi 2546; Tiemco 811S
Thread: Black
Tail: Yellow hackle; red Krystal Flash
Body: Thread
Collar: Yellow bucktail
Wing: Chartreuse bucktail
Throat: Red Krystal Flash
Eyes: Painted black on white
AVAILABLE THROUGH THE FLY SHOP

ROCKFISH MUDDLER

Hook: Tiemco 9394, size 2
Tag: Red thread
Body: Gold Mylar tubing
Wing: Marabou, yellow, orange; gold Flashabou; peacock herl
Collar: Deer hair, yellow, orange, black
Head: Deer hair, yellow, orange, black
AVAILABLE THROUGH THE FLY SHOP

ROCKIN' ROLLER (BLACK)—C. Boyd Pfeiffer

Hook: Mustad 34011; Tiemco 511S; size 1-1/0
Thread: Cover hook shank
Tail: Brown craft fur; purple Fire Flash
Body: Black soft hair roller foam; epoxy glue
Eyes: Optional
Variations: Cut head for popper (flat), slider (slope face up), skipper (slope face down), or spouter (cut sides like prow of ship); paint body with fabric paint; vary tail materials; vary eyes: prism, dressmaker pins, doll eyes, plastic stem eyes, dots of fabric paint
TIED BY C. BOYD PFEIFFER

ROCKIN' ROLLER (YELLOW)—C. Boyd Pfeiffer

Hook: Mustad 34011; Tiemco 511S; size 2
Thread: Cover hook shank
Tail: Bucktail, white, red; silver Fire Flash
Body: Yellow soft hair roller foam; epoxy glue
Eyes: Plastic, orange on red
Variations: Cut head for popper (flat), slider (slope face up), skipper (slope face down), or spouter (cut sides like prow of ship); paint body with fabric paint; vary tail materials; vary eyes: prism, dressmaker pins, doll eyes, plastic stem eyes, dots of fabric paint
TIED BY C. BOYD PFEIFFER

ROGERS' BIG-EYE BAITFISH (BLACK)—Page Rogers

Hook: Tiemco 800S
Thread: Danville's flat waxed nylon, black
Body: Black hackle; pearlescent black Fly Flash,
Throat: Black bucktail
Topping: Black bucktail
Eyeplate: Black prismatic tape
Eyes: Witchcraft adhesive, black on yellow
Variations: Herring, chartreuse, mackerel, yellow, hot tamale, bunker
TIED BY PAGE ROGERS/UMPQUA FEATHER MERCHANTS

ROGERS' BIG-EYE BAITFISH (BUNKER)—Page Rogers

Hook: Tiemco 800S
Thread: Danville's flat waxed nylon, white
Body: White hackle; pearlescent and silver Fire Fly Tie
Throat: White bucktail; red wool
Shoulder: Super dark blue bucktail
Topping: Black bucktail; purple pearlescent Fly Flash; blue Umpqua Streamer Hair
Eyeplate: Dark blue prismatic tape
Eyes: Witchcraft adhesive, black on yellow
Variations: Herring, chartreuse, black, yellow, hot tamale, mackerel
TIED BY PAGE ROGERS/UMPQUA FEATHER MERCHANTS

Redfish Murky Habit
(flash/orange)

Rio Chico Crystal

Rockin' Roller
(black)

Redfish Murky Habit
(red/white)

Roadkill

Rockin' Roller
(yellow)

Rockfish Charley
(chartreuse)

Red White Tarpon

Rockfish Charley
(red)

Roger's Big-Eye Baitfish
(black)

Reef Demon
(Wholly Mackerel)

Rockfish Deceiver

Reefsalt Squid
(white)

Rockfish Muddler

Roger's Big-Eye Baitfish
(bunker)

ROGERS' BIG-EYE BAITFISH (CHARTREUSE)—Page Rogers

Hook: Tiemco 800S
Thread: Danville's flat waxed nylon, chartreuse
Body: Chartreuse hackle; lime pearlescent Fly Flash; silver Flashabou
Throat: White bucktail; red wool
Shoulder: Chartreuse bucktail
Eyeplate: Chartreuse prismatic tape
Eyes: Witchcraft adhesive, black on orange
Variations: Herring, yellow, mackerel, black, hot tamale, bunker
TIED BY PAGE ROGERS/UMPQUA FEATHER MERCHANTS

ROGERS' BIG-EYE BAITFISH (HERRING)—Page Rogers

Hook: Tiemco 800S
Thread: Danville's flat waxed nylon, white
Body: White hackle; pearl and silver Fire Fly Tie
Throat: White bucktail; red wool
Shoulder: Gray bucktail
Topping: Olive and black pearlescent Fly Flash; peacock herl
Eyeplate: Silver prismatic tape
Eyes: Witchcraft adhesive, black on orange
Variations: Chartreuse, yellow, mackerel, black, hot tamale, bunker
TIED BY PAGE ROGERS/UMPQUA FEATHER MERCHANTS

ROGERS' BIG-EYE BAITFISH (HOT TAMALE)—Page Rogers

Hook: Tiemco 800S
Thread: Danville's flat waxed nylon, fluorescent fire orange
Body: Fluorescent orange and fluorescent red hackle; red pearlescent Fly Flash
Throat: Fluorescent yellow bucktail
Shoulder: Yellow grizzly hackle
Topping: Copper Flashabou; peacock herl
Eyeplate: Fluorescent yellow prismatic tape
Eyes: Witchcraft adhesive, black on orange
Variations: Herring, chartreuse, black, yellow, bunker, mackerel
TIED BY PAGE ROGERS/UMPQUA FEATHER MERCHANTS

ROGERS' BIG-EYE BAITFISH (MACKEREL)—Page Rogers

Hook: Tiemco 800S
Thread: Danville's flat waxed nylon, white
Body: White hackle; pearlescent and silver Fire Fly Tie
Throat: White bucktail; red wool
Shoulder: Light green bucktail
Topping: Black bucktail; kelly green Flashabou; kelly green Umpqua Streamer Hair, barred black
Eyeplate: Kelly green prismatic tape

Eyes: Witchcraft adhesive, black on yellow
Variations: Herring, chartreuse, black, yellow, hot tamale, bunker
TIED BY PAGE ROGERS/UMPQUA FEATHER MERCHANTS

ROGERS' BIG-EYE BAITFISH (YELLOW)—Page Rogers

Hook: Tiemco 800S
Thread: Danville's flat waxed nylon, buttercup yellow
Body: Yellow hackle; yellow pearlescent Fly Flash; gold Flashabou
Throat: Yellow bucktail; red wool
Shoulder: Yellow bucktail
Topping: Olive bucktail
Eyeplate: Yellow prismatic tape
Eyes: Witchcraft adhesive, black on orange
Variations: Herring, chartreuse, mackerel, black, hot tamale, bunker
TIED BY PAGE ROGERS/UMPQUA FEATHER MERCHANTS

ROGERS' DOGFISH DEMON—Page Rogers

Hook: Tiemco 511S size 6
Tail: White wool
Body: Livebody foam; pearl Mylar tubing; Dave's Flexament
Gills: Painted, Testors gloss red
Eyes: Witchcraft adhesive, black on silver
TIED BY PAGE ROGERS/UMPQUA FEATHER MERCHANTS

ROGERS' MENEMSHA MINNOW (BABY BUNKER)—Page Rogers

Hook: Tiemco 511S, size 2/0 or 2
Thread: Danville flat waxed nylon, white
Tail: White calf tail or marabou; fountain blue Flashabou
Body: Prismatic tape, silver, blue; black permanent marker (Sharpie); epoxy
Gills: Painted, Testors gloss red
Eyes: Witchcraft 5EY, black on yellow
Variations: Mackerel, Herring
TIED BY PAGE ROGERS/UMPQUA FEATHER MERCHANTS

ROGERS' MENEMSHA MINNOW (HERRING)—Page Rogers

Hook: Tiemco 511S, size 2/0 or 2
Thread: Danville flat waxed nylon, white
Tail: Black calf tail or marabou
Body: Prismatic tape, silver, black; epoxy
Gills: Black permanent marker (Sharpie)
Eyes: Witchcraft 5EY, black on yellow
Variations: Baby Bunker, Mackerel
TIED BY PAGE ROGERS/UMPQUA FEATHER MERCHANTS

ROGERS' MENEMSHA MINNOW (MACKEREL)—Page Rogers

Hook: Tiemco 511S, size 2/0 or 2
Thread: Danville flat waxed nylon, white

Tail: White calf tail or marabou; kelly green Flashabou
Body: Prismatic tape, silver, kelly green; black permanent marker; epoxy
Gills: Painted, Testors gloss red
Eyes: Witchcraft 5 EY, black on yellow
Variations: Baby Bunker, Herring
TIED BY PAGE ROGERS/UMPQUA FEATHER MERCHANTS

ROGERS' SHIMMERING SHRIMP (GOLD)—Page Rogers

Hook: Tiemco 811S
Thread: Danville's fine clear mono
Mouth: Yellow Ultra Hair; hot yellow and gold Flashabou dubbing
Body: Livebody foam, yellow; dubbing of gold Fly Fur, hot yellow and gold Flashabou dubbing
Carapace: Yellow Ultra Hair; wide pearl cellophane
Rib: Clear mono
Eyes: Burned 25-pound mono painted black
Variations: Pink, gray, white, olive
TIED BY PAGE ROGERS/UMPQUA FEATHER MERCHANTS

ROGERS' SHIMMERING SHRIMP (GRAY)—Page Rogers

Hook: Tiemco 811S
Thread: Danville's fine clear mono
Mouth: Smoke Ultra Hair; silver, gun metal and pearl Flashabou dubbing
Body: Livebody foam, gray; dubbing of gray Fly Fur, silver, gunmetal and pearl Flashabou dubbing
Carapace: Smoke Ultra Hair; wide pearl cellophane
Rib: Clear mono
Eyes: Burned 25-pound mono painted black
Variations: Pink, white, gold, olive
TIED BY PAGE ROGERS/UMPQUA FEATHER MERCHANTS

ROGERS' SHIMMERING SHRIMP (OLIVE)—Page Rogers

Hook: Tiemco 811S
Thread: Danville's fine clear mono
Mouth: Olive Superhair; olive Lite Brite; chartreuse Flashabou dubbing
Body: Livebody foam, olive; dubbing of olive Fly Fur, olive Lite Brite, chartreuse Flashabou dubbing
Carapace: Olive Superhair; wide pearl cellophane
Rib: Clear mono
Eyes: Burned 25-pound mono painted black
Variations: Gray, white, gold, pink
TIED BY PAGE ROGERS/UMPQUA FEATHER MERCHANTS

SALTWATER FLIES

Rogers' Big-Eye Baitfish
(chartreuse)

Rogers' Big-Eye Baitfish
(yellow)

Rogers' Dogfish Demon

Rogers' Big-Eye Baitfish
(herring)

Rogers' Shimmering Shrimp
(gold)

Rogers' Menemsha
Minnow
(baby bunker)

Rogers' Shimmering Shrimp
(gray)

Rogers' Big-Eye Baitfish
(hot tamale)

Rogers' Menemsha
Minnow
(Herring)

Rogers' Shimmering Shrimp
(olive)

Rogers' Big-Eye Baitfish
(mackerel)

Rogers' Menemsha Minnow
(Mackerel)

ROGERS' SHIMMERING SHRIMP (PINK)—Page Rogers

Hook: Tiemco 811S
Thread: Danville's fine clear mono
Mouth: Pink Superhair; Salmon pink Lite Brite and silver Flashabou dubbing
Body: Livebody foam, pink; dubbed with pink Fly Fur, salmon pink Lite Brite and silver Flashabou dubbing
Carapace: Pink Superhair; wide pearl cellophane
Rib: Clear mono
Eyes: Burned 25-pound mono painted black
Variations: Gray, white, gold, olive
TIED BY PAGE ROGERS/UMPQUA FEATHER MERCHANTS

ROGERS' SHIMMERING SHRIMP (WHITE)—Page Rogers

Hook: Tiemco 811S
Thread: Danville's fine clear mono
Mouth: Polar Bear Ultra Hair; gunmetal and pearl Flashabou dubbing
Body: Livebody foam, white; dubbing of polar white Fly Fur, gunmetal and pearl Flashabou dubbing
Carapace: Polar Bear Ultra Hair; wide pearl cellophane
Rib: Clear mono
Eyes: Burned 25-pound mono painted black
Variations: Pink, gray, gold, olive
TIED BY PAGE ROGERS/UMPQUA FEATHER MERCHANTS

ROGERS' SIMPLE SQUID—Page Rogers

Hook: Mustad 34011
Tail: White hackle; fluorescent cerise Krystal Flash; white marabou skirt
Body: Wide white Everglow tubing, end unraveled; epoxy
Eyes: Witchcraft adhesive, black on yellow
TIED BY PAGE ROGERS

ROGERS' SLIM JIM (BLACK)—Page Rogers

Hook: Mustad 34011, size 2
Tail: Fly Fur or FisHair, black
Body: Livebody Foam, black; epoxy; glitter
Eyes: Witchcraft adhesive, black on silver
Variations: Olive/white, black/white, black/yellow
TIED BY PAGE ROGERS/UMPQUA FEATHER MERCHANTS

ROGERS' SLIM JIM (BLACK/WHITE)—Page Rogers

Hook: Mustad 34011, size 2
Tail: Fly Fur, white, black; pink pearlescent Fly Flash
Body: Livebody Foam, white; permanent marker, black (Sharpie); epoxy
Lateral Line: Wide pearl Mylar tinsel
Eyes: Witchcraft adhesive, black on silver
Variations: Olive/white, black, black/yellow
TIED BY PAGE ROGERS/UMPQUA FEATHER MERCHANTS

ROGERS' SLIM JIM (BLACK/YELLOW)—Page Rogers

Hook: Mustad 34011, size 2
Tail: Fly Fur, hot yellow, black; yellow pearlescent Fly Flash
Body: Livebody Foam, yellow; permanent marker, black (Sharpie); epoxy
Lateral Line: Wide pearl Mylar tinsel
Eyes: Witchcraft adhesive, black on silver
Variations: Olive/white, black, black/white
TIED BY PAGE ROGERS/UMPQUA FEATHER MERCHANTS

ROGERS' SLIM JIM (OLIVE/WHITE)—Page Rogers

Hook: Mustad 34011, size 2
Tail: Fly Fur, polar white, olive; olive pearlescent Fly Flash; silver Flashabou
Body: Livebody Foam, white; permanent marker, sides yellow chartreuse, top olive green; epoxy
Lateral Line: Wide pearl Mylar tinsel
Eyes: Witchcraft adhesive, black on silver
Variations: Black/white, black, black/yellow
TIED BY PAGE ROGERS/UMPQUA FEATHER MERCHANTS

ROGERS' SPARKLE WORM—Page Rogers

Hook: Tiemco 811S
Thread: Danville's flat waxed nylon, black
Tail: Fluorescent red Zonker strip
Body: Fluorescent red Estaz
Head: Black/green Lite Brite
TIED BY PAGE ROGERS

ROGERS' TASHMOO WORM FLY—Page Rogers

Hook: Tiemco 811S
Thread: Danville's flat waxed nylon, fluorescent fire orange
Tail: Marabou, fluorescent pink, fluorescent red
Body: Fluorescent red chenille
Body Hackle: Fluorescent red
TIED BY PAGE ROGERS

ROGERS' VELVET CINDER WORM—Page Rogers

Hook: Tiemco 811S
Thread: Danville's flat waxed nylon, black
Body: Red/orange velvet tubing
Head: Black/green Lite Brite
TIED BY PAGE ROGERS/UMPQUA FEATHER MERCHANTS

RON'S EEL—Ron Ayotte

Hook: Mustad 34007; Tiemco 811S, sizes 4/0-2
Thread: 3/0 monocord

Tail: Blonde badger hackle; black saddle hackle; bronze Crystal Hair
Body Hackle: Black saddle
Head: Thread overlayered with iridescent black Buggy Nymph braided tinsel #201
Eyes: Large or medium doll eyes, black on yellow
Finish: Devcon 5-minute epoxy
TIED BY RON AYOTTE

ROYAL FERGIE—Ron Ayotte

Hook: Mustad 34011/92608; Tiemco 9394, sizes 2/0-8
Thread: 3/0 monocord, white or green
Tail: White polar bear or bucktail; red marabou
Body: Braided silver tinsel rear 2/3; bright green chenille forward 1/3
Wing: Peacock herl; white polar bear or buck tail
Front Hackle: Guinea dyed blue, red, or orange
Cheeks: Jungle cock eyes
TIED BY RON AYOTTE

RUIZ'S BEACH BUM (ORANGE, FEMALE SAND FLEA)—Anthony Ruiz

Hook: Mustad 34007/3407; Daiichi 2546; Tiemco 811S
Thread: Orange
Tail: White C-D-C; Crystal Hair, pearl, orange
Body: Vernille, chartreuse, orange; orange micro tinsel; epoxy top
Body Hackle: White ostrich herl
Eyes: Adhesive 3/32, black on white
Variations: White, sand flea
TIED BY ANTHONY RUIZ

RUIZ CALAMARA—Anthony Ruiz

Hook: Tiemco 9394; size 2
Tail: Krystal Flash, pearl blue, pearl pink; white hackle; blue/silver metal flake living rubber skirt
Body: Pearl blue Lite Brite; epoxy
Eyes: Adhesive 9/32, black on red
TIED BY ANTHONY RUIZ

RUIZ FLATS WORM—Anthony Ruiz

Hook: Mustad 34007/3407; Daiichi 2546; Tiemco 811S; sizes 4-8
Thread: Tan
Wing: Tan vernille; pearl Krystal Flash
TIED BY ANTHONY RUIZ

RUIZ LIL' BIT (HOG FRY MINNOW)—Anthony Ruiz

Hook: Mustad 34007/3407; Daiichi 2546; Tiemco 811S; sizes 6-10
Body: Pearl flat braid; epoxy
Wing: Krystal Flash, silver, pearl; gray qcraft fur
Eyes: Adhesive, 7/32, 9/32, black on gold
Mouth: Red permanent marker
TIED BY ANTHONY RUIZ

Rogers' Shimmering Shrimp (pink)

Rogers' Slim Jim (black/yellow)

Royal Fergie

Rogers' Shimmering Shrimp (white)

Rogers' Slim Jim (olive/white)

Ruiz's Beach Bum (orange, female sand flea)

Rogers' Sparkle Worm

Rogers' Simple Squid

Ruiz Calamar

Rogers' Slim Jim (black)

Ruiz Flats Worm

Rogers' Tashmoo Worm Fly

Rogers' Slim Jim (black/white)

Rogers' Velvet Cinder Worm

Ron's Eel

Ruiz Lil' Bit (hog fry minnow)

RUIZ'S REVENGE—Anthony Ruiz

Hook: Mustad 34007/3407; Daiichi 2546;
Tiemco 811S; size 2/0
Wing: FisHair, moss green, white; silver
Flashabou; peacock Krystal Flash
Eyes: Adhesive 7/32, black on yellow;
epoxy
TIED BY ANTHONY RUIZ

RUIZ'S ULTIMATE CRAB—Anthony Ruiz

Hook: Mustad 34007/3407; Daiichi 2546;
Tiemco 811S; sizes 2-6
Claws: Olive calftail; Krystal Flash, olive,
black
Body: Olive vernille; epoxy
Body Hackle: Living rubber legs, knotted
olive metal flake
Eyes: Black plastic bead
TIED BY ANTHONY RUIZ

RUOFF'S BACKCOUNTRY BONEFISH FLY—Rick Ruoff

Hook: Mustad 34007; sizes 4-6
Tail: Grizzly hackle; pearl Krystal Flash;
Body: Spun deer hair
Front Hackle: Deer hair
Eyes: Lead painted red on yellow
TIED BY ORVIS

RUOFF'S BACKCOUNTRY POPPER— Rick Ruoff

Hook: Mustad 34011, size 1
Tail: White hackle
Body: Hard foam
Body Hackle: Green
Eyes: Painted, black on yellow
TIED BY ORVIS

RUOFF'S BARRACUDA FLY—Rick Ruoff

Hook: Mustad 34007, size 1
Thread: Chartreuse
Tail: Fish Hair, chartreuse, white; pearl
Krystal Flash
Body: Chartreuse chenille
Body Hackle: Chartreuse
TIED BY ORVIS

RUOFF LAY-UP TARPON FLY (BROWN)—Rick Ruoff

Hook: Mustad 34007; sizes 1/0-2/0
Tail: Badger hackle; yellow Fish Hair;
Krystal Flash, red, yellow
Body: Tan dubbing
Body Hackle: Badger
Eyes: Plastic black bead
Weedguard: Single strand wire
Variations: Yellow, chartreuse, pink
TIED BY ORVIS

SALSA SHRIMP—Craig Mathews

Hook: Mustad 3407; Daiichi 2546; Tiemco
800S; sizes 1/0-6
Thread: White 3/0 monocord
Tail: Red deer or elk hair; grizzly hackle
clipped

Body: Zelon, gray, pink dubbing; gray
Zelon over
Body Hackle: Grizzly
Wing: Gray Zelon
Eyes: Black plastic bead
TIED BY CRAIG MATHEWS/BLUE RIBBON FLIES

SALT SHRIMP (GRAY)—Dave Whitlock

Hook: Mustad 34007/3407; Daiichi 2546;
Tiemco 811S; sizes 4-1/0
Thread: Gray
Tail: Natural deer hair
Body: Gray sparkle dubbing; wire rib
Shellback: Clear plastic
Antennae: Grizzly hackle stem
Body Hackle: Grizzly
Eyes: Black plastic
Variations: Gold, olive
TIED BY UMPQUA FEATHER MERCHANTS

SALTY INDIAN SUMMER— Walter Johnson

Hook: Mustad 34011, sizes 4/0-1/0
Thread: Fluorescent pink or orange
monocord
Tail: Red hackle fibers or marabou
Butt: Red dubbing
Body: Orange dubbing
Rib: Copper wire
Wing: Hot pink polar bear or bucktail
Throat: Red hackle fibers or marabou
Head: Thread cemented or epoxy
TIED BY RON AYOTTE

SANDSTOM'S SHRIMP (PINK/AMPHIPOD)—Garry Sandstom

Hook: Mustad 34007; Tiemco 811S; sizes
6-10
Thread: Larva Lace, clear, fine thread
Antennae: Pink Krystal Flash
Body: Salmon pink Lite Brite or #37
Flashabou dubbing
Eyes: Small black mono
Variations: See White/Euphasid
TIED BY GARY SANDSTROM

SANDSTOM'S SHRIMP (WHITE/EUPHASID)—Garry Sandstom

Hook: Mustad 34007; Tiemco 811S; sizes
4-6
Thread: Danville hot orange; Larva Lace,
clear, fine thread for head
Antennae: Pearl Krystal Flash
Body: Polar pearl Lite Brite
Eyes: Small black mono
Variations: See Pink/Amphipod
TIED BY GARY SANDSTROM

SANDY'S TARPON MUDDLER— Sandy Moret

Hook: Mustad 3407SS, size 3/0
Tail: Marabou, orange, black; pearl

Krystal Flash
Body: Brown yarn
Wing: Pearl Krystal Flash
Front Hackle: Deer hair
Eyes: Silver bead chain
Head: Deer hair
TIED BY FLORIDA KEYS SCHOOL & OUTFITTERS

SAR-MUL-MAC (ANCHOVY, BLUE)— Dan Blanton

Hook: Mustad 34007/3407; Daiichi 2546;
Tiemco 811S; size 3/0
Wing: Bucktail, white, blue; hackle, white;
silver Flashabou; peacock Crystal
Flash; peacock herl
Gills: Red chenille
Head: White chenille
Eyes: Plastic black on yellow
Variations: Mullet/red
TIED BY UMPQUA FEATHER MERCHANTS/THE FLY SHOP

SAR-MUL-MAC (MULLET, RED)— Dan Blanton

Hook: Mustad 34007/3407; Daiichi 2546;
Tiemco 811S; size 3/0
Wing: Bucktail, white; hackle, white,
grizzly; silver Flashabou; gray
marabou
Cheeks: Teal
Gills: Red chenille
Head: White chenille
Eyes: Plastic black on yellow
Variations: Anchovy/blue
TIED BY UMPQUA FEATHER MERCHANTS/THE FLY SHOP

SCATES SHRIMP, PINK (Turrall)

Hook: Mustad 34007/3407; Daiichi 2546;
Tiemco 811S
Thread: White
Tail: Brown bucktail
Body: Chenille, hot pink
Body Hackle: Black
Shellback: Krystal Flash, pearl
Rib: Monofilament
Front Hackle: Krystal Flash, pearl
Eyes: Plastic bead, black
Variations: With weedguard
TIED BY TURRALL

SCATES SHRIMP, RED (Turrall)

Hook: Mustad 34007/3407; Daiichi 2546;
Tiemco 811S
Thread: Red
Tail: Brown bucktail
Body: Chenille, red
Body Hackle: Black
Shellback: Krystal Flash, orange
Rib: Monofilament
Front Hackle: Krystal Flash, orange
Eyes: Plastic bead, black
Variations: With weedguard
TIED BY TURRALL

Ruiz's Revenge

Ruiz's Ultimate Crab

Salt Shrimp
(gray)

Sar-Mul-Mac
(anchovy, blue)

Ruoff's Backcountry Bonefish
Fly

Ruoff's Backcountry Popper

Salty Indian Summer

Sar-Mul-Mac
(mullet, red)

Sandstom's Shrimp
(pink/amphipod)

Ruoff's Barracuda Fly

Scates Shrimp, Pink

Sandstom's Shrimp
(white/euphasid)

Ruoff's Lay-Up Tarpon Fly
(brown)

Scates Shrimp, Red

Salsa Shrimp

Sandy's Tarpon Muddler

SCATES SHRIMP, WHITE (Turrall)
Hook: Mustad 34007/3407; Daiichi 2546; Tiemco 811S
Thread: White
Tail: Brown bucktail
Body: Chenille, white
Body Hackle: Black
Shellback: Krystal Flash, pearl
Rib: Monofilament
Front Hackle: Krystal Flash, pearl
Eyes: Plastic bead, black
Variations: With weedguard
TIED BY TURRALL

SCRAPPY—Ron Ayotte
Hook: Mustad 34007 size 2/0; stinger loop optional for trolled fly
Tail: Layered colors of Crystal Hair scraps, random lengths ok
Throat: Red Crystal Hair
Head: Overlay 3/0 monocord with micro tinsel or braided tinsel
Eyes: Doll eyes
Finish: Devcon 5-minute epoxy
Variations:
TIED BY RON AYOTTE

SEA BUNNY (RUST)—Mike Wolverton
Hook: Mustad 3407, sizes 2/0-3/0
Thread: Fluorescent orange
Tail: Rabbit strip, rust; pearl Krystal Flash
Body: Thread under epoxy
Collar: Rust colored rabbit
Eyes: Painted, black on yellow
Variations: (Tail/collar) Black/red, white/red, yellow/orange, yellow/gray.
TIED BY MIKE WOLVERTON

SEA BUNNY (WHITE/RED)— Mike Wolverton
Hook: Mustad 3407, sizes 2/0-3/0
Thread: White
Tail: Rabbit strip, white; pearl Crystal Flash
Body: Thread under epoxy
Collar: Red rabbit
Eyes: Painted, black on yellow
Variations: (Tail/collar) Black/red, white/red, yellow/orange, yellow/gray.
TIED BY UMPQUA FEATHER MERCHANTS

SEA DEVIL (White)—Doug Swisher
Hook: Mustad 34007/3407; Daiichi 2546; Tiemco 811S
Thread: White
Tail: Tasmanian devil hair, white; pearl Krystal Flash
Body: Mohlon, white
Wing: Tasmanian devil hair, white; pearl Krystal Flash
Variations: Pink and white, yellow and white
TIED BY DOUG SWISHER

SEADUCER (YELLOW/RED)— Riverborn Fly Company
Hook: Mustad 3407, sizes 3/0-1/0
Thread: Danville Flymaster 6/0 red
Tail: Yellow hackle; yellow Krystal Flash
Body Hackle: Yellow
Front Hackle: Red
Variations: Chartreuse/orange, orange/red, white/red
TIED BY LANCE GRAY/RIVERBORN FLY COMPANY

SEA-DUCER (WHITE/RED)— Chico Fernandez
Hook: Mustad 34007/3407; Daiichi 2546; Tiemco 811S; size 2/0
Tail: White hackle; silver Flashabou
Body Hackle: White
Front Hackle: Red
Variations: Yellow/red, white/yellow/-grizzly
TIED BY UMPQUA FEATHER MERCHANTS

SEA-DUCER, RED AND YELLOW (Turrall)
Hook: Mustad 34007/3407; Daiichi 2546; Tiemco 811S
Thread: Black
Tail: Yellow and grizzly hackle
Body Hackle: Red and yellow hackle
TIED BY TURRALL

SEAFOAM POPPER (CHARTREUSE)— A.J. Hand
Hook: Eagle Claw 2044-SS Kink shank
Thread: White
Tail: Bucktail, chartreuse, white; Crystal Flash, pearl
Body: Foam
Eyes: Doll, black over yellow
Variations: Fluorescent pink
TIED BY MYSTIC BAY FLIES

SEAFOAM POPPER (PINK)—A.J. Hand
Hook: Eagle Claw 2044-SS Kink shank
Thread: White
Tail: Bucktail, fluorescent pink, white; Krystal Flash, pearl
Body: Foam
Eyes: Doll, black over yellow
Variations: Chartreuse
TIED BY MYSTIC BAY FLIES

SEAFOAM SPARKLE BUG
Hook: Eagle Claw 2044-SS Kink shank
Tail: Flashabou, pearl
Body: Foam; pearlescent tubing
Eyes: Black over yellow
TIED BY MYSTIC BAY FLIES

SEAFOOD—Bill & Kate Howe
Hook: Tiemco 511S, 2/0
Thread: Red

Claws: Red crinkle nylon
Body: Holographic Mylar; crinkle nylon, red, brown, orange
Eyes: Black plastic bead chain
Head: Finished with Jolly Glaze and holographic powder
Variations: Blue and red, chartreuse
TIED BY BILL AND KATE HOWE

SEA LICE—Craig Mathews
Hook: Mustad 3407; Daiichi 2546; Tiemco 800S; sizes 6-10
Thread: White 6/0 or 3/0
Body: Fine white yarn, chenille or dubbing
Body Hackle: Grizzly or white hackle, trimmed
Head: Chartreuse dubbing
TIED BY CRAIG MATHEWS/BLUE RIBBON FLIES

SEA SERPENT (BLACK/RED)— Chris Windram
Hook: Mustad 34007, sizes 4-1/0
Thread: Flat black nylon
Tail: Rabbit, black
Body: Rabbit, black
Body Hackle: Deer hair, red
Collar: Deer hair, red
Head: Deer hair, red
Variations: Chartreuse/white
TIED BY CHRIS WINDRAM/TIGHT LINES

SEA SERPENT (CHARTREUSE/WHITE)— Chris Windram
Hook: Mustad 34007, sizes 2-1/0
Thread: Cream nylon
Tail: Rabbit, chartreuse
Body: Rabbit, chartreuse
Body Hackle: Deer hair, white
Collar: Deer hair, white
Head: Deer hair, white
Variations: Black/red
TIED BY CHRIS WINDRAM/TIGHT LINES

SEA SPRITE—Tom Kintz
Hook: Tiemco 811S size 2
Thread: White size A flat nylon
Tail: Cream hackle; pearl Flashabou
Collar: White bucktail
Body: Pearl Mylar braid
Eyes: Silver bead chain
TIED BY TOM KINTZ

SEDOTTI FLOUNDER (8")—Mark Sedotti
Hook: Tiemco 811S, size 3/0
Thread: White
Tail: Extension, 100-pound mono
Underbody: .030 lead wire plus lead keel
Body: Bottom, white saddle hackle; top, tan bucktail
Eyes: 10mm doll eyes
TIED BY MARK SEDOTTI

SALTWATER FLIES

Scates Shrimp, White

Seaducer (yellow/red)

Sea Lice

Sea Serpent (black/red)

Scrappy

Sea-ducer (white/red)

Sea Serpent (chartreuse/white)

Sea Bunny (rust)

Sea-ducer, Red and Yellow

Sea Sprite

Sea Bunny (white/red)

Seafoam Popper (chartreuse)

Seafoam Popper (pink)

Seafoam Sparkle Bug

Sea Devil (white)

Seafood

Sedotti Flounder (8")

SEDOTTI MACKEREL (10")—
Mark Sedotti
Hook: Eagle Claw 254SS, size 6/0
Thread: White
Tail: Schlappen, green, white or white saddle hackle
Underbody: .030 lead wire plus lead keel
Mid-Fly: Bucktail on sides covered with Schlappen or saddle hackle
Flash: Pearl Flashabou
Back: Peacock herl
Head: Top, green bucktail; sides and bottom, white bucktail
Eyes: 12mm doll eyes
Markings: Black Pantone marker
TIED BY MARK SEDOTTI

SEDOTTI'S SLAMMER
(8"—MENHADEN)—Mark Sedotti
Hook: 6/0 Eagle Claw 254SS; Daiichi size 6/0; Owner size 8/0
Thread: White
Weight: .030 lead wire plus lead keel
Tail: Schlappen, white, green
Mid-Fly: White bucktail
Side: White bucktail; Schlappen, white, pink
Flash: Krystal Flash, pearl, pink
Back: Peacock herl
Head: Top, olive bucktail; sides and bottom, white bucktail
Eyes: 12mm doll eyes
Variations: Also 12-inch-plus; see 6"; 4" for peanut bunker, shad, alewife.
TIED BY MARK SEDOTTI

SEDOTTI'S SLAMMER (6"—MENHADEN, HERRING, ALEWIFE, SHAD)—
Mark Sedotti
Hook: Tiemco size 3/0
Thread: White
Weight: .030 lead wire plus lead keel
Tail: Schlappen, white
Mid-Fly: White bucktail
Side: White bucktail
Flash: Krystal Flash, pink; silver Flashabou
Back: Peacock herl
Head: Top, olive bucktail; sides and bottom, white bucktail
Eyes: 10mm doll eyes
Variations: See 8"; 4" for peanut bunker, shad, alewife.
TIED BY MARK SEDOTTI

SEDOTTI'S SLAMMER (4"—PEANUT BUNKER, ALEWIFE, SHAD)—
Mark Sedotti
Hook: Tiemco size 1/0
Thread: White
Weight: .030 lead wire plus lead keel
Tail: Schlappen, white
Mid-Fly: White bucktail
Side: White bucktail
Flash: Krystal Flash, pearl
Back: Peacock herl
Head: Top, olive bucktail; sides and bottom, white bucktail
Eyes: 10mm doll eyes

Variations: See 8"; 6" for menhaden, herring, shad, alewife.
TIED BY MARK SEDOTTI

SENGEKONTACKET SAND EEL—
Chris Windram
Hook: Mustad 34011, size 6-1
Thread: Light olive nylon 6/0
Tail: Fly fur, white, lavender, olive
Body: Mylar tubing; epoxy
Gills: Painted red
Eyes: Painted, black on white
TIED BY CHRIS WINDRAM/CASTLE ARMS

SHIMMER BACK SPOON—Terry Baird
Hook: Gamakatsu
Thread: Orange
Tail: Silver Flashabou
Shellback: Shimmerback Mylar sheeting
Body: Pearl Flashabou Mylar
Wing: Orange squirrel; silver Flashabou
Weedguard: 40-pound test wire, single strand
Eyes: Adhesive black on silver
TIED BY TERRY BAIRD/BIGHORN FLY TRADING

SHINING SARDINE—Bill Black
Hook: Mustad 34011, size 3/0
Tail: Super Hair, white
Body: White thread
Wing: Super Hair, white, smoke; Fly Flash, black, olive, pearl, dark blue
Throat: Red Fly Flash
Eyes: Doll eyes
TIED BY SPIRIT RIVER, INC

SHINY STREAMER (BLACK/BLUE)—
C. Boyd Pfeiffer
Hook: Mustad 34011
Tail: Synthetic hair: Ultra Hair, Super Hair, Cascade Toothy Hair, FisHair, or Permatron; black over blue
Body: Same as wing material
Eyes: Optional, adhesive black on gold
Variations: White, neon yellow, black, royal blue, kelly green, pink, red
TIED BY C. BOYD PFEIFFER

SHINY STREAMER (BLUE)—
C. Boyd Pfeiffer
Hook: Mustad 34011
Tail: Synthetic hair: Ultra Hair, Super Hair, Cascade Toothy Hair, FisHair, or Permatron; blue
Body: Same as wing material
Variations: White, neon yellow, black, kelly green, pink, red
TIED BY C. BOYD PFEIFFER

SHINY STREAMER (GREEN)—
C. Boyd Pfeiffer
Hook: Mustad 34011
Tail: Synthetic hair: Ultra Hair, Super Hair, Cascade Toothy Hair, FisHair, or Permatron; green
Body: Same as wing material

Variations: White, neon yellow, black, blue, pink, red; cut tail into forked shape
TIED BY C. BOYD PFEIFFER

SHINY STREAMER (PINK CRYSTAL)—
C. Boyd Pfeiffer
Hook: Mustad 34011
Tail: Pink Krystal Flash
Body: Same as wing material
Variations: White, neon yellow, black, blue, pink, red; cut tail into forked shape
TIED BY C. BOYD PFEIFFER

SHORT TAILED DECEIVER—
Marc Mousseau
Hook: Mustad 34007/3407; Daiichi 2546; Tiemco 811S
Thread: Black
Body: Black thread
Wing: Silver metallic thread; bucktail, white, royal blue; white hackle
Throat: Red metallic thread
Eyes: 4mm moveable doll eyes, black on white; or painted on
TIED BY MARC MOUSSEAU/WOODS AND WATER

THE SHRIMP—Peter Masters
Hook: Partridge double salmon size 6
Thread: White Kevlar
Tail: White poly nylon
Body: Fluorescent orange floss; orange Krystal Flash; 5-minute epoxy
Body Hackle: White poly yarn
Feelers: Brown poly yarn
Eyes: Burned black nylon
Legs: Brown rubber legs
TIED BY PETER MASTERS, ENGLAND

SHRIMP WOBBLER—Jon Cave
Hook: Mustad 34007/3407; Daiichi 2546; Tiemco 800S; sizes 4-3/0 ("C" Series on straight shank hook; "S" Series on bend back style hook)
Thread: 6/0, color matches color of Mylar tubing
Tail: Orange bucktail or polar bear, craft fur, kiptail, marabou, etc.; gold Krystal Flash
Body: Gold Mylar tubing (3/8" for 1/0-3/0; 1/4" for sizes 4-1 hooks); epoxy
Eyes: Large or extra large bead chain painted black
Weedguard: .014 trolling wire or 20# mono
TIED BY JON CAVE

SHRIMPY GRIZ APTE TOO—Stu Apte
Hook: Mustad 34007/3407; Daiichi 2546; Tiemco 811S
Thread: Red
Tail: Grizzly hackle, orange, yellow; pearl Crystal Hair
Body: Thread
Body Hackle: Red fox squirrel tail
Head: Epoxy over thread
Eyes: Painted black on yellow
Weedguard: Anti-foul mono rear loop
TIED BY MCKENZIE FLY TACKLE

**Sedotti Mackerel
(10")**

**Shiny Streamer
(pink crystal)**

Sengekontacket Sand Eel

Shimmer Back Spoon

Short Tailed Deceiver

**Sedotti's Slammer
(8"—menhaden)**

The Shrimp

Shining sardine

**Sedotti's Slammer
(6"—menhaden, herring,
alewife, shad)**

**Shiny Streamer
(black/blue)**

Shrimp Wobbler

**Shiny Streamer
(blue)**

**Sedotti's Slammer
(4"—peanut bunker, alewife, shad))**

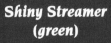

**Shiny Streamer
(green)**

Shrimpy Griz Apte Too

SILICLONE (CHARTREUSE)— Bob Popovics

Hook: Mustad 34007/3407; Daiichi 2546; Tiemco 811S; size 3/0
Tail: Chartreuse bucktail; chartreuse ostrich; chartreuse Flashabou
Body: Chartreuse wool; silicone; glitter
Eyes: Adhesive black on silver
Variations: Black, yellow
TIED BY UMPQUA FEATHER MERCHANTS/THE FLY SHOP

SILVER DARTER—Peter Masters

Hook: Lure chromed size 10
Thread: Fluorescent red Kevlar
Body: none
Wing: Dark feather or hair
Front Hackle: Light blue cock
TIED BY PETER MASTERS, ENGLAND

SIR MANTIS SHRIMP—Craig Mathews

Hook: Mustad 3407; Daiichi 2546; Tiemco 800S; sizes 1/0-6
Thread: Monocord 3/0, white or olive
Tail: Olive rabbit; olive Krystal Flash; olive deer hair
Body: Olive Zelon over olive rabbit strip
Body Hackle: Orange grizzly
Front Hackle: Olive Zelon
Eyes: Black bead
Tag: Orange dubbing
TIED BY CRAIG MATHEWS/BLUE RIBBON FLIES

SKINNY MINNIE (HACKLE WING)— Ron Ayotte

Hook: Mustad 34007, sizes 1/0-8
Thread: 3/0 monocord or uni-thread to match wing color
Tail: Hackle cut "V"; extension of body tubing
Body: Mylar tubing, color to match bait fishbeing imitated, usually pearl or silver
Wing: Hackle
Topping: Peacock herl, optional
Head: Thread or overwrapped with micro tinsel
Eyes: Prism
TIED BY RON AYOTTE

SKINNY MINNIE (HAIRWING)— Ron Ayotte

Hook: Mustad 34007, sizes 1/0-8
Thread: 3/0 monocord or uni-thread to match wing color
Tail: Frayed Mylar tubing; extension of body tubing
Body: Mylar tubing, color to match bait fish being imitated, usually pearl or silver
Wing: Bucktail or polar bear, color of intended imitation; Flashabou or Crystal Hair optional
Topping: Peacock herl, optional

Head: Thread or overwrapped with micro tinsel
Eyes: Prism
TIED BY RON AYOTTE

SKINNY MINNIE (HAIRWING WITH MARKINGS, GREEN)—Ron Ayotte

Hook: Mustad 34007, sizes 1/0-8
Thread: 3/0 monocord or uni-thread to match wing color
Tail: Frayed green pearl Mylar tubing; extension of body tubing
Body: Pearl green Mylar tubing; permanent black marker
Wing: Bucktail or polar bear, green; Flashabou or Crystal Hair optional
Topping: Peacock herl, optional
Head: Thread or overwrapped with micro tinsel
Eyes: Prism
TIED BY RON AYOTTE

SKINNY MINNIE (HAIRWING WITH MARKINGS, ORANGE)—Ron Ayotte

Hook: Mustad 34007, sizes 1/0-8
Thread: 3/0 monocord or uni-thread to match wing color
Tail: Frayed orange pearl Mylar tubing; extension of body tubing
Body: Pearl orange Mylar tubing; permanent black marker
Wing: Bucktail or polar bear, orange; Flashabou or Crystal Hair optional
Topping: Peacock herl, optional
Head: Thread or overwrapped with micro tinsel
Eyes: Prism
TIED BY RON AYOTTE

SKINNY MINNIE (HAIRWING WITH STINGER)—Ron Ayotte

Hook: Mustad 34007, sizes 1/0-8; stinger hook
Thread: 3/0 monocord or uni-thread to match wing color
Tail: Frayed Mylar tubing; extension of body tubing
Body: Mylar tubing, color to match bait fish being imitated, usually pearl or silver
Wing: Bucktail or polar bear, color of intended imitation; Flashabou or Crystal Hair optional
Topping: Peacock herl, optional
Head: Thread or overwrapped with micro tinsel
Eyes: Prism
TIED BY RON AYOTTE

SKIRTED BUCKTAIL—Ron Ayotte

Hook: Mustad 34007/34011; Tiemco 811S/800S, sizes 6/0-4
Skirting: Witchhair prism strips or wide Flashabou
Wing: One or more colors bucktail; Crystal Hair optional

Head: Overwrap with micro tinsel
Eyes: Prism
Finish: Devcon 5-minute epoxy
TIED BY RON AYOTTE

SKOK'S BABY BUNKER—Dave Skok

Hook: Mustad 34007/3407; Daiichi 2546; Tiemco 811S
Thread: White
Tail: White bucktail; Krystal Flash, pearl; Flashabou, pearl; olive streamer hair
Body: Lite Brite, polar pearl; tail materials; covered with silicone
Head: White deer hair; covered with silicone
Eyes: Prismatic
TIED BY MYSTIC BAY FLIES

SKOK'S SEE-THRU SHRIMP—Dave Skok

Hook: Mustad 34007/3407; Daiichi 2546; Tiemco 811S
Thread: Clear
Legs, Feelers: Polar Super Hair, white
Rostrum: Polar white craft fur
Antennae: Pearl Krystal Flash
Eyes: Orange plastic bead chain
Thorax: Polar white craft fur
Tail: White Polar Super Hair
Abdomen: Polar White craft fur under epoxy
TIED BY MYSTIC BAY FLIES

SLAMAROO—Lenny Moffo

Hook: Mustad 34007/3407; Daiichi 2546; Tiemco 811S
Tail: Brown Krystal Flash
Body: Brown Krystal Flash
Wing: White rubber legs; brown permanent marker; tips red or orange, permanent marker; brown sili legs
Head: Variegated brown chenille
Eyes: Lead barbell
Variations: Can vary head colors
TIED BY LENNY MOFFO

SLIDING POPPER (FLUORESCENT PINK/SILVER)

Hook: Long shank size 2/0
Tail: White hackle
Body: Foam, fluorescent pink, silver
Body Hackle: White
Eyes: Painted black on yellow
Variations: Black/silver
AVAILABLE THROUGH THE FLY SHOP

SLIDING POPPER (BLACK/SILVER)

Hook: Long shank size 2/0
Tail: White hackle
Body: Foam, black, silver
Body Hackle: White
Eyes: Painted black on yellow
Variations: fluorescent pink/silver
AVAILABLE THROUGH THE FLY SHOP

SALTWATER FLIES

Siliclone
(chartreuse)

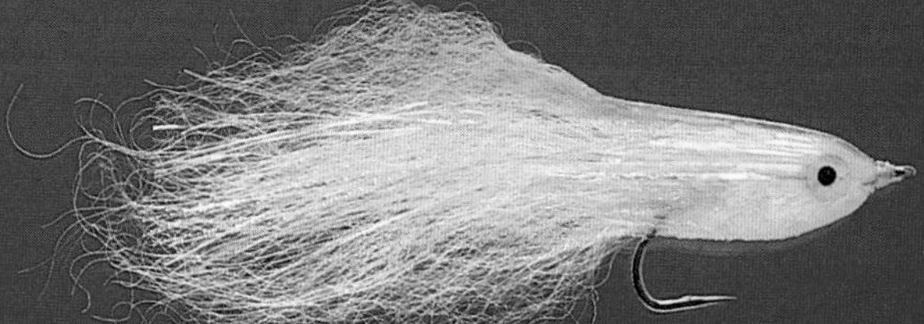

Skinny Minnie
(hairwing with markings, green)

Silver Darter

Skinny Minnie
(hairwing with markings, orange)

Skok's Baby Bunker

Skok's See-Thru Shrimp

Sir Mantis Shrimp

Skinny Minnie
(hairwing with stinger)

Slamaroo

Skinny Minnie
(hackle wing)

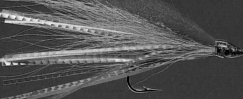

Skirted Bucktail

Sliding Popper
(flourescent pink/silver)

Skinny Minnie
(hairwing)

Sliding Popper
(black/silver)

SMILEY NEEDLEFISH (GREEN)—Scott Walker

Hook: Tiemco 811S; sizes 1/0-4
Thread: White
Tail: Polar bear hair, olive, highlander green; Mylar tubing picked out
Body: Diamond braid, silver; pearl Mylar tubing; epoxy
Eyes: Adhesive black on green
Variations: Substitute bucktail for polar bear; Purple version
TIED BY SCOTT WALKER, CANADA

SMILEY NEEDLEFISH (PURPLE)—Scott Walker

Hook: Tiemco 811S; sizes 1/0-4
Thread: White
Tail: Polar bear hair, purple, silver; Mylar tubing picked out
Body: Diamond braid, silver; pearl Mylar tubing; epoxy
Eyes: Adhesive black on amber
Variations: Substitute bucktail for polar bear; Green version
TIED BY SCOTT WALKER, CANADA

SNAPPING CRAB—Bighorn Fly Trading

Hook: Gamakatsu
Body: White chenille; fluorescent orange yarn
Claws: Olive yarn, knotted, trimmed, glued
Underwing: Olive yarn
Eyes: Black plastic bead chain
TIED BY BIGHORN FLY TRADING

SNAPPING SHRIMP—Chico Fernandez

Hook: Mustad 34007/3407; Daiichi 2546; Tiemco 811S; sizes 4-6
Thread: Black
Body: Dubbing, orange, gray
Wing: Brown craft fur
TIED BY UMPQUA FEATHER MERCHANTS

SNOOK SLIDER—Randy L. Morgan

Hook: Mustad 34007, size 1/0
Tail: Chartreuse saddle hackle; chartreuse Krystal Flash
Rear Collar: Chartreuse marabou
Front Collar: Deer hair, chartreuse, red
Head: Chartreuse deer hair
Eyes: 4mm plastic doll eyes
Weedguard: 22-pound Mason
TIED BY RANDY L. MORGAN/THE FLY FISHERMAN

SON OF CLOUSER—John Kumiski

Hook: Mustad 34007/3407; Daiichi 2546; Tiemco 811S
Thread: Black
Wing: Squirrel tail; copper Krystal Flash; brown marabou
Head: Brown chenille
Eyes: Lead barbell
TIED BY JOHN KUMISKI

SOGGY HEAD (CHARTREUSE)—Greg Miheve

Hook: Mustad 34011, sizes 2-4/0
Body: Cloisonne braid, chartreuse
Wing: Bucktail, chartreuse; Flashabou, chartreuse
Collar: Yellow deer hair
Head: Deer hair, chartreuse
Eyes: Doll eyes, black on yellow
Variations: White, green/white, blue/white, yellow, red/white, red/yellow, red/orange, purple, and black.
TIED BY GREG MIHEVE

SOGGY Head (ORANGE/YELLOW)—Greg Miheve

Hook: Mustad 34011, sizes 2-4/0
Body: Cloisonne braid, orange
Wing: Bucktail, orange, yellow; Flashabou, yellow, orange
Collar: Yellow deer hair
Head: Deer hair, yellow, red
Eyes: Doll eyes, black on yellow
Variations: White, green/white, blue/white, yellow, red/white, red/yellow, chartreuse, purple, and black.
TIED BY GREG MIHEVE

SPINSTER (PEPPERMINT)—Steve Shiba

Hook: Mustad 34011
Tail: Marabou, white; hackle, red; Crystal Flash, pearl; bucktail, red
Body: Foam, red/white
Eyes: Black on yellow post
Variations: Black, white, chartreuse, yellow, blue.
TIED BY EDGEWATER

SQUIRREL TARPON—Jon Olch

Hook: Mustad 34007/3407; Daiichi 2546; Tiemco 811S
Thread: Red
Tail: Squirrel tail; grizzly hackle
Body: Thread under epoxy
Eyes: Painted black on yellow
TIED BY JON OLCH/UMPQUA FEATHER MERCHANTS

SRI ULTRA EPOXY SEA SHRIMP—Bill Black

Hook: Mustad 34007/3407; Daiichi 2546; Tiemco 811S
Thread: White
Tail: Lite Brite, pearl; Crystal Twist, pearl, copper
Body: Tan Dazl-tron dubbing; epoxy over tail material
Front Hackle: Pearl Crystal Twist
Eyes: Burnt mono
TIED BY BILL BLACK/SPIRIT RIVER, INC

SRI EPOXY SUPER STREAMER (ANCHOVIE)—Bill Black

Hook: Mustad 34007/3407; Daiichi 2546; Tiemco 811S
Tail: Silver Flashabou; polar white Polar Aire; Super Hair, smoke, olive
Body: Epoxy
Eyes: Adhesive black on silver
Variations: Baby Herring, Sand Eel
TIED BY BILL BLACK/SPIRIT RIVER, INC

SRI EPOXY SUPER STREAMER (BABY HERRING)—Bill Black

Hook: Mustad 34007/3407; Daiichi 2546; Tiemco 811S
Tail: Polar white Polar Aire; Magnum Lite Brite, pearl; Super Hair, dark blue, black
Body: Epoxy
Eyes: Adhesive black on silver
Variations: Anchovie, Sand Eel
TIED BY BILL BLACK/SPIRIT RIVER, INC

SRI EPOXY SUPER STREAMER (SAND EEL)—Bill Black

Hook: Mustad 34007/3407; Daiichi 2546; Tiemco 811S
Tail: Polar White Polar Aire; Magnum Lite Brite, pearl; Super Hair, light olive, black
Body: Epoxy
Eyes: Adhesive black on silver
Variations: Anchovie, Baby Herring
TIED BY BILL BLACK/SPIRIT RIVER, INC

SST FLY (SUPER STEALTH TAILER FLY)—Capt Kevin Guerin

Hook: Mustad 34007/3407; Daiichi 2546; Tiemco 811S
Thread: Brown
Tail: Brown hackle; pearl Krystal Flash; red fox squirrel tail
Body: Epoxy over thread
Body Hackle: Brown
Eyes: Black plastic bead
Weedguard: Two strands monofilament
TIED BY CAPT KEVIN GUERIN

STEVE HUFF TARPON FLY (BROWN/GRIZZLY)—Steve Huff

Hook: Mustad 34011; size 2/0-4/0
Thread: Fluorescent pink
Tail: Grizzly hackle; pearl Flashabou
Body Hackle: Brown marabou
Variations: Red/black, tan, yellow/white
TIED BY ORVIS

STIR FRY—Bill & Kate Howe

Hook: Mustad 34007/3407; Eagle Claw 254/354; Tiemco 800S/811S; Pate; Owner SSW; size 6-2/0
Thread: White
Wing: Lite Brite, polar pearl; crinkle nylon, red; Ocean Hair, white; Ultra Hair, smoke, olive, black; Krystal Flash, peacock; Flashabou, silver
Head: Thread colored with black felt tip, coated with Hot Stuff Special T glue with Kick-it accelerator, Jolly Glaze
Eyes: Prismatic
Variations: FLATS FLY
TIED BY BILL HOWE

Smiley Needlefish
(green)

Soggy Head
(chartreuse)

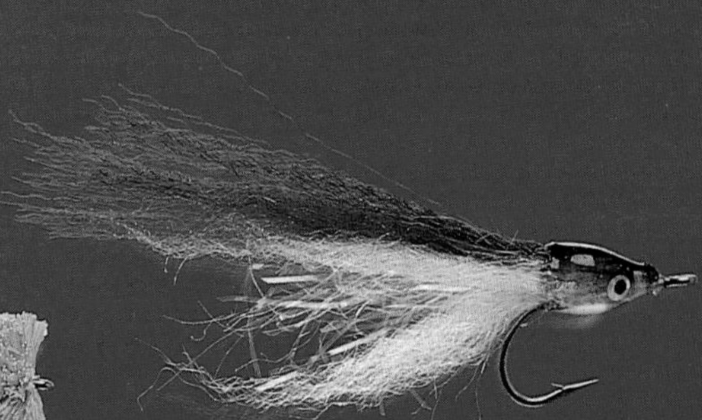

Sri Epoxy Super Streamer
(baby herring)

Smiley Needlefish
(purple)

Soggy Head
(orange/yellow)

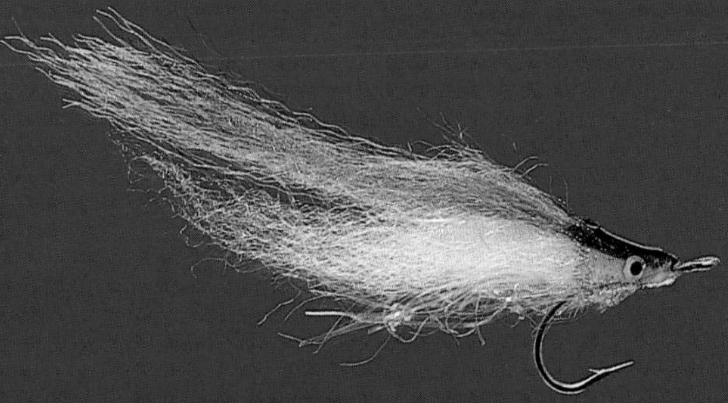

Snapping Crab

Sri Epoxy Super Streamer
(sand eel)

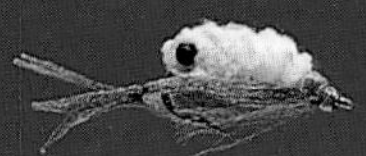

Spinster
(peppermint)

SST Fly
(Super Stealth Tailer Fly)

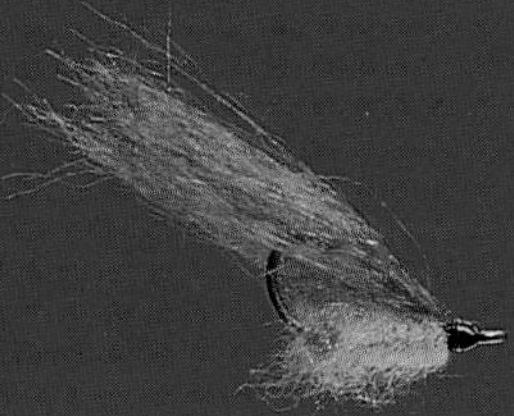

Snapping Shrimp

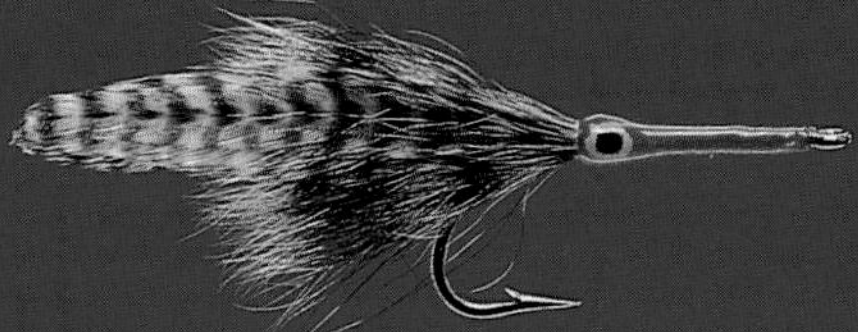

Squirrel Tarpon

Steve Huff Tarpon Fly
(brown/grizzly)

Snook Slider

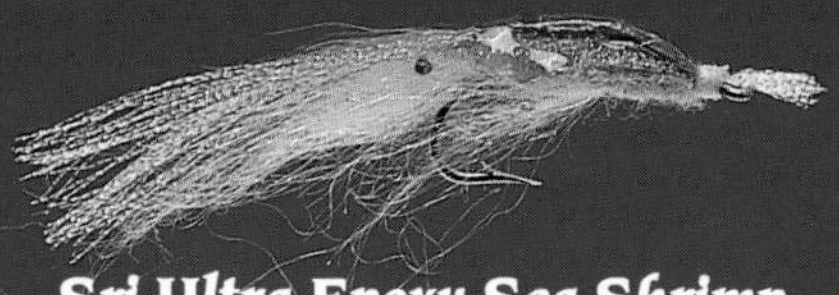

Sri Ultra Epoxy Sea Shrimp

Son of Clouser

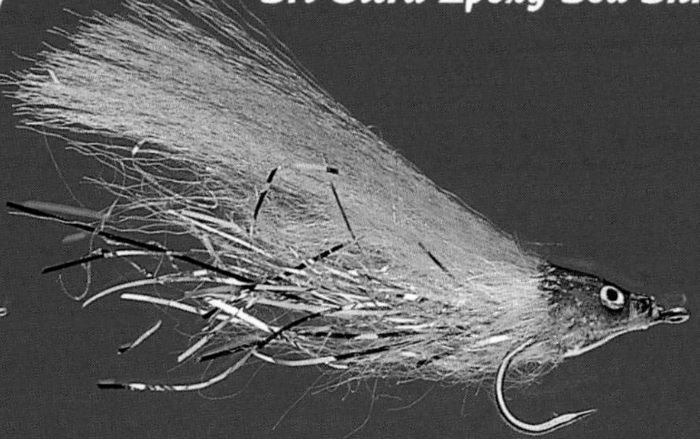

Sri Epoxy Super Streamer
(Anchovie)

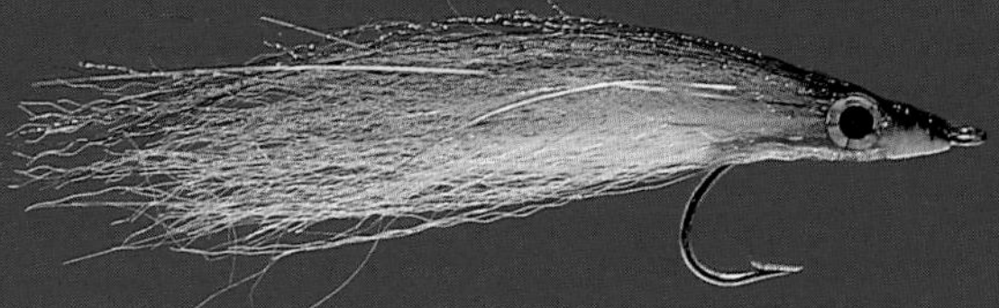

Stir Fry

STRETCH POPPER (YELLOW)—
Edgewater

Hook: Mustad 34011
Tail: Marabou, yellow; Krystal Flash, pearl
Body: Foam
Eyes: Black on yellow post
Variations: Chartreuse, white, black, blue, peppermint, purple.
TIED BY EDGEWATER

STRIP TEASE—Tom Kintz

Hook: Tiemco 811S, size 4/0
Thread: White size A flat nylon
Tail: Hackle, cream, grizzly
Underbody: .032" lead wire
Body: Pearl Mylar braid; 40-pound pink mono
Collar: White bucktail; pearl Flashabou
Eyes: 9mm plastic, black on red
TIED BY TOM KINTZ

SURF PLUG (WHITE)—Edgewater

Hook: Bendback style; Mustad 34011; on a pivot
Thread: White
Tail: Bucktail, white; Flashabou, pearl
Body: Foam, white/red
Eyes: Black on yellow post
Variations: Chartreuse, black.
TIED BY EDGEWATER

SWIMMING SHRIMP—
Bramblett Bradham

Hook: Mustad 34011
Thread: White
Tail: Grizzly hackle
Body: Gray sparkle yarn
Rib: Gray monofilament
Head: White sparkle yarn
Shellback: Pearl Krystal Flash
Front Hackle: White
Eyes: Burnt mono
Antennae: Grizzly hackle stems
TIED BY BRAMBLETT BRADHAM

SUPERFLY—Jon Fisher

Hook: Tiemco 800S, size 2, tandem
Thread: Black
Tail: Black marabou; pearl Krystal Flash
Body Hackle: Black marabou
Wing: Pearl Krystal Flash
Front Hackle: Grizzly
Eyes: Nickel-plated brass or lead
TIED BY JON FISHER/URBAN ANGLER LTD.

SURF CANDY (LIME GREEN)—
Bob Popovics

Hook: Mustad 34007/3407; Daiichi 2546; Tiemco 811S; size 1/0
Tail: Ultra Hair, white, green; silver Mylar tubing; trimmed hackle
Body: Epoxy over tail materials
Gills: Painted
Eyes: Adhesive black on chartreuse
Variations: Light blue, olive, yellow

TIED BY UMPQUA FEATHER MERCHANTS/THE FLY SHOP

SURFLEECH—John Shewey

Hook: Mustad 34007/3407; Daiichi 2546; Tiemco 811S; size 1-1/0
Thread: Red
Tail: Red rabbit strip; red Flashabou; orange Krystal Flash
Body Hackle: Red rabbit strip
Collar: Yellow hackle
Eyes: Silver bead chain
Variations: Substitute red Krystal Flash
TIED BY JIM SYNDER

TABORY'S BIG EYE SPEARING—
Lou Tabory

Hook: Mustad 34007, size 1/0
Thread: Green
Tail: Nylon crinkle, white, lavender, pale olive; pearl Flashabou
Body: Epoxy
Eyes: Doll eyes, black on yellow
TIED BY ORVIS

TABORY'S SAND EEL—Lou Tabory

Hook: Mustad 34007/3407; Daiichi 2546; Tiemco 811S
Thread: Black
Tail: Black bucktail
Body: Black chenille coated with epoxy
TIED BY LOU TABORY

TABORY'S SAND LANCE—Lou Tabory

Hook: Mustad 34007, size 2
Thread: Green
Tail: Nylon crinkle, white, lavender, pale olive; pearl Flashabou
Body: Epoxy
Eyes: Painted black on yellow
TIED BY ORVIS

TABORY'S SEA RAT (BLACK)—
Lou Tabory

Hook: Mustad 34007, size 2/0
Tail: Black hackle; black marabou
Body: Black deer hair
Body Hackle: Black deer hair
Head: Black chenille
Eyes: Non-toxic black on yellow
Variations: White, red/white
TIED BY ORVIS

TABORY'S SEA RAT (RED/WHITE)—
Lou Tabory

Hook: Mustad 34007/3407; Daiichi 2546; Tiemco 811S
Thread: Yellow
Tail: White saddle hackle
Body Hackle: Red deer hair
Wing: White marabou
Front Collar: Red deer hair
Eyes: Lead; black on yellow
Head: Red chenille
Variations: Black, white, chartreuse.
TIED BY LOU TABORY

TABORY'S SLAB FLY—Lou Tabory

Hook: Mustad 34007; size 2/0 or 4/0
Tail: Bucktail, white, red, yellow; pearl Flashabou; peacock herl
Body: White deer hair
Body Hackle: White deer hair
Eyes: Plastic black on yellow
TIED BY ORVIS

TABORY'S SLAB SIDE—Lou Tabory

Hook: Mustad 34007/3407; Daiichi 2546; Tiemco 811S
Wing: Bucktail, white, red; Krystal Flash, pearl; peacock herl
Front Hackle: White deer hair
Eyes: Lead; black on yellow
Head: White deer hair
TIED BY LOU TABORY

TABORY'S SNAKE FLY (BLACK)—
Lou Tabory

Hook: Mustad 34007/3407; Daiichi 2546; Tiemco 811S
Tail: Black ostrich
Body: Black tying thread
Wing: Black marabou
Front Hackle: Black deer hair collar
Variations: White, red/white, chartreuse.
TIED BY LOU TABORY

TABORY'S SNAKE FLY (CHARTREUSE)—
Lou Tabory

Hook: Mustad 34007, size 1
Tail: Chartreuse ostrich; chartreuse marabou; pearl Krystal Flash
Body: Chartreuse deer hair
Body Hackle: Chartreuse deer hair
Variations: Black, white
TIED BY ORVIS

TANDEM POLAR BEAR
HAIR STREAMER—Ken Durrant

Hook: Tandem
Thread: Black
Tail: Polar bear, red
Body: Red yarn
Rib: Embossed flat silver tinsel
Wing: Polar bear, white, purple, gray
Front Hackle: Polar bear, red
Eyes: Painted white on black
TIED BY KEN DURRANT, CANADA

TARPON, PINK (Turrall)

Hook: Mustad 34007/3407; Daiichi 2546; Tiemco 811S
Thread: Black
Tail: Hackle, black and hot pink
Body: Thread, black
Body Hackle: Marabou, hot pink
TIED BY TURRALL

TARPON, RED AND WHITE (Turrall)

Hook: Mustad 34007/3407; Daiichi 2546; Tiemco 811S
Thread: Red
Tail: Hackle, white
Body: Thread, red
Body Hackle: Marabou, red
TIED BY TURRALL

**Stretch Popper
(yellow)**

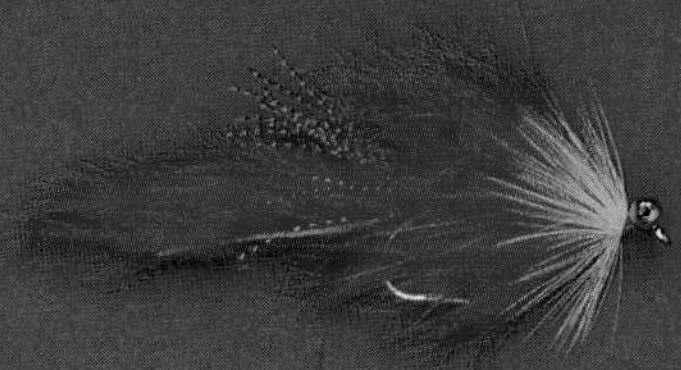

Surfleech

Tabory's Slab Fly

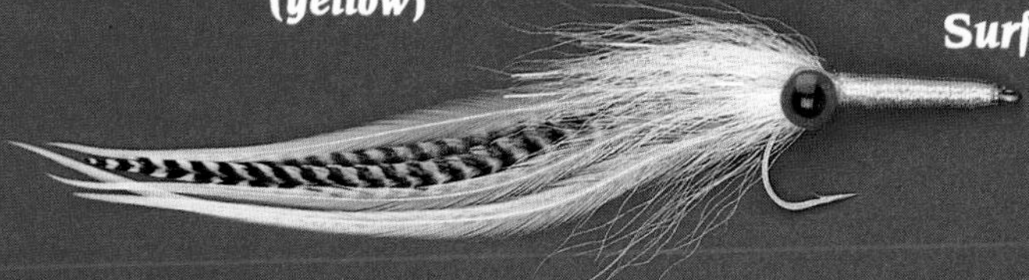

Strip Tease

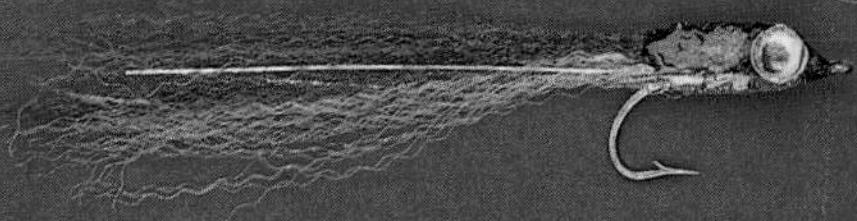

Tabory's Big Eye Spearing

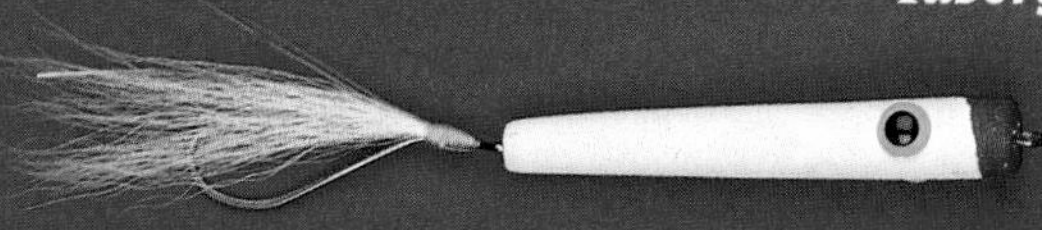

Tabory's Slab Side

**Surf Plug
(white)**

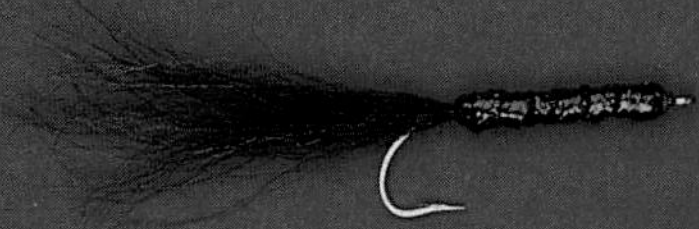

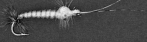

Tabory's Sand Eel

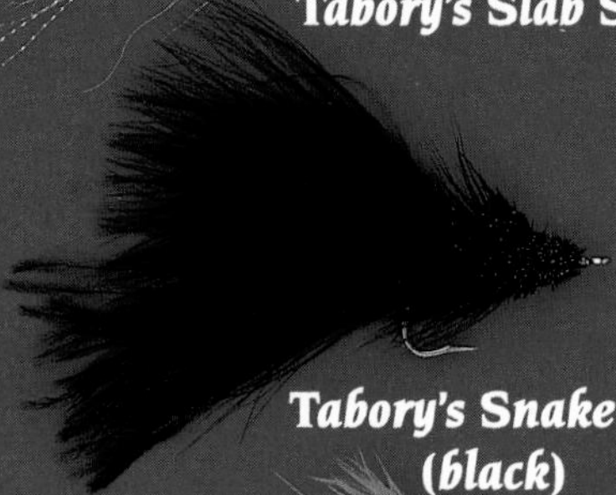

**Tabory's Snake Fly
(black)**

Swimming Shrimp

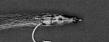

Tabory's Sand Lance

**Tabory's Snake Fly
(chartreuse)**

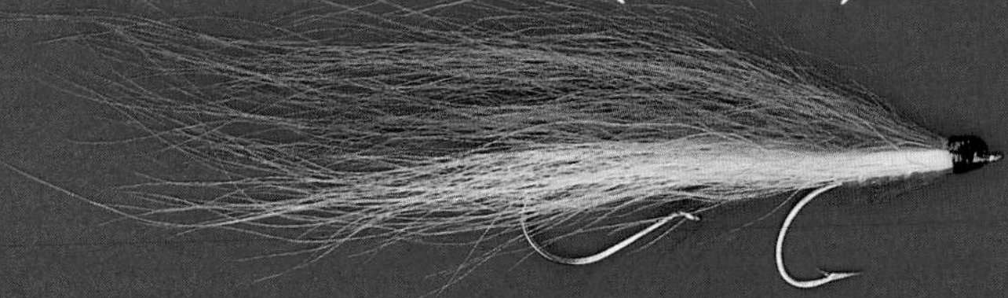

Tandem Polar Bear Hair Streamer

Superfly

**Tabory's Sea Rat
(black)**

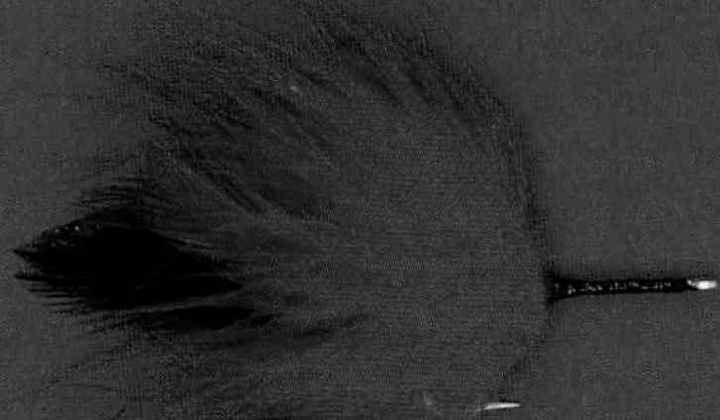

Tarpon, Pink

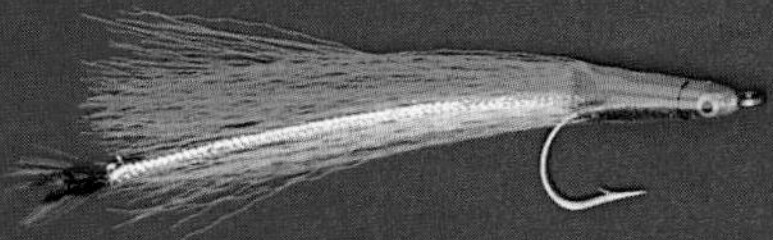

**Surf Candy
(lime green)**

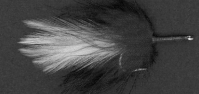

**Tabory's Sea Rat
(red/white)**

Tarpon, Red and White

TARPON, YELLOW (Turrall)

Hook: Mustad 34007/3407; Daiichi 2546;
Tiemco 811S
Thread: Yellow
Tail: Hackle, yellow
Body: Thread, yellow
Body Hackle: Marabou, yellow
Eyes: Painted black
TIED BY TURRALL

TARPON BUNNY

Hook: Mustad 34007/3407; Daiichi 2546;
Tiemco 811S; size 3/0
Thread: Orange
Tail: Badger hackle
Body: Epoxy over thread
Body Hackle: Brown marabou
Eyes: Painted black on yellow
TIED BY JOE BRANHAM/THE FLY SHOP

TARPON FLY

Hook: Mustad 34011, size 5/0
Thread: Fluorescent red
Tail: Badger hackle
Body: Fluorescent red thread
Body Hackle: Silver gray squirrel
Wing: Pearl Flashabou
Front Hackle: Brown
Variations: Grizzly hackle tail; pearl
Krystal Flash
TIED BY ELIOT NELSON/NORTHWEST
TIES

TARPON GRIZZLY (RED/WHITE)— Riverborn Fly Company

Hook: Mustad 3407, sizes 4/0-2/0
Thread: Danville Flymaster 6/0
fluorescent red
Tail: White hackle; red squirrel tail
Body: Thread
Body Hackle: Red grizzly
Eyes: Painted black on yellow
Variations: Tarpon Grizzly: blue, green,
olive, orange, red, purple, yellow
TIED BY LANCE GRAY/RIVERBORN FLY
COMPANY

TARPON RABBIT (BLACK)

Hook: Mustad 34007/3407; Daiichi 2546;
Tiemco 811S; size 3/0
Body: Black chenille; copper wire rib
Wing: Black rabbit strip
Front Hackle: Black
Eyes: Painted black on yellow
Variations: Orange, gray
TIED BY JOE BRANHAM/THE FLY SHOP

TARPON RABBIT (ORANGE)

Hook: Mustad 34007/3407; Daiichi 2546;
Tiemco 811S; size 3/0
Body: Brown chenille; copper wire rib
Wing: Orange rabbit strip
Front Hackle: Brown
Eyes: Painted black on yellow
Variations: Black, gray
TIED BY JOE BRANHAM/THE FLY SHOP

T-BONE—Tim Tollett

Hook: Mustad 34007; Tiemco 800S
Thread: White flat size A nylon
Tail: Pearl Mylar tubing
Body: Pearl Mylar tubing
Underbody: 2-amp lead wire
Wing: Calf hair, sand or white or pink;
grizzly hackle
Eyes: Umpqua black mono eyes
TIED BY TIM TOLLETT/FRONTIER
ANGLERS

TIM'S DOUBLE DOG POPPER— Tim Tollett

Hook: Tiemco 511S
Tail: Ocean Hair, white; Crystal Hair,
pearl, yellow; peacock herl; grizzly hackle
Body: Edgewater foam; permanent markers
Eyes: Moveable doll eyes, black in white
TIED BY TIM TOLLETT/FRONTIER
ANGLERS

TIM'S DEEP FRIED PRAWN— Tim Tollett

Hook: Mustad 34007; Tiemco 800S
Thread: Flat white nylon size A
Tail: Ocean Hair, white, olive; Crystal
Hair, pearl; rabbit hair, cream, olive
Body: Rabbit hair, cream, olive; Lite Brite,
cream, olive
Wingcase: Plastic bag
Rib: Clear monofilament, 6-pound
Front Wing: Ocean Hair, olive, white
Eyes: 80-pound Ande monofilament,
burned, painted black
TIED BY TIM TOLLETT/FRONTIER ANGLERS

TIN LIZZIE—Liz Stelle

Hook: Mustad 34007; sizes 4-1/0
Thread: White
Tail: Red floating yarn
Body: .020 lead wire; silver tinsel yarn
Wing: White bucktail; white marabou;
silver Flashabou
Variations: Copper, lime, gold
TIED BY LIZ STEELE/THE FLY FISHERMAN

TINSEL PLUG (SILVER)—Edgewater

Hook: Mustad 34011
Tail: Marabou, white; hackle, grizzly;
witch hair, silver
Body: Foam; witch tape, silver
Eyes: Black on silver
Variations: Pearl, electric blue, light blue,
chartreuse, green, red, peacock black,
pink.
TIED BY EDGEWATER

TINSEL TEASE (BLACK/PEARL)— C. Boyd Pfeiffer

Hook: Mustad 34011/34007/3407; Daiichi
2546; Tiemco 811S
Tail: Touch of Glitz tassel material, pearl
Body: Bump Chenille, black; tail material,
pearl
Variations: Body: Bump Tinsel, Cactus
Chenille, Estaz, etc; tail: Fire Fly, Ultra
Hair, Super Hair, Krystal Flash,

Kreinek Metallic Strands, etc; varied
color schemes
TIED BY C. BOYD PFEIFFER

TINSEL TEASE (COPPER)— C. Boyd Pfeiffer

Hook: Mustad 34011/34007/3407; Daiichi
2546; Tiemco 811S
Tail: Krystal Flash, copper
Body: Bump Tinsel; tail material, copper
Variations: Body: Bump Chenille, Cactus
Chenille, Estaz, etc; tail: Fire Fly, Ultra
Hair, Super Hair, Touch of Glitz tassel
material, Kreinek Metallic Strands,
etc; varied color schemes
TIED BY C. BOYD PFEIFFER

TINSEL TEASE (SILVER/BLUE)— C. Boyd Pfeiffer

Hook: Mustad 34011/34007/3407; Daiichi
2546; Tiemco 811S
Tail: Ultra Hair, light blue-green
Body: Bump Tinsel, silver; tail material
Variations: Body: Bump Chenille, Cactus
Chenille, Estaz, etc; tail: Touch of
Glitz tassel, Fire Fly, Super Hair,
Krystal Flash, Kreinek Metallic
Strands, etc; varied color schemes
TIED BY C. BOYD PFEIFFER

TOM'S BUBBLE BAIT—Tom Piccolo

Hook: Mustad 34007/3407; Daiichi 2546;
Tiemco 811S; Partridge Sea Prince
CS52; sizes 1-1/0
Thread: Ultra fine clear mono
Tail: White bucktail; pearl Flashabou;
pearl Krystal Flash; red streamer hair
Body: White lamb's wool; white bucktail;
pearl Flashabou; pearl Krystal Flash;
red streamer hair; silicone
Eyes: Adhesive, black on silver
Variations: Olive/white; blue/green/white;
black; white.
TIED BY TOM PICCOLO

TOM'S FINGER MULLET—Tom Lentz

Hook: Mustad 34007 size 1/0
Tail: Grizzly hackle; silver and gold
Flashabou
Body: Deer hair; permanent marker
Body Hackle: Deer hair
Eyes: Large bead chain painted black
TIED BY TOM LENTZ/THE FLY FISHERMAN

TOM'S TUBE EEL—Tom Piccolo

Hook: Mustad 34011, size 2-2/0
Thread: Fine clear mono
Tail: White streamer hair; pearl Krystal Flash;
pearl Lite Brite; red streamer hair
Body: White streamer hair; pearl Crystal
Flash; pearl Lite Brite; red streamer
hair; red grizzly; silicone; ultra fine
glitter
Eyes: Prizmatic, black on red
Variations: Various color combinations such
as olive/white; blue/white; white/white.
TIED BY TOM PICCOLO

Tarpon, Yellow

T-Bone

Tinsel Tease (copper)

Tim's Double Dog Popper

Tinsel Tease (silver/blue)

Tarpon Bunny

Tim's Deep Fried Prawn

Tom's Bubble Bait

Tarpon Fly

Tin Lizzie

Tarpon Grizzly (red/white)

Tom's Finger Mullet

Tinsel Plug (silver)

Tarpon Rabbit (black)

Tom's Tube Eel

Tarpon Rabbit (orange)

Tinsel Tease (black/pearl)

TOM'S WIDE BODY BUNKER—
Tom Piccolo
Hook: Mustad 34007/3407; Daiichi 2546; Tiemco 811S; Partridge Sea Prince CS52; sizes 3/0-6/0
Thread: Clear fine mono
Tail: White bucktail; pearl Krystal Flash; white Ultra Hair; pearl Flashabou; mixed pink and purple Ultra Hair; rainbow Krystal Flash: yellow Ultra Flash; pearl Flashabou; mixed light blue, smoke, olive Ultra Hair
Body: Tail materials; white bucktail blended with green pearl Lite Brite; saltwater pearl Flashabou; purple Lite Brite; pink bucktail; peacock herl
Cheeks: Silver pheasant (outline edges), colored with red Pantone marker
Head: Silicone and fine glitter
Eyes: Large prizmatic, black on silver
TIED BY TOM PICCOLO

TRADITIONAL
POLAR BEAR STREAMER—Ken Durrant
Hook: Mustad 34007/3407; Daiichi 2546; Tiemco 811S
Thread: Black
Tail: Red marabou
Body: Chartreuse chenille
Rib: Embossed flat silver tinsel
Wing: Polar bear, white, purple, pale green
Front Hackle: Red marabou
Eyes: Painted black on white
TIED BY KEN DURRANT, CANADA

TRAVIS OCTOPUS—Tom Travis
Hook: Mustad 34011, size 3/0
Tail: Badger hackle; red marabou
Body: Variegated chenille
Head: Variegated chenille
Eyes: Doll eyes, black on white
TIED BY ORVIS

TROPICAL PUNCH—Dan Blanton
Hook: Mustad 34007/3407; Daiichi 2546; Tiemco 811S; size 2/0
Tail: Yellow bucktail; gold Flashabou
Body: Gold Mylar tinsel
Wing: Orange grizzly; yellow Crystal Flash; peacock herl
Front Hackle: Yellow
Head: Fluorescent pink chenille
Eyes: Silver bead chain
TIED BY UMPQUA FEATHER MERCHANTS/THE FLY SHOP

TUBE FLY—Greg Tompkins
Hook: Varies
Thread: Black
Tail: Silver Mylar picked out
Body: Silver Mylar over plastic tube
Wing: Bucktail, white, green, dark blue; silver Mylar; peacock herl
Gills: Red bucktail
Eyes: Adhesive, black on silver
Variations: Red thread, wing color

variations such as chartreuse, pearl Mylar over tube.
TIED BY GREG TOMPKINS

TURNEFFE CRAB (BROWN)—
Craig Mathews
Hook: Mustad 3407; Daiichi 2546; Tiemco 800S; sizes 4-8
Thread: 6/0, brown
Body: Furry foam, brown
Body Hackle: Pantone marker; round rubber legs, brown
Wing: Deer hair
Eyes: Gold bead chain or mini-lead eyes
TIED BY CRAIG MATHEWS/BLUE RIBBON FLIES

TURNEFFE CRAB (CREAM)—
Craig Mathews
Hook: Mustad 3407; Daiichi 2546; Tiemco 800S; sizes 4-8
Thread: 6/0, cream
Body: Furry foam, cream
Body Hackle: Pantone marker; round rubber legs, cream
Wing: Deer hair
Eyes: Gold bead chain or mini-lead eyes
TIED BY CRAIG MATHEWS/BLUE RIBBON FLIES

TURNEFFE CRAB (GREEN)—
Craig Mathews
Hook: Mustad 3407; Daiichi 2546; Tiemco 800S; sizes 4-8
Thread: 6/0, green
Body: Furry foam, green
Body Hackle: Pantone marker; round rubber legs, green
Wing: Deer hair
Eyes: Gold bead chain or mini-lead eyes
TIED BY CRAIG MATHEWS/BLUE RIBBON FLIES

TURNEFFE CRAB (OLIVE)—
Craig Mathews
Hook: Mustad 3407; Daiichi 2546; Tiemco 800S; sizes 4-8
Thread: 6/0, olive
Body: Furry foam, olive
Body Hackle: Pantone marker; round rubber legs, olive
Wing: Deer hair
Eyes: Gold bead chain or mini-lead eyes
TIED BY CRAIG MATHEWS/BLUE RIBBON FLIES

TWISTED SISTER (Yellow)—A.J. Hand
Hook: Mustad 34007/3407; Daiichi 2546; Tiemco 811S
Thread: Red
Tail: Yellow hackle under silicone
Body: Pearlescent tinsel under silicone
Wing: Bucktail, yellow
Head: Red thread
Eyes: Painted, black on yellow
Variations: Grizzly/brown
TIED BY MYSTIC BAY FLIES

ULTRA CLOUSER (JOHNNY GLENN)—
Bob Clouser
Hook: Mustad 34011, size 4
Thread: Fluorescent orange flat waxed nylon
Body: Thread, gloss coated
Wing: Light blue kid goat hair; yellow Krystal Flash; yellow kid goat hair
Eyes: Lead dumbbell painted black on yellow
TIED BY JOHNNY GLENN/ORVIS NEW YORK

ULTRA SHRIMP—Bob Popovics
Hook: Mustad 34007/3407; Daiichi 2546; Tiemco 811S; sizes 1/0-4
Thread: Tan
Tail: Ultra Hair, tan; copper Krystal Flash
Body: Epoxy over tail materials, tan thread
Body Hackle: Tan
Front Hackle: Tan Ultra Hair
Eyes: Burnt mono, painted black
TIED BY UMPQUA FEATHER MERCHANTS/THE FLY SHOP

UMPQUA SWIMMING BAITFISH
(RED/YELLOW)
Hook: Mustad 34007/3407; Daiichi 2546; Tiemco 811S; size 1/0
Tail: Hackle, yellow, grizzly; yellow Crystal Flash
Body: Deer hair, natural, red, orange, yellow
Collar: Red Flashabou; deer hair, natural, yellow
Eyes: Plastic black on amber
Weedguard: Mono loop
Variations: Red/white, shad
TIED BY UMPQUA FEATHER MERCHANTS/THE FLY SHOP

UMPQUA SWIMMING BAITFISH (SHAD)
Hook: Mustad 34007/3407; Daiichi 2546; Tiemco 811S; size 1/0
Tail: Hackle, gray, white; rainbow Crystal Flash
Body: Deer hair, natural, gray, blue, white
Collar: Red Flashabou; deer hair, natural, white
Eyes: Plastic black on amber
Weedguard: Mono loop
Variations: Red/white, red/yellow
TIED BY UMPQUA FEATHER MERCHANTS/THE FLY SHOP

WALKER'S PINK SQUID—Scott Walker
Hook: Tiemco 811S
Thread: Pink
Tail: Hackle, pink; pink sili legs
Rear Collar: Deer hair, fluorescent pink
Body: Deer hair, fluorescent pink
Fins: Deer hair, fluorescent pink
Eyes: Silver bead chain
Variations: White
TIED BY SCOTT WALKER/UMPQUA FEATHER MERCHANTS

Ultra Clouser

Tom's Wide Body Bunker

Traditional Polar Bear Streamer

Turneffe Crab (brown)

Ultra Shrimp

Travis Octopus

Turneffe Crab (cream)

Umpqua Swimming Baitfish (red/yellow)

Turneffe Crab (green)

Tropical Punch

Turneffe Crab (olive)

Umpqua Swimming Baitfish (shad)

Tube Fly

Twisted Sister (yellow)

Walker's Pink Squid

WALKER'S WHITE SQUID—
Scott Walker
Hook: Tiemco 811S
Thread: White
Tail: Hackle, white; black/gray sili legs
Rear Collar: Deer hair, white
Body: Deer hair, white
Fins: Deer hair, white
Eyes: Silver bead chain
Variations: Pink
TIED BY SCOTT WALKER/UMPQUA
FEATHER MERCHANTS

WALLACE BLACK
'LECTRIC EELWORM—Jon Wallace
Hook: Mustad 36890
Thread: Black
Tail: Saddle hackle, black
Body: Crystal Chenille, black
Eyes: Lead, painted fluorescent red on black
Weedguard: Mono loop
Variations: Chartreuse, purple
TIED BY MCKENZIE FLY TACKLE

WALLACE CHARTREUSE
'LECTRIC EELWORM—Jon Wallace
Hook: Mustad 36890
Thread: Black
Tail: Saddle hackle, chartreuse
Body: Crystal Chenille, chartreuse
Eyes: Lead, painted black on fluorescent red
Weedguard: Mono loop
Variations: Black, purple
TIED BY MCKENZIE FLY TACKLE

WALLACE PURPLE
'LECTRIC EELWORM—Jon Wallace
Hook: Mustad 36890
Thread: Black
Tail: Saddle hackle, purple
Body: Crystal Chenille, purple
Eyes: Lead, painted black on fluorescent red
Weedguard: Mono loop
Variations: Black, chartreuse
TIED BY MCKENZIE FLY TACKLE

WHISTLER, RED AND WHITE
(TURRALL)—Dan Blanton
Hook: Mustad 34007/3407; Daiichi 2546; Tiemco 811S
Thread: Black
Wing: White bucktail; grizzly hackle; silver Flashabou
Front Hackle: Red marabou
Eyes: Silver bead chain
TIED BY TURRALL

WHISTLER, WHITE (GREG MIHEVE)—
Dan Blanton
Hook: Mustad 9175; Eagle Claw 254SS, sizes 1/0-6/0
Thread: 3/0 Monocord, white
Tail: Bucktail, white; silver Krystal Flash

Body: Fluorescent red chenille, two turns
Hackle: White saddle hackle
Eyes: Silver bead chain; lead wire
Variations: Yellow, red/white, chartreuse; red head with white or yellow or chartreuse or grizzly tail. Grizzly saddle to side of tail.
TIED BY GREG MIHEVE

WHISTLER, YELLOW (GREG MIHEVE)—
Dan Blanton
Hook: Mustad 9175; Eagle Claw 254SS, sizes 1/0-6/0
Thread: 3/0 Monocord, yellow
Tail: Bucktail, yellow; yellow Krystal Flash
Body: Fluorescent red chenille, two turns
Hackle: Yellow saddle hackle
Eyes: Silver bead chain; lead wire
Variations: White, red/white, chartreuse; red head with white or yellow or chartreuse or grizzly tail. Grizzly saddle to side of tail.
TIED BY GREG MIHEVE

WHOPPER STOPPER TUBE POPPER—
Tom Kintz
Hook: Mustad 34011 size 2/0; snelled
Thread: Size A flat nylon
Tail: Ultra Hair, brown; Krystal Flash, gold
Body: Plastic tube, 1/4" diameter aft, 1/8" diameter forward; 5/8" foam, cupped face; gold prizm tape
Eyes: Adhesive black on silver
TIED BY TOM KINTZ

WIGGLE BUG (PURPLE)—Steve Shiba
Hook: Mustad 34011
Thread: Black
Tail: Marabou, purple; Krystal Flash, pearl
Body: Underbody, chenille, black; over body, foam, purple
Body Hackle: Black
Eyes: Black on yellow post
Variations: White, chartreuse, yellow, black/chartreuse, blue, black.
TIED BY EDGEWATER

WIGGLE WHAM—Mark Petrie
Hook: Mustad 34011, sizes 2-1/0
Tail: Marabou, olive, white; pearl Krystal Flash
Body: Deer hair, white, olive
Lip: Black closed cell foam
Eyes: Doll eyes or solid plastic
TIED BY MARK PETRIE/SALTWATER SPE-CIALTIES

WINDRAM'S BASS BUNNY
(BLACK/RED)—Chris Windram
Hook: Mustad 34007, sizes 2-1/0
Thread: Red nylon
Tail: Rabbit, black
Body: Rabbit, black; red
Front Hackle: Red
Variations: Olive/white, red/white,

white/red, yellow/red
TIED BY CHRIS WINDRAM/TIGHT LINES

WINDRAM'S BASS BUNNY
(OLIVE/WHITE)—Chris Windram
Hook: Mustad 34007, sizes 2-1/0
Thread: White nylon
Tail: Rabbit, olive
Body: Rabbit, olive; white
Front Hackle: White
Variations: Black/red, red/white, white/red, yellow/red
TIED BY CHRIS WINDRAM/TIGHT LINES

WINDRAM'S BASS BUNNY
(RED/WHITE)—Chris Windram
Hook: Mustad 34007, sizes 2-1/0
Thread: White nylon
Tail: Rabbit, red
Body: Rabbit, red; white
Front Hackle: White
Variations: Black/red, olive/white, white/red, yellow/red
TIED BY CHRIS WINDRAM/TIGHT LINES

WINDRAM'S BASS BUNNY
(WHITE/RED)—Chris Windram
Hook: Mustad 34007, sizes 2-1/0
Thread: Red nylon
Tail: Rabbit, white
Body: Rabbit, white; red
Front Hackle: Red
Variations: Black/red, olive/white, red/white, yellow/red
TIED BY CHRIS WINDRAM/TIGHT LINES

WINDRAM'S BASS BUNNY
(YELLOW/RED)—Chris Windram
Hook: Mustad 34007, sizes 2-1/0
Thread: Red nylon
Tail: Rabbit, yellow
Body: Rabbit, yellow; red
Front Hackle: Red
Variations: Black/red, olive/white, red/white, white/red
TIED BY CHRIS WINDRAM/TIGHT LINES

WINNIE TARPON—Capt Kevin Guerin
Hook: Mustad 34007/3407; Daiichi 2546; Tiemco 811S
Thread: Black
Tail: Badger hackle; pearl Krystal Flash; tan wool
Body: Mottled tan yarn
Body Hackle: Tan and brown marabou
Eyes: Black plastic
TIED BY CAPT KEVIN GUERIN

WINSLOW'S WHISPER—Pip Winslow
Hook: Mustad 34007, size 6
Thread: White
Wing: Silver Krystal Flash; bucktail, white, olive
Front Hackle: Mallard
Gills: Red Krystal Flash
Eyes: Adhesive black on silver
TIED BY ORVIS

Walker's White Squid

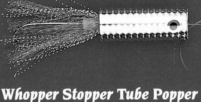

Whistler, Yellow

**Windram's Bass Bunny
(olive/white)**

Wallace Black 'Lectric Eelworm

**Windram's Bass Bunny
(red/white)**

Whopper Stopper Tube Popper

Wallace Chartreuse 'Lectric Eelworm

**Windram's Bass Bunny
(white/red)**

Wallace Purple 'Lectric Eelworm

**Wiggle Bug
(purple)**

**Windram's Bass Bunny
(yellow/red)**

Wiggle Wham

Whistler, Red and White

Winnie Tarpon

**Windram's Bass Bunny
(black/red)**

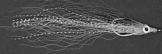

Winslow's Whisper

Whistler, White

WINSTON'S CARIBE

Hook: Mustad 34007/3407; Daiichi 2546;
Tiemco 811S; sizes 6-8
Thread: Black
Body: Olive chenille
Wing: Grizzly hackle; blue calf tail
AVAILABLE THROUGH THE FLY SHOP

WINSTON'S URCHINS (AMBER)—
Craig Mathews

Hook: Mustad 3407; Daiichi 2546; Tiemco
800S;size 6 or 8
Thread: 3/0 white monocord
Body Hackle: Sili-Legs or Spandex, amber
Wing: Deer hair; Zelon, amber
Head: Hot glue bubble head
Variations: Orange, olive, pink, lime
TIED BY CRAIG MATHEWS/BLUE RIB-
BON FLIES

WINSTON'S URCHINS (LIME)—
Craig Mathews

Hook: Mustad 3407; Daiichi 2546; Tiemco
800S; size 6 or 8
Thread: 3/0 white monocord
Body Hackle: Sili-Legs or Spandex, lime
Wing: Deer hair; Zelon, lime
Head: Hot glue bubble head
Variations: Orange, olive, pink, amber
TIED BY CRAIG MATHEWS/BLUE RIB-
BON FLIES

WINSTON'S URCHINS (OLIVE)—
Craig Mathews

Hook: Mustad 3407; Daiichi 2546; Tiemco
800S; size 6 or 8
Thread: 3/0 white monocord
Body Hackle: Sili-Legs or Spandex, olive
Wing: Deer hair; Zelon, olive
Head: Hot glue bubble head
Variations: Orange, pink, lime, amber
TIED BY CRAIG MATHEWS/BLUE RIB-
BON FLIES

WINSTON'S URCHINS (ORANGE)—
Craig Mathews

Hook: Mustad 3407; Daiichi 2546; Tiemco
800S; size 6 or 8
Thread: 3/0 white monocord
Body Hackle: Sili-Legs or Spandex, orange
Wing: Deer hair; Zelon, orange
Head: Hot glue bubble head
Variations: Olive, pink, lime, amber
TIED BY CRAIG MATHEWS/BLUE RIB-
BON FLIES

WINSTON'S URCHINS (PINK)—
Craig Mathews

Hook: Mustad 3407; Daiichi 2546; Tiemco
800S; size 6 or 8
Thread: 3/0 white monocord
Body Hackle: Sili-Legs or Spandex, pink
Wing: Deer hair; Zelon, pink
Head: Hot glue bubble head
Variations: Orange, olive, lime, amber
TIED BY CRAIG MATHEWS/BLUE RIB-
BON FLIES

YOSHI'S FUR EEL—Yoshi Sato

Hook: Mustad 34007, size 1-2/0
Thread: Black
Tag: Black bucktail
Tail: Black rabbit
Body: Black rabbit
Gills: Red wool
Collar: Black deer hair
Head: Black deer hair
Eyes: Painted lead eyes, black on yellow
TIED BY YOSHI SATO/TIGHT LINES

YOSHI'S SEA ZONKER—Yoshi Sato

Hook: Mustad 34011, sizes 1-2/0
Thread: Black
Tail: Black rabbit
Tag: Silver Mylar strands
Body: Silver Mylar tubing
Gills: Red wool
Wing: Black rabbit
Front Hackle: Black rabbit
Eyes: Lead eyes, painted black on white
TIED BY YOSHI SATO/TIGHT LINES

YOSHI'S SLIDING BAITFISH—
Yoshi Sato

Hook: Mustad 34011, sizes 1-1/0
Thread: White
Tail: Bucktail, white; marabou, white,
olive; pearl Krystal Flash; silver
Flashabou; peacock herl
Body: Packing foam; silver Flashabou;
olive marabou; peacock herl; glitter
fabric paint, silver, green; epoxy
Gills: Painted red
Eyes: Doll eyes, black on white, moveable
TIED BY YOSHI SATO/TIGHT LINES

YUCATAN CHARLIE—Capt Jan Isley

Hook: Mustad 34007/3407; Daiichi 2546;
Tiemco 811S; sizes 2-6
Thread: Olive
Tail: Pink yarn or marabou
Body: Fluorescent green Amnesia
monofilament
Wing: Fine white hair
Eyes: Silver bead chain
TIED BY BOB NAUHEIM

YUCATAN SPECIAL

Hook: Mustad 34007/3407; Daiichi 2546;
Tiemco 811S
Thread: Black
Tag: Red thread
Body: Chartreuse chenille
Wing: Chartreuse FisHair; permanent
black marker
AVAILABLE THROUGH THE FLY SHOP

Z-SMELT

Hook: Mustad 34007/3407; Daiichi 2546;
Tiemco 811S; size 6
Thread: White
Tail: White FisHair; Krystal Flash, red,
pearl
Body: Epoxy over tail materials
Eyes: Painted black
AVAILABLE THROUGH THE FLY SHOP

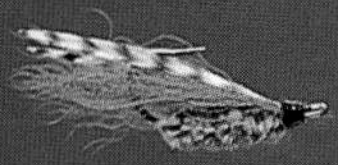

Winston's Caribe

**Winston's Urchins
(orange)**

Yoshi's Sliding Baitfish

**Winston's Urchins
(amber)**

**Winston's Urchins
(pink)**

Yucatan Charlie

**Winston's Urchins
(lime)**

Yoshi's Fur Eel

Yucatan Special

**Winston's Urchins
(olive)**

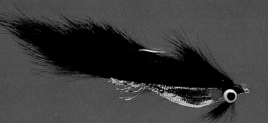

Yoshi's Sea Zonker

Z-Smelt

COMMERCIAL FLY SOURCES

A
AMERICAN ANGLING SUPPLIES
23 MAIN STREET
SALEM, NH 03079
1-800-264-5378

ANGLERS WORKSHOP
1350 ATLANTIC
WOODLAND, WA 98674
(206) 225-6359
(WHOLESALE OR RETAIL)

B
BIGHORN FLY TRADING CO.
1517 14TH ST, SUITE 229
BILLINGS, MT 59102
1-800-FISH FLY
(406) 652-1557
(WHOLESALE ONLY)

BLUE HERON TRADING COMPANY
RON AYOTTE
3551 ORLANDO SE
PORT ORCHARD, WA 98366
(206) 871-0151

BLUE RIBBON FLIES
BOX 1037
WEST YELLOWSTONE, MT 59758
(406) 646-9365
FAX (406) 646-9045

C
CARRILON UK
23 RAGLAN RD
RETFORD, KNOTTINGHAM
ENGLAND

CASTLE ARMS
PHIL CASTLEMAN
PO BOX 30070
SPRINGFIELD, MA 01103
1-800-525-4866
FAX (413) 731-1292
(WHOLESALE ONLY)

CATHERWOOD, BILL
399 MARSHALL ST
TEWKSBURY, MA 01876
(508) 851-3359

CLEARWATER ANGLER
620 AUBURN WAY SOUTH,
SUITE J
AUBURN, WA 98002
(206) 939-1484

CUSTOM TIED FLIES
5612 NE 62ND AVE
VANCOUVER, WA 98661
(206) 694-7734
FAX (206) 695-0205
(WHOLESALE AND RETAIL)

D
DIXON'S SPORTING LIFE
PAUL DIXON
74 MONTAUK HWY.
EASTHAMPTON, NY 11937
(516) 324-7979

E
EDGEWATER
35 NORTH 1000 WEST
CLEARFIELD, UT 84015
1-800-584-7647
FAX (801) 773-2758
(WHOLESALE AND RETAIL)

ELLEN'S
PO BOX 1205
ISLAMORADA, FL 33036
(305) 664-8050

F
FLORIDA KEYS SCHOOL &
OUTFITTERS
PO BOX 603
MILE MARKER 82, BAYSIDE
ISLAMORADA, FL 33036
(305) 664-5423
FAX (305) 664-5501

FLY FISHERMAN, THE
1400 S. WASHINGTON AVE
TITUSVILLE, FL 32780
(407) 267-0348

FLY SHOP, THE
4140 CHURN CREEK ROAD
REDDING, CA 96002
1-800-669-3474
(916) 222-3555
FAX (916) 222-3572

FRONTIER ANGLERS
680 N. MONTANA ST
PO BOX 11
DILLON, MT 59725
1-800-228-5263
FAX (406) 683-6736

G
GLENN, JOHNNY
870 PEQUOT TRAIL
STONINGTON, CT 06378
(203) 535-1910

GODDARD, D.L.
8013 SHIPSHEAD CREEK
DRIVE
EASTON, MD 21601
(410) 820-9762

H
HOWE, BILL & KATE
CLASSIC ANGLERS
18047 DOTY RD
CASSEL, CA 96016
(WHOLESALE ONLY)
(916) 335-2665
FAX (916) 335-2014
Some Howe flies available
through retail at:
THE FLY SHOP
1-800-669-FISH

HUNTERS ANGLING SUPPLIES
CENTRAL SQUARE
NEW BOSTON, NH 03070
1-800-331-8558
FAX (603) 487-3939

J
JACKSON CARDINAL FLIES
525 WEST KELLY
BOX 1280
JACKSON, WY 83001
1-800-346-4339
FAX (307) 733-7791
(WHOLESALE ONLY)

K
KINTZ CUSTOM FLY FISHING
EQUIP.
TOM KINTZ
13 MORIAH DRIVE
WESTERLY, RI 02891
(401) 596-7716

M
MANHATTAN CUSTOM TACKLE
913 BROADWAY
NEW YORK, NY 10010
(212) 505-6690

MCKENZIE FLY TACKLE
1075 SHELLY ST
SPRINGFIELD, OR 97477
(503) 741-8161
FAX (503) 741-7565
(WHOLESALE ONLY)

MIHEVE, GREG
507 DORY AVE
FT. WALTON BEACH, FL 32548
(904) 244-1602

MYSTIC BAY FLIES
85 TURKEY HILL ROAD,
SOUTH
WESTPORT, CT 06880
1-800-255-4310
FAX (203) 256-1213
(WHOLESALE; RETAIL BY
MAIL ORDER ONLY)

N
NORTHWEST TIES
48582 MCKENZIE HWY
NIMROD, OR 97488
1-800-334-8437
FAX (503) 896-3781
(WHOLESALE AND RETAIL)

O
ORVIS
1711 BLUE HILLS DRIVE
PO BOX 12000
ROANOKE, VA 24022-8001
1-800-548-9548
(703) 345-4606
FAX (703) 343-7053

ORVIS NEW YORK
45TH & MADISON
NEW YORK, NY 10017
(212) 697-3133

ORVIS TYSONS CORNER
8334-A LEESBURG PIKE
VIENNA, VA 22182
(703) 556-8634
FAX (703) 556-4450

P
PICCOLO, TOM
313 DELANCEY AVE
MAMARONECK, NY 10543
(914) 698-3798

R
RIVERBORN FLY COMPANY
PO BOX 65
68 SOUTH IDAHO ST
WENDELL, ID 83355
1-800-354-5534
(208) 536-2355
(WHOLESALE ONLY)

RIVERS END TACKLE CO
MARK LEWCHIK
141 BOSTON POST RD
OLD SAYBROOK, CT 06475
(203) 388-2283

RUIZ, ANTHONY
ROUTE 2, BOX 1503
WILLISTON, FL 32696
(904) 528-4698

S
SALTWATER SPECIALTIE
MARK PETRIE
PO BOX 924332
HOUSTON, TX 77018
(713) 686-4606

SEDOTTI, MARK
59 SOUTH REGENT ST
PORT CHESTER, NY 10573
(914) 939-5960

SIGLER, CAM
11061 PATTEN LANE SW
PO BOX 656
VASHON ISLAND, WA 98070
(206) 567-4836
FAX (206) 567-4940
(WHOLESALE ONLY)

SPARTON FISHING TACKLE
STEVE PARTON
UNIT 2, FIELDS FARM ROAD
LONG EATON, NOTTS NG10
3FZ
ENGLAND
PHONE 011 44 602 463 572
FAX 011 44 602 463 571

SPIRIT RIVER, INC
2405-68 NE DIAMOND LAKE
BLVD
ROSEBURG, OR 97470
1-800-444-6916 (ORDER
ONLY)
(503) 440-6916
FAX 1-800-550-6916
(WHOLESALE ONLY)

SWISHER, DOUG
29 SAN REMO CIRCLE
NAPLES, FL 33962
(813) 793-7438

T
TIGHT LINES
CHRIS WINDRAM
1100 MAIN STREET
PO BOX 362
HOUSATONIC, MA 01236
(413) 274-6143

TRACER LIGHTS
DAVID WOODHOUSE
19 DAVID AVE
WICKFORD, ESSEX SS11 7BE
ENGLAND
(Available in small quantities,
$.50 to $1.50 each; large lot
information available from
the UK manufacturer, AVRO)

TROUT FISHER, THE
DARREL SICKMON
2020 SOUTH PARKER ROAD
DENVER, CO 80231
(303) 369-7970

TURRALL USA
STEVE PRANSKY
45 KNOBHILL STREET
SHARON, MA 02067
PHONE AND FAX (617) 784-3732
(WHOLESALE ONLY)

U
UMPQUA FEATHER MERCHANTS
17537 N. UMPQUA HWY
GLIDE, OR 97443
1-800-547-3699
(503) 496-3512
FAX (503) 496-0150
(WHOLESALE ONLY)

URBAN ANGLER LTD.
118 EAST 25TH STREET
NEW YORK, NY 10010
1-800-255-5488
FAX (212) 473-4020

W
WALKER, SCOTT
835 IRONWOOD PLACE
DELTA, BC
CANADA V4L 2K6
(604) 943-4367

WOODS AND WATER
127 LAURENS ST NW
AIKEN, SC 29801
(803) 649-4361

Y
YOSHI'S FLIES
YOSHI SATO
24 HILLSIDE AVE
GT BARRINGTON, MA 01230
(413) 528-5476

BIBLIOGRAPHY

Favorite Flies and Their Histories, Mary Orvis Maybury, 1892

Complete Book of Fly Fishing, Joe Brooks, 1958

Salt Water Fly Fishing, George X. Sand, 1969

Salt Water Flies, Kenneth Bay, 1972

Master Fly-Tying Guide, 1972, Art Flick

Dressing Flies for Fresh and Salt Water, Poul Jorgensen, 1973

The Fly Tier's Almanac, Boyle and Whitlock, 1975

Fly Fishing Strategy, Swisher and Richards, 1975

The Essential Fly Tier, J. Edson Leonard, 1976

The Second Fly Tier's Almanac, Boyle and Whitlock, 1978

Lee Wulff on Flies, Lee Wulff, 1980

American Fly Fishing, Paul Schullery, 1987

INDEX

LEARN MORE ABOUT FLY FISHING AND FLY TYING WITH THESE BOOKS

If you are unable to find the books shown below at your local book store
or fly shop you can order direct from the publisher below.

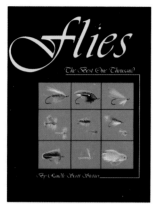

Flies: The Best One Thousand
Randy Stetzer
$24.95

Fly Tying Made Clear and Simple
Skip Morris
$19.95 (HB: $29.95)

The Art of Tying the Dry Fly
Skip Morris
$29.95(HB:$39.95)

Curtis Creek Manifesto
Sheridan Anderson
$7.95

American Fly Tying Manual
Dave Hughes
$9.95

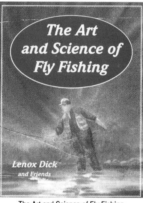

The Art and Science of Fly Fishing
Lenox Dick
$19.95

Western Hatches
Dave Hughes, Rick Hafele
$24.95

Lake Fishing with a Fly
Ron Cordes, Randall Kaufmann
$26.95

Advanced Fly Fishing for Steelhead
Deke Meyer
$24.95

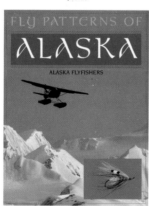

Fly Patterns of Alaska
Alaska Flyfishers
$19.95

Fly Tying & Fishing for Panfish and Bass
Tom Keith
$19.95

Float Tube Fly Fishing
Deke Meyer
$11.95

VISA, MASTERCARD or AMERICAN EXPRESS ORDERS CALL TOLL FREE: 1-800-541-9498
(9-5 Pacific Standard Time)

Or Send Check or money order to:

Frank Amato Publications
Box 82112
Portland, Oregon 97282

(Please add $3.00 for shipping and handling)